Volume 1:
From the Stone Age to 1500

Volume 1:
From the Stone Age to 1500

World History

Original and Secondary Source Readings

Charles A. Frazee, professor of history, California
State University, Fullerton, Book Editor

David L. Bender, Publisher
Bruno Leone, Executive Editor
Bonnie Szumski, Editorial Director
James Miller, Series Editor

Editorial Advisory Board
Michael Doyle, Ocean County College
Patrick Manning, Northeastern University
Richard Lewis, St. Cloud State University
Sara Tucker, Washburn University
Heidi Roupp, President, World History Association
Harry Wade, Texas A&M University

Perspectives on History

GREENHAVEN PRESS, INC., SAN DIEGO, CA

Library of Congress Cataloging-in-Publication Data

World history : original and secondary source readings / Charles A. Frazee, book editor.
       p.   cm. — (Perspectives on history)
   Includes bibliographical references and index.
   Contents: v. 1. From the Stone Age to 1500
   ISBN 1-56510-985-6 (lib. : alk. paper). — ISBN 1-56510-984-8 (pbk. : alk. paper)
   1. World history. 2. History—Sources. I. Frazee, Charles A. II. Series
   D20.W886   1999
   909—dc21
                                        98-8852
                                          CIP

CONTENTS

UNIT 1
Forming the First Civilizations

UNIT 2
The Early European Experience

UNIT 3
Asian Cultural Supremacy
and European Recovery

UNIT 4
African and American Centers of Early Civilization

TO THE INSTRUCTOR

This collection of readings is designed to supplement a textbook on world history from the Stone Age to A.D. 1500. It follows a chronological order and provides the student with guided access to both primary sources and extracts from the scholarly literature. Volume 2 carries the story from 1500 to the present.

No book of this size, of course, can offer complete coverage of every fascinating issue in world history. The topics that I have selected, however, are among those that every introductory treatment of world history must confront, whatever approach the instructor chooses. *World History: Perspectives on History* offers a balance of political, religious, economic, and cultural topics, and it encompasses the experiences of the entire range of historical actors: the powerful and the weak, men and women.

A major objective of this collection is to encourage students to think critically about history. Accordingly, the title of each chapter poses a question. Questions are embedded in the introductions to each chapter and to many selections, and after each selection the student's critical thinking is tested. By asking such questions, both of the historical sources and of the scholarly literature, students cease to be passive consumers of "facts" and begin to regard history as an inquiry into what has shaped the human experience.

Charles A. Frazee

TO THE STUDENT

In beginning your world history course, you are embarking on an exciting voyage through time, one that will take you from the dawn of humanity until our own time. You will meet a great variety of cultures and peoples; you will witness terrible tragedies and inspiring triumphs of the human spirit. You will encounter ideas that have changed the course of history and spoken profoundly of the human condition—ideas that people have believed worth dying for. Above all, you will encounter change, for that is what history is all about. How do people respond to new challenges in their lives? How do they react to changes that are forced upon them? How do they interpret an environment that threatens familiar patterns of life? Do they welcome change, or flee from it? Explaining and interpreting change is what the historian does. You will encounter plenty of examples as you move through this course; if your encounters help you understand events that are happening in our own society, then the time you spend with world history will be a valuable lifetime investment.

This book is not a complete history of the world. The textbook that your instructor has probably assigned will provide you with a connected narrative of world history, and it is on that narrative, as well as on your instructor's lectures, that you should rely for the "big picture." This book has a different purpose: to take you closer to certain key events in world history. Taking these closer looks will give you two opportunities. First, you will hear actual participants in past events tell their stories. Second, you can benefit from the interpretations of these events that experts who have devoted their working lives to studying the past can share with you.

History does not write itself. It is written by historians who use evidence to construct an account of what happened. If there is no evidence, there can be no history. Whatever account the historian writes, remember that it is that historian's interpretation, based on the evidence that he or she has critically examined. New evidence is constantly turning up, sometimes causing historians to revise radically their understanding of the past. (Some of the most dramatic instances of such revisions occur in the case of very ancient cultures and civilizations, for which evidence is sparse; a single new discovery can overturn much of what historians thought they knew.) More commonly, interpretations change subtly, as historians begin to ask other questions or to consider different kinds of evidence. For example, historians today are much more interested in the experiences of ordinary men and women of the past than they were a generation ago,

11

when "history" mainly meant the doings of kings, generals, and other such leaders.

What is the evidence that historians use? Written documents, of course, reveal what someone said or did. But historians cannot accept such evidence at face value: Not only is forgery a possibility, but the trustworthiness of the source must be questioned. What motivated the person who wrote this report or recorded this list or ordered this inscription carved in stone? In asking such questions, the historian does the job that a good detective must do in investigating a case.

But there are far more varieties of historical evidence than written documents. Works of art and literature can reveal much about the values of past societies and cultures. Religious traditions, philosophical ideas, political attitudes, and all the complex patterns of thought and behavior that anthropologists call culture must come within the historian's field of vision. Oral traditions, passed by word of mouth through many generations who could not read or write, become important sources for understanding cultures of the past.

Sometimes "material culture" provides the only direct evidence that has survived the ages. Did certain ruins result from a natural disaster, from abandonment of the site by its inhabitants, or from devastation by some enemy? Do scraps of broken pottery suggest who made them, and when, and how wealthy their society was, and who did the work? How was labor divided between men and women? What tools and weapons did these people use? How did they get their food? What did they eat? (Archaeologists love to poke through ancient garbage heaps!)

Historians also rely on the evidence that experts in other disciplines can provide. Languages change, but according to patterns that can be scientifically analyzed; what does this tell us about how a certain ethnic group arose, and how it is related to other peoples? Scientific analyses of very old textiles, of ancient deposits of pollen in the soil, of glacial ice, or even of DNA and of the isotopes of fossils, can reveal surprisingly important information about the distant past.

All of what we have mentioned so far historians consider their primary sources. These are the fundamental building blocks of history, from which the historian hopes to extract reliable data. Included among these primary sources are historians' accounts written in the distant past, which can useful for suggesting what past generations thought about their own historical traditions, or for narrating events. But obviously the writings of, for example, ancient Greek, Roman, or Chinese historians, or of medieval Christian or Islamic chroniclers, have to be judged with the same highly critical eye that the historian casts upon an Egyptian pharaoh's boasts in his victory monuments of the enemies he has destroyed, or upon a thousand-year-old account of a visitor to a Japanese city.

In contrast to the primary sources of history are the writings that modern historians themselves produce, usually called "secondary sources." They are not primary sources because historians cannot use them as direct evidence of what happened. Instead, they are just what the working historian is trying to produce: an interpretation of the past. Historians build on the accomplishments of their colleagues and predecessors. Whatever they publish must withstand the critical scrutiny of other historians, both their contemporaries and those who will come later. New questions are continually asked, new interpretations advanced, and older interpretations either refined or rejected.

As you read the selections in the chapters that follow, keep in mind the nature of the source and keep your critical eyes open. If the text is a primary source, ask yourself how this evidence should be interpreted, both in light of other evidence available to you and from the perspective of historians' interpretations of this period. If it is a secondary source, ask yourself how persuasive is the modern historian's case. What kind of evidence has the historian considered? Has the historian asked the right questions?

The readings in this book have been chosen to provide a useful and interesting collection of primary and secondary sources for the study of world history.

Timeline:
From the Stone Age to 1500

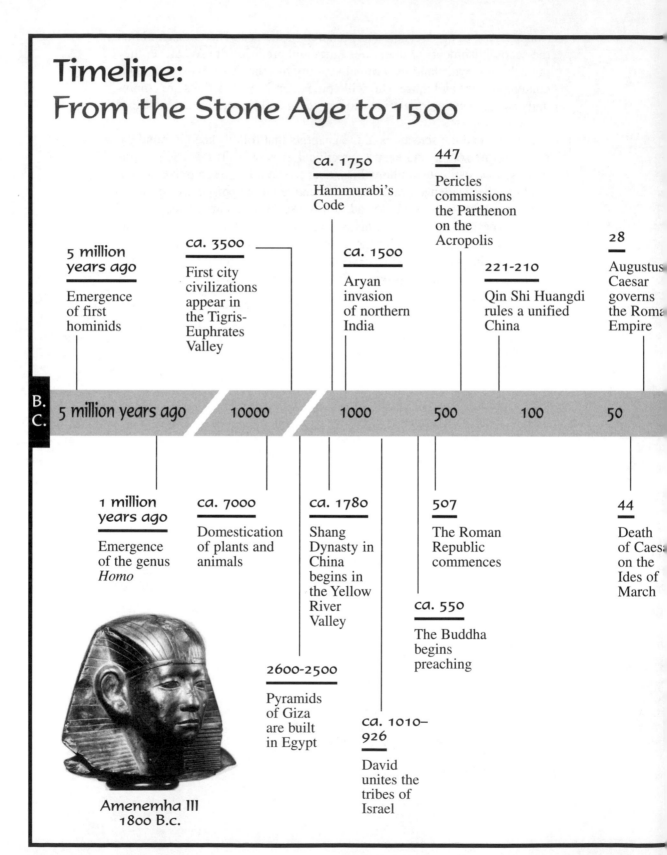

ca. 1750

Hammurabi's Code

447

Pericles commissions the Parthenon on the Acropolis

5 million years ago

Emergence of first hominids

ca. 3500

First city civilizations appear in the Tigris-Euphrates Valley

ca. 1500

Aryan invasion of northern India

221-210

Qin Shi Huangdi rules a unified China

28

Augustus Caesar governs the Roma Empire

B. C.

5 million years ago   10000   1000   500   100   50

1 million years ago

Emergence of the genus *Homo*

ca. 7000

Domestication of plants and animals

ca. 1780

Shang Dynasty in China begins in the Yellow River Valley

507

The Roman Republic commences

ca. 550

The Buddha begins preaching

44

Death of Caes: on the Ides of March

2600-2500

Pyramids of Giza are built in Egypt

ca. 1010– 926

David unites the tribes of Israel

Amenemha III
1800 B.c.

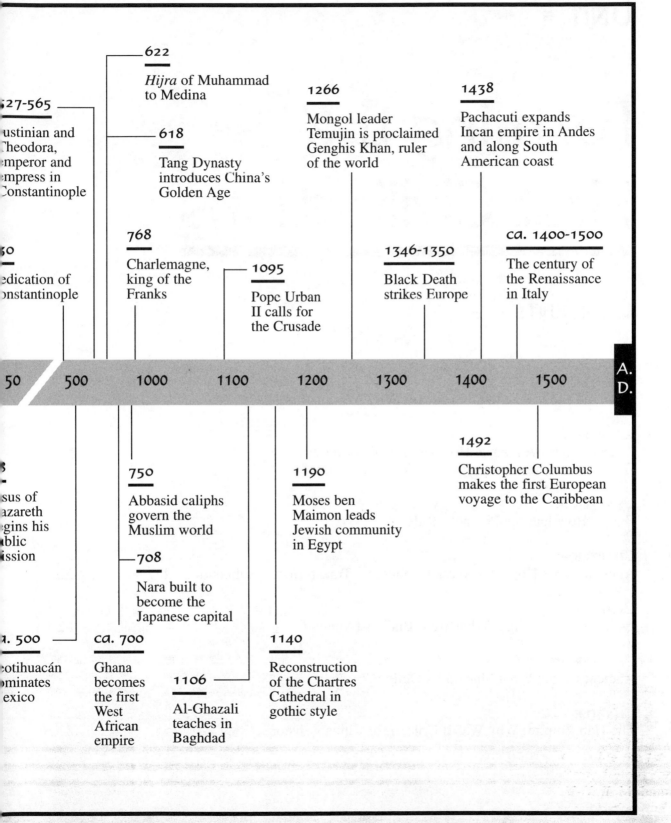

622

Hijra of Muhammad to Medina

527-565

ustinian and Theodora, emperor and empress in Constantinople

618

Tang Dynasty introduces China's Golden Age

1266

Mongol leader Temujin is proclaimed Genghis Khan, ruler of the world

1438

Pachacuti expands Incan empire in Andes and along South American coast

50

edication of onstantinople

768

Charlemagne, king of the Franks

1095

Pope Urban II calls for the Crusade

1346-1350

Black Death strikes Europe

ca. 1400-1500

The century of the Renaissance in Italy

| 50 | 500 | 1000 | 1100 | 1200 | 1300 | 1400 | 1500 | A.D. |

1492

Christopher Columbus makes the first European voyage to the Caribbean

sus of azareth egins his blic ission

750

Abbasid caliphs govern the Muslim world

708

Nara built to become the Japanese capital

1190

Moses ben Maimon leads Jewish community in Egypt

a. 500

eotihuacán ominates exico

ca. 700

Ghana becomes the first West African empire

1106

Al-Ghazali teaches in Baghdad

1140

Reconstruction of the Chartres Cathedral in gothic style

UNIT 1

Forming the First Civilizations

CONTENTS

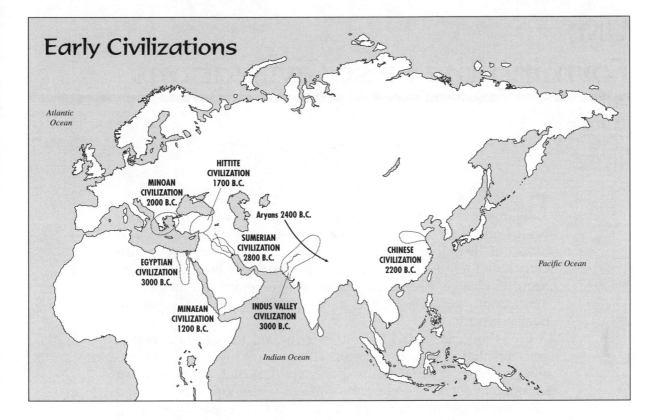

Early Civilizations

Atlantic Ocean

MINOAN CIVILIZATION 2000 B.C.

HITTITE CIVILIZATION 1700 B.C.

Aryans 2400 B.C.

EGYPTIAN CIVILIZATION 3000 B.C.

SUMERIAN CIVILIZATION 2800 B.C.

CHINESE CIVILIZATION 2200 B.C.

Pacific Ocean

MINAEAN CIVILIZATION 1200 B.C.

INDUS VALLEY CIVILIZATION 3000 B.C.

Indian Ocean

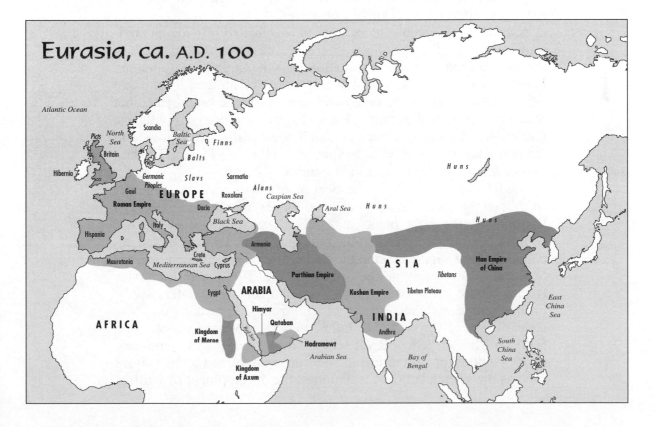

Eurasia, ca. A.D. 100

Atlantic Ocean

Picts

North Sea

Scandia

Baltic Sea

Finns

Britain

Balts

Hibernia

Germanic Peoples

Slavs

Sarmatia

Huns

Gaul

EUROPE

Roxolani

Alans

Roman Empire

Dacia

Caspian Sea

Aral Sea

Huns

Huns

Italy

Black Sea

Hispania

Armenia

ASIA

Han Empire of China

Mauretania

Crete

Cyprus

Parthian Empire

Tibetans

Mediterranean Sea

Egypt

ARABIA

Kushan Empire

Tibetan Plateau

East China Sea

AFRICA

Himyar

INDIA

Kingdom of Meroe

Qataban

Andhra

South China Sea

Hadramawt

Arabian Sea

Bay of Bengal

Kingdom of Axum

Unit 1
Forming the First Civilizations

Beginning with the first hominids millions of years ago, human beings and their immediate ancestors were social creatures who lived out their lives as members of hunting and foraging bands. Only about ten thousand years ago did this basic condition of life begin to change. The developments of agriculture and animal domestication were among the most significant turning points in human history.

Five thousand years after this Agricultural Revolution, another great revolution in history began. This occurred when agricultural areas became, in certain parts of the world, sufficiently productive to support centers of civilization—places where kings, priests, and the artisans and merchants who catered to their needs could begin to produce written records, artistic traditions, organized religious cults, and coercive mechanisms of power.

A number of circumstances worked together to provide an environment for civilization about 3500 B.C. The most important factor must have been related to population growth. Coupled with human initiative to devise a new tool or implement or an idea to improve their lives, as well as increased willingness to take on projects that required communal action, people began to cluster in villages. Eventually the villages became small towns filled with men and women who were skilled in buying and selling and in the production of articles to trade with their neighbors.

Town life rested on the domestication of plants and animals needed to feed the specialists who were no longer hunters and gatherers. Fortunately, the right plants and animals were found in the hill country of southeastern Anatolia, now in modern Turkey. With a dependable food supply at hand the first of the world civilizations, the Sumerian, developed in the valley of the Tigris and Euphrates Rivers, where irrigation methods assured a sufficient water supply. From there the characteristics of civilization spread to the Nile River valley of Egypt, to the Indus plain of modern Pakistan, and lastly to China's Yellow River region. Tools, seeds, and young animals essential for agriculture and herding were joined by inventions such as the wheel, building techniques, the development of writing, and complex religious structures. Eventually societies were built on class lines, with rulers who had power to make laws and lead armies against hostile neighbors.

The selections in unit 1 follow the development of the civilizations of these four geographic regions. Each took products and ideas from Mesopotamia and shaped them to fit their own conditions. Egyptians, the Indus Valley people, and the Chinese discovered and utilized plants and animals suited to their own environment. They thought of unique ways to worship their gods, to organize their societies, and to develop writing systems. In India the Aryans organized their states in quite different ways than the Chinese or the Egyptians.

As you read these selections keep in mind:

1. What was common to ancient civilizations?
2. What was unique to each of them?
3. How were values taught and enforced?
4. How did ruling elites, those people who held power in their states, hold their position?
5. What role did religion play, and why?

CHAPTER 1
From the Stone Age to Civilization: What Was the Price?

Modern human beings (*Homo sapiens* or "wise man") are today the sole surviving representatives of a larger biological classification known as hominids. Almost every year, scientists announce a new discovery that extends knowledge of our hominid ancestors further into the past. According to DNA analysis, the hominids branched off from the apes at least 5 million years ago. The oldest known hominid fossils have been dated to 3.9 million years ago. At least 2 million years ago, the earliest biological human beings, known as *Homo erectus* ("upright man"), appeared in Africa.

What distinguishes a human being? Intellectually, it is the ability to think in abstract ways, to use language, to understand that one has a personality, to recall the past, and to plan for the future. In material terms it is the ability to make tools, to build fires, and to leave evidence of paintings or carvings. These abilities did not appear at once—in fact, they probably were not completely evolved until about 100,000 years ago, with the appearance on earth of *Homo sapiens*. But the earliest signs of such development can be traced back some 2.5 million years to the earliest toolmakers, whose material traces have recently been found in Ethiopia (selection 1).

The readings in this chapter will take you from these earliest known prehuman toolmakers to the dawn of what we call civilized life, about 5,500 years ago. That journey covers a huge span of time, and for most of that time change occurred very slowly. Think of the 2.5 million years that have passed since the earliest toolmakers fashioned their crude implements as a single twenty-four-hour day that runs from midnight to midnight. In that imaginary day, *Homo sapiens* would not appear until about 11 P.M., the eve of civilization not until 11:55 P.M. The entire history of the world since then would speed by in the last five minutes!

Historians call the enormous period from the first toolmakers to the appearance of civilization the Stone Age, subdivided into the Old Stone Age (or Paleolithic) and the New Stone Age (Neolithic). The Old Stone Age designates the period in which human beings depended on relatively crude stone tools and weapons and lived as wandering bands of hunter-gatherers. It was in the Neolithic, which began (in some parts of the world) about ten thousand years ago, that human beings experienced those crucial revolutions that made civilization possible: They discovered agriculture; learned to raise animals for food, for power, and for transportation; made tools and weapons from finely worked stone; and began to live in settled villages and to channel water to irrigate their crops. Eventually they discovered how to smelt metals (especially copper) and began to live in cities that were fed by surrounding villages. Between 4000 and 3000 B.C., in present-day Iraq, human life had become so closely organized that historians speak of the patterns of life there as constituting a civilization. For these people, the Neolithic had ended and the age of civilization—in which we ourselves live—had begun. (In some parts of the world, such as the Amazon basin, New Guinea, and the deserts of southern Africa and Australia, the Stone Age way of life has continued into the twentieth century, and remnants of it still survive.)

What was gained, and what was lost, in this transition from the Stone Age to civilization? How have human beings learned to master their environment, and in what ways have they remained dependent on nature? What forms of cooperation have they had to learn? How have differences of wealth and power arisen as civilized life became more complex? And how have human beings explained their place in the world?

Think about these questions as you study the six selections that follow, and indeed throughout this book.

SELECTION 1:

The Oldest Tools

In the following selection, a contemporary anthropologist describes the discoveries that have extended our knowledge of toolmaking by hominids to 2.5 million years ago, and tells us something of how these creatures lived. From this selection you will also learn about how modern scientists investigate humanity's ancestors.

Modern human technology had humble beginnings. The earliest signs of this are the ability to select a suitable pebble from a stream bed, and to

strike it with an appropriate stone to produce either sharp-edged flakes or a crude chopping tool. Sileski Semaw and others present new evidence from Gona in Ethiopia which pushes the date for the onset of tool manufacture back to at least 2.5 million years ago. And in December 1996 in the

Bernard Wood, "The Oldest Whodunnit in the World," *Nature*, vol. 385, no. 6614 (Jan. 23, 1997), p. 292.

Journal of Human Evolution, Kimbel and others reported that at the nearby 2.3-million-years-old site at Hadar, similar-looking stone tools were found in "close association" with a jawbone from one of the earliest examples of the genus *Homo*. But how secure is the claim that hominid technology is so deeply rooted in the past, and how justified is the assumption that the first technologists were members of our own genus?

The assertion that stone-tool manufacture goes back 2.5 million years is based on evidence from the Gona River, which is in the Awash Valley in Ethiopia. The Awash Valley is best known for the collections of fossil hominids that have been found at Hadar, to the northeast of Gona, and at the Middle Awash, which is to the south. Thus far, work in the Awash Valley has concentrated on strata that are between 2.9 and 3.9 million years old. Although these efforts have yielded an impressive collection of an early hominid species known as *Australopithecus afarensis*, even after many years of field work there have been no signs of stone tools in these earlier strata.

There is no doubt that the two teams have recovered genuine and remarkably sophisticated artefacts. Of the several thousand tools that were discovered by Semaw at Gona, more than a thousand were found *in situ* at two excavations. Kimbel recovered a more modest haul from Hadar— just 34 artefacts—but 14 of these were from an excavation. The geological context of the artifacts at both sites is reassuring: at neither location is there any evidence that the tools might have been made more recently and then deposited in the beds of stream channels that had cut into the older layers. The sediments are too fine-grained to be channel deposits, and the edges on the tools are fresher than they would have been if they had been rolled in stream beds. Stone-on-stone percussion can occur naturally, but it is inconceiv-

able that random impacts could mimic the uniform flaking patterns of many of these artefacts.

Archaeologists use the term 'industry' for distinctive collections of stone tools, and both the Gona and the Hadar artefacts have been assigned to the 'Oldowan industry'. This was the name given by Mary Leakey to the 1.8 million-year-old stone tools that she recovered from Bed I at Olduvai Gorge in Tanzania. Oldowan-like artefacts have been found at sites elsewhere, but until the new discoveries at Gona, the earliest evidence came from the Lokalalei site at West Turkana which, like at Hadar, is around 2.3 million years old.

Stone tools of this antiquity cannot be dated directly—their ages have to be inferred from the strata that contain them. Semaw used two dating methods and they relied on the ability to trace distinctive, reliably dated, strata from site to site and from one locality to another. A stratum below the two excavations is apparently equivalent to the tuff-derived layer from Hadar, and single-crystal argon/argon dates confirmed that it results from a volcanic eruption that took place around 2.9 million years ago.

After reading this selection, consider these questions:

1. How convincing is the evidence that the artifacts discovered in the Awash Valley were really made by early hominids?

2. What can you deduce from this evidence about the way of life and level of intelligence of early hominids?

3. What other kinds of evidence might scientists be able to find that could tell us more about the early hominids? What kinds of evidence are likely to have been lost forever?

SELECTION 2:

Tracing the Past Through DNA

Archaeology is not the only way we have of gaining insights into earliest human history. DNA, the biochemical substance that is present in all living things and carries the genetic code, has certain unique characteristics shared by each member of a given genus (for example, Homo*) or species (for example,* Homo sapiens*). Recently developed procedures enable scientists to analyze the rate of evolutionary change in DNA, and thus to establish an approximate date for its separation from its biological relatives as described in the following selection. Such analysis throws startling light on the emergence of modern human beings, although conclusions based on it thus far remain highly controversial.*

Since the 19th century, scientists have been studying fossils to reconstruct our past. But there was no evidence to tell them definitely whether these represented our direct ancestors or were merely dead branches on the family tree. So scientists did the logical thing. They arranged them with the oldest and most dissimilar hominids first, leading up to the most recent and close-to-human types. It was a convenient time line, familiar from textbook illustrations and museum dioramas. And then came Eve.

She debuted before the world in the winter of 1988: a naked woman holding an apple on the cover of *Newsweek*. The article explained that a team of biochemists at Berkeley had discovered the single female ancestor of the entire human race. The scientists, led by Rebecca Cann, had done so by looking at the DNA found in a specific part of the cell called the mitochondria. Unlike other DNA, mitochondrial DNA isn't a combination of both parents' genes; it is inherited only from the mother. This means that the only changes to the mitochondrial genes, as they pass from generation to generation, are occasional mutations. By calculating the rate of these muta-

tions, and comparing the mitochondrial DNA of people from around the world, the Berkeley researchers had come up with a surprisingly young common ancestress: Eve, as the scientists dubbed her, was only 200,000 years old. "Genetically speaking," writes James Shreeve in *The Neandertal Enigma*, "there was not all that much difference between a [modern] New Guinean highlander, a South African !Kung tribeswoman, and a housewife from the Marin County hills. . . . Whatever appearances might suggest, they simply hadn't had time enough to diverge."

The Eve discovery shocked evolutionary historians. It meant the hominids that spread out of Africa 1.2 million years ago were not modern humans' direct ancestors. Instead they and their descendants had been supplanted by a far more recent out-of-Africa migration—perhaps only 100,000 years ago. That would mean that all the old standbys of the museum diorama—Peking Man, Java Man, Neanderthal Man—were evolutionary dead ends.

Not surprisingly, traditional paleontologists have attacked Eve with vigor, arguing that Cann's sample was skewed, her computer program flawed, and that even if all humans share a recent female ancestor, it doesn't mean there weren't other contributions to our gene pool. Eve's partisans counterattacked: A number of independent

Adam Goodheart, "Mapping the Past," *Civilization*, vol. 3, no. 2 (March/April 1996), pp. 45, 47.

researchers have looked at different parts of the DNA and arrived at similar dates for our divergence from a common ancestor. In 1995, a geneticist at the University of Arizona claimed to have found a common male ancestor who lived 188,000 years ago.

Now scientists are trying to resolve the Eve debate by looking in the most logical place of all: ancient DNA. "If we had even one Neanderthal DNA sample we could be sure of, it would quickly emerge how closely related it was to modern *Homo sapiens*," says Sir Walter Bodmer, former president of the Human Genome Organisation. Just a few years ago, the idea of finding a sample of Neanderthal DNA would have seemed about as probable as the idea of finding a live Neanderthal living deep in some cave, since scientists believed that the fragile DNA molecule decayed rapidly after death. But now geneticists are reading DNA recovered from ancient human remains. Despite skepticism from many scientists, their results are winning acceptance. . . .

Our genes cannot wholly account for our diversity. In fact, the work of genetic historians would be far easier were it not for the fact that the peoples of the world are so similar under the skin. "It is because they are external that . . . racial differences strike us so forcibly, and we automatically assume that differences of similar magnitude exist below the surface, in the rest of our genetic makeup," [Luigi-Luca] Cavalli-Sforza has written. "This is simply not so: the remainder of our genetic makeup hardly differs at all." Indeed, research has shown that culture usually drives the spread of genes and not vice versa. "In the history of human development," Cavalli-Sforza says, "whenever there has been a major expansion geographically or demographically, it has been because one people has had an increase in food or power or transportation. . . . Whenever I see an expansion, I start looking for the innovation that made it." The invention of agriculture or the wheel makes history; genes only reflect it.

Even so, the story that the genes' tiny gradations tell is altering the way we think about the past. "Genetics changed something fundamental about our view of history," says Jones. "It shows us that history is largely the story of love, not war." The genetic historians suggest that it's time we started asking, with E.M. Forster: Who *did* go to bed with whom in the year 1400? And as we consider the possibilities—a Mongol chieftain and his Chinese bride, say; an Aztec woman and her husband; a fumbling pair of teenagers on a French hillside—it is pleasing to think that those ancient acts of love left their mark somewhere within each of us.

After reading this selection, consider these questions:
1. In what ways does DNA analysis offer an unexpected and controversial explanation of the evolution of modern humans?
2. Why is DNA analysis controversial?
3. Do you find the analysis presented in selection 2 convincing? Why or why not?

SELECTION 3:
Tensions in the Neolithic

Most scholars regard the Agricultural Revolution—the process by which human beings learned to cultivate plants rather than simply gather their food from wild plants—as the single most important change in history. From this change flowed virtually everything else that has made the society in which we live: food production sufficient to support growing populations, new gender relationships, the impetus to develop more efficient tools, villages and cities, trade and money, economic divisions into rich and poor, governments, wars, the leisure and money to support the arts. The list could go on and on.

But, as Professor D. Brendan Nagle of the University of Southern California argues in the following selection, there was a price for this progress.

Hunters and gatherers place a low value on possessions and a high value on mobility. Always on the move, they carry only a few tools and weapons with them. Agriculture reverses this way of life. It cannot be practiced without a commitment to permanence and the accumulation of large amounts of material goods. Homes, villages, and storage facilities have to be constructed; fields cleared, divided, and fenced; herds built up and maintained; and implements and tools fabricated. Constant effort is required to maintain all of these. Once settled, farmers may not move again for generations. Pastoralists are equally committed to their flocks and herds.

For practical purposes, hunting-gathering bands always remained small, in the range of approximately 30 to 50 people. Larger groups would have been difficult for most environments to sustain; smaller ones could not reproduce themselves. Agriculture, by contrast, knew no limits insofar as population growth was concerned. Thus where hunting-gathering bands restricted their numbers, agricultural communities tended to expand them. Children could be put to work in the fields or gardens at an early age, and at harvest time it was essential to maximize the number of people who could be mobilized. Overpopulation was solved by emigration and opening up new land for cultivation. By about 6000 B.C., villages with populations in the thousands were common throughout the Middle East.

The growth of population and the accumulation of material goods forever changed the way human beings lived. Under hunting-gathering conditions a rough egalitarianism prevailed; no one had—or needed—any more than anyone else. What was the point of accumulating things that could not be carried from place to place during long, nomadic treks? In the settled conditions of agriculture, however, this was not the case. Now there was a point—and an incentive—to expanding one's possessions, whether farm or flock. Wealth was its own self-evident justification. Material goods could be accumulated, enjoyed during one's lifetime, and then passed on to the next generation. With the Agricultural Revolution inequality became, for the first time, an aspect of the human condition since not everyone could be equally successful in the quest for material possessions.

The new way of life had a powerful impact on gender relations. With the introduction of agriculture, the role and status of women changed. It is estimated, for instance, that in some present-day hunting-gathering groups, women contribute over 70 percent of the daily food supply and as a result have a higher status than their counterparts in agrarian societies. In hunting-gathering bands children are usually spaced at three- to four-year intervals (by means of late weaning), whereas in agricultural societies women have frequent pregnancies and spend more time caring for small children. Finally, men dominate agriculture wherever it involves the use of the plow and herding. As their roles changed and as they lost the ability to contribute directly to the economic well-being of the community, the status of women declined.

Another factor contributing to this decline was the emergence of a form of public life. In hunting-gathering bands there was little need for the exercise of authority; everyone was related to everyone else, and everyone knew each other intimately. Conflicts could be resolved informally. This changed with the development of large villages where more formal and less personal methods of administering justice and maintaining

D. Brendan Nagle, *The Ancient World* (Englewood Cliffs, NJ: Prentice-Hall, 1989), pp. 4–6.

order became necessary. Men easily assumed the new roles of judges, which complemented their responsibility for defending villages from outside marauders and policing the more unruly members of the village community; the power of coercion and patriarchal control went hand in hand. The realm of justice, administration, and warfare was defined as an arena of public concern under male control in opposition to, and superior to, the private realm of the family and the household to which women, along with children, servants, and, for the first time, slaves were assigned. This distinction between public and private realms is a key to understanding all of ancient society.

The results of the Agricultural Revolution were thoroughly mixed. It is usually regarded as a great leap forward for humankind, as indeed it is if we focus only on its ability to provide large food surpluses and to create new and more varied jobs for men. But in other respects it posed challenges in terms of cooperation and the ownership of goods that have never been adequately solved.

Apart from its lowering of the status of women, the agricultural way of life created new stresses and tensions for everyone. Herds and farms had to be maintained; there could be no relaxation in that task. There were new sources of friction over boundary lines, possessions, and the equitable distribution of goods and responsibilities. Relations between men and women and between children and their parents changed. New relations between haves and have-nots, masters and servants, owners and nonowners, freemen and slaves, came into being. Warfare was now a much more serious business than in the past. There was now something worth fighting over

beyond mere disputes about hunting territory. There was booty worth taking in the form of movable goods and people who could be put to work for their new masters. Herds and farms could be appropriated and their previous owners enslaved.

It is undoubtedly true that plain superiority in force allowed agriculturists to overwhelm hunting-gathering peoples everywhere in the world. It was not a peaceful process. Even when not in direct confrontation, agriculturists always encroached aggressively on the territories of hunters and gatherers. Rapid population growth was solved by the expedient of encouraging surplus population to move on—into the territories of hunters and gatherers. In all of the sustained confrontations between agriculturists and hunters and gatherers, the latter have always lost. Today, what was once the only way of life for the human race is practiced by a tiny and ever-shrinking percentage of people in the most distant and inaccessible parts of the globe. In the great sweep of human history the only two other events that can be compared to the Agricultural Revolution in terms of their capacity to revolutionize human relations are the State and Urban Revolution and the Industrial Age Revolution—the age in which we live.

After reading this selection, consider these questions:
1. What determined the size of hunting-gathering bands?
2. Contrast the life of the hunter with that of the farmer.
3. How did the agricultural revolution affect women?

SELECTION 4:

Farming

Learning how to grow plants for food was the crucial breakthrough; it affected every other aspect of Neolithic life. Many historians theorize that *women, who in hunter-gatherer bands bear primary responsibility for finding edible plants while the men are tracking game, played the largest role in perfecting the techniques of cultivation. As the clearing of fields and the growing of crops began to demand greater physical strength, and as hunting yields declined, men gradually took control of farming. In the following selection, American historian William McNeill explains some of the implications of Neolithic farming.*

As to how farming was invented, we have to guess. The real breakthrough was the discovery of how to make seed-bearing grasses—ancestors of our wheat and barley—grow in places where they did not grow naturally. By preparing fields in forested land, where grasses did not ordinarily grow at all, people could plant suitable kinds of seeds and be sure that only food crops would grow. In such locations natural competitors (weeds) could not mix with and partly crowd out the seed-bearing wheat and barley because weed seeds could not easily pass through the forest barrier and establish themselves on the artificially cleared land.

The trick, then, was to be able to create at will special environments where useful plants could thrive. Men did this by cutting a ring of bark around trees of the forest. Slashing the bark killed the trees and opened the forest floor to sunlight. In such a specially prepared place, wheat and barley could grow very well indeed.

But before agriculture could flourish, still another change had to take place. When shaken by the wind or by some passing animal, wild wheat and barley scattered their ripe seeds on the ground. This made harvesting difficult. But human action soon selected strains with tougher husks, so that seed no longer shook out of the ripened ears, even when the stalks were grasped by human hands and cut with a sickle. After all, only those seeds that stayed in the ear could be carried home by the farmers, and only seeds that had been safely harvested could be planted the next year. Rapid selection therefore took place in favor of varieties that suited human needs.

After forest clearings had been cultivated for

two or three years, the cultivators found it helpful to burn the dead tree trunks and scatter the ashes over the soil. This fertilized the ground for one or two more crops. But after five or six years such fields usually became choked with thistles and other weeds (whose seeds had come in on the wind), so that the soil was no longer worth cultivating. Instead, the early farmers killed the trees somewhere else in the forest and started the cycle of slash-and-burn cultivation all over again. Their old fields, abandoned, so filled with trees again.

The soft soil of the forest floor scarcely needed to be dug. A pointed stick to stir up the leaf mold and make sure the seeds were in contact with moist ground beneath was all that was necessary to make the seeds grow. Special sickles for cutting grain stalks had already been invented to aid in harvesting wild-growing grain. None of these implements required any fundamental change in tool types.

But cutting the bark around tree trunks was a different matter. An ax sharp enough to bite through into the wood, and tough enough not to shatter on impact against the tree trunk, demanded a different kind of stone from that used in making hunting tools. Arrowheads, knives, and spears could be made of brittle stone, for they were designed to cut soft animal tissues. They needed to be sharp, and even prehumans had discovered how to shatter a stone in such a way as to produce suitable cutting edges. But the techniques for shaping brittle stone would not do for an ax. Tough unchippable kinds of stones were needed to withstand the impact against a tree trunk. The problem was solved by grinding and polishing basalt and similar varieties of hard, dense stone.

Tools produced by this method look very different from those made by chipping brittle pieces of flint. Slow, patient work of grinding and pol-

William McNeill, *A History of the Human Community,* 4th ed., (Englewood Cliffs, NJ: Prentice-Hall, 1993), pp. 10–11.

ishing the natural surfaces of the stone produced smooth, keen, cutting edges. Obviously this took much longer than chipping tools into shape; but a well-made stone ax might last a lifetime and could be resharpened over and over again in exactly the same way that it had been made in the first place. Such axes were quite efficient. Modern experiments have shown that, when put onto a proper handle, ancient stone axes can cut down a tree almost as fast as a modern steel-bladed ax.

After reading this selection, consider these questions:

1. How does seed selection affect farming?
2. How did slash-and-burn agriculture get its name?
3. Why was the invention of the stone ax important for the first farmers?

SELECTION 5:

Counting

Once there was an agricultural surplus and a need for storage, people had to devise a way to count the inventory and determine the amount of space needed. This very simple operation soon became more complex.

In Mesopotamia (present-day Iraq), where as we will see in chapter 2 the first genuine civilization appeared sometime between 4000 and 3000 B.C., large temple complexes were established that depended on collecting enough grain to sustain and satisfy the priests whose full-time job was to please the gods and interpret their wishes. These temples had rooms for storing food reserves and agricultural tools. Naturally, the scribes who kept the records had to learn how to count accurately.

Tally stones are one ancient method of aiding the memory while counting. While a herd of animals was being counted, for example, a stone was thrown on a pile or dropped into a container for every tenth or xth animal. By this method only the number can be fixed, and this only for as long as the stones or tokens are kept together. Every other aspect of the process, such as the kind of animals, the place, the time, or the people involved, must be obtained by recourse to the memory of the people taking part.

This system, whose "stones," already in earlier times—especially in Babylonia where there were no stones—had been made of clay and could thus easily be made into different shapes, was refined by having "stones" of different shapes represent different counting units: something numerous finds attest to. A further step was taken by shaping some of the pieces of clay to help one to recognize what was being counted. If such pieces of clay were kept together in containers, it was possible to carry out something like the simplest form of bookkeeping, although this clearly still meant going without a record of all the other important information involved.

The next step, shown by the material we have found, combined this token method and the system of cylinder seals, which had been set up in the meantime. The precise number of clay pieces collected together for a specific operation were now encased in a lump of clay that was molded into a ball, the outside of which was then covered

Hans J.Nissen, *The Early History of the Ancient Near East, 9000–2000 B.C.*, Elizabeth Lutzeier and Kenneth Northcott, trans. (Chicago: University of Chicago Press, 1988), pp. 85, 87.

with impressions, mostly from only one seal. In this way, two important further aspects could be recorded: (a) since it was possible to identify the seal of a particular person, it became possible to name those who took part in or were responsible for an operation; and (b) here, for the first time, there was a protection against manipulation. It must, however, be conceded that this method was exceedingly laborious, which meant that it was scarcely of use for all the operations involved in economic administration.

However, there is a direct line of development from here on, insofar as in some cases there are oblong impressions on the outside of such balls that represent numbers, to judge from further developments, and that were intended to make visible on the outside the numbers encased within the ball.

The next development is linked with this one because now, for the first time, we see the emergence of flat clay slabs with the oblong signs for numbers on their surfaces, which may be completely covered by impressions of cylinder seals.

The same matters could now be dealt with in a much simpler way than with the use of the sealed balls. And there was an added advantage, which would later be one of the most important preconditions for the formulation of lengthier texts— with the help of simple incised lines such clay tablets could be subdivided into compartments, each of which could hold a different number. This meant that several operations could be recorded on one tablet. Obviously, what was actually being counted and the time, place, and so forth still had either to be retained in the memory or distinguished by the use of particular storage places for the tablets.

After reading this selection, consider these questions:
1. What steps were taken to make counting easier?
2. What other ways can you think of to make counting possible?
3. Where would the need for record keeping have been most urgent?

SELECTION 6:

Herding

Once men and women began farming, their gardens attracted animals. Young sheep and goats could easily be captured and kept as a handy source of meat. Keeping animals had another advantage , for sheep and goats can eat coarse grasses that humans cannot digest, thereby indirectly increasing the overall food supply. In the selection below, historian Charles Keith Maisels discusses how important the discovery of animal husbandry was for the Neolithic revolution.

Maintaining herds of wild animals may have been practiced very early on. The fact that among the bones found during excavations of the prepot-

Charles Keith Maisels, *The Emergence of Civilization* (London: Routledge, 1990), pp. 24–26.

tery Neolithic period there are cases of definite concentration as regards the sex and age of the slaughtered animals of a particular type indicates that early humans had the sort of exact control of the animals' age and sex that it is impossible for hunters to have. After these early examples of keeping herds of wild animals, it probably took a much longer time to arrive at some sort of planned breeding that aimed at more strongly reproducing characteristics of the animals useful to people.

An example is the development of the wool sheep, which differs in one important aspect from the wild sheep, namely in the type of coat. The wild sheep has a coat like a goat's, made up chiefly of long hairs, between which a light, woolly undercoat can be found. There are two different types of hair root that are responsible for this. Under normal conditions there are more roots for long hair, so that a thick coat of hair prevents the further development of the lighter covering of wool. But there is also a variant in which the relationship of the two different hair roots is reversed, enabling a thick pile of wool to develop unhindered by the hair. After a long interval, planned breeding of this variant finally produced the prototype of our present-day wool sheep.

Keeping herds of animals that will reproduce while they are in captivity requires great experience if the herd is to develop uniformly once the animals taken for human consumption have been removed, since a complex balance must be maintained between the sexes and age groups in any herd. There was also a great danger of things going wrong on another level. Apparently, the process of domestication led to animals becoming less resistant, and, to make matters worse, when they were being cared for by man in a herd, it was possible for more animals to live together in the open country than ever before. Epidemics could therefore spread much more quickly among the animals and have much more serious consequences, so that long years of work could be wiped out in a very short space of time. This must have had a critical impact on people who would have depended on animal husbandry as their only means of livelihood.

After reading this selection, consider these questions:
1. What is needed for the selective breeding of animals?
2. What is a major disadvantage of herding?
3. Why would some people prefer keeping animals to farming?

CHAPTER 2
Ancient Southwest Asia: How Did People of the First Civilization Understand Life, Death, and the Gods?

Civilization began in ancient Mesopotamia. For the first time in history, written documents rather than archaeological artifacts alone can be used to reconstruct the past. From about 3400 B.C., when cuneiform tablets first appeared, to the death of Alexander the Great in 323 B.C., Southwest Asia was almost always at the center of world history.

There are many reasons to explain this. First, it was here that the domestication of plants and animals allowed food surpluses to grow large enough to support increased populations. Men and women formed not only agricultural villages but also cities in the Tigris-Euphrates valley, wherever the soil was well watered either by natural springs or where there was ready access to the rivers once levies were cut into their banks. The people who inhabited these cities followed such specialized occupations as metalwork, weaving, carpentry, and performing religious rites. Kings with great powers appeared, financed public works, and with their civil servants and armies created a monarchical political system that produced the first law codes. Much attention went to irrigation projects, for access to water for farming was a matter of life and death.

Writers in ancient Mesopotamia wrote down the oral traditions of their people so that they should not be lost to memory. This literature encouraged men and women to think about the origins of humans and the purpose of life. As you read the selections that follow, try to imagine yourself back in the world of Mesopotamia during the third and second millennia B.C. and try to block out all that we, five thousand years later, have learned from modern science. What hopes and fears would you have had as an ancient Mesopotamian? How would your thinking be different from that of an intelligent person today? Do you think that ancient Mesopotamians were too pessimistic? What hope did their religion hold out?

SELECTION 1:

Thinking in the Ancient World

In the following selection, Henri Frankfort, a pioneering archaeologist who taught in both the United States and Great Britain during the mid–twentieth century, explains how ancient people viewed the world around them.

It is likely that the ancients recognized certain intellectual problems and asked for the "why" and "how," the "where from" and "where to." Even so, we cannot expect in the ancient Near Eastern documents to find speculation in the predominantly intellectual form with which we are familiar and which presupposes strictly logical procedure even while attempting to transcend it. We have seen that in the ancient Near East, as in present-day primitive society, thought does not operate autonomously. The whole man confronts a living "Thou" in nature; and the whole man—emotional and imaginative as well as intellectual—gives expression to the experience. All experience of "Thou" is highly individual; and early man does, in fact, view happenings as individual events. An account of such events and also their explanation can be conceived only as action and necessarily take the form of a story. In other words, the ancients told myths instead of presenting an analysis or conclusions. We would explain, for instance, that certain atmospheric changes broke a drought and brought about rain. The Babylonians observed the same facts but experienced them as the intervention of the gigantic bird Imdugud which came to their rescue. It covered the sky with the black storm clouds of its wings and devoured the Bull of Heaven, whose hot breath had scorched the crops.

In telling such a myth, the ancients did not intend to provide entertainment. Neither did they

seek, in a detached way and without ulterior motives, for intelligible explanations of the natural phenomena. They were recounting events in which they were involved to the extent of their very existence. They experienced, directly, a conflict of powers, one hostile to the harvest upon which they depended, the other frightening but beneficial: the thunderstorm reprieved them in the nick of time by defeating and utterly destroying the drought.

The images had already become traditional at the time when we meet them in art and literature, but originally they must have been seen in the revelation which the experience entailed. They are products of imagination, but they are not mere fantasy. It is essential that true myth be distinguished from legend, saga, fable, and fairy tale. All these may retain elements of the myth. And it may also happen that a baroque or frivolous imagination elaborates myths until they become mere stories. But true myth presents its images and its imaginary actors, not with the playfulness of fantasy, but with a compelling authority. It perpetuates the revelation of a "Thou."

The imagery of myth is therefore by no means allegory. It is nothing less than a carefully chosen cloak for abstract thought. The imagery is inseparable from the thought. It represents the form in which the experience has become conscious. . . .

Our view of causality, then, would not satisfy primitive man, because of the impersonal character of its explanations. It would not satisfy him, moreover, because of its generality. We understand phenomena, not by what makes them peculiar, but by what makes them manifestations of

H. Frankfort et al., *Before Philosophy* (Baltimore: Penguin Books, 1951), pp. 14–15, 24–25.

general laws. But a general law cannot do justice to the individual character of each event. And the individual character of the event is precisely what early man experiences most strongly. We may explain that certain physiological processes cause a man's death. Primitive man asks: Why should *this* man die *thus* at *this* moment? We can only say that, given these conditions, death will always occur. He wants to find a cause as specific and individual as the event which it must explain. The event is not analysed intellectually; it is experienced in its complexity and individuality, and these are matched by equally individual causes. Death is *willed*. The question, then, turns once more from the "why" to the "who," not to the "how."

This explanation of death as willed differs from that given a moment ago, when it was viewed as almost substantialized and especially created. We meet here for the first time in these chapters a curious multiplicity of approaches to problems which is characteristic for the mythopoeic mind. In the Gilgamesh Epic death was specific and concrete; it was allotted to mankind.

Its antidote, eternal life, was equally substantial; it could be assimilated by means of the plant of life. Now we have found the view that death is caused by volition. The two interpretations are not mutually exclusive, but they are nevertheless not so consistent with each other as we would desire. Primitive man, however, would not consider our objections valid. Since he does not isolate an event from its attending circumstances, he does not look for one single explanation which must hold good under all conditions.

After reading this selection, consider these questions:

1. What are the differences in thinking between the ancient and modern worlds?
2. Why was storytelling or myth making important to people in ancient times?
3. Why does the author argue that imagery was a reality for ancient men and women? Why were generalities avoided?

SELECTION 2:

The Mesopotamian Myth of Creation

*O*ne of the earliest attempts to tell how the world began is written on a Mesopotamian clay tablet called the Enuma Elish *(a translation of its opening words: "When above . . ."). In the form in which we now possess it, the* Enuma Elish *dates from between 1550 and 1150 B.C., but the ideas that it expresses are much older. Describing how the gods and the earth originally arose out of a watery chaos before the beginning of time, the* Enuma Elish *was publicly chanted at the beginning of each year by Mesopotamian priests. Two of the earliest myths in world literature, contained in the* Enuma Elish, *tell how the original gods were created out of the mingling of freshwater (*apsu), *saltwater, and clouds.*

When above the heaven had not (yet) been
  named,
(And) below the earth had not (yet) been
  called by a name;
(When) Apsû primeval, their begetter,
Mummu, (and) Ti'âmat, she who gave birth
  to them all,
(Still) mingled their waters together,
And no pasture land had been formed (and)
  not (even) a reed marsh was to be seen;
When none of the (other) gods had been
  brought into being,
(When) they had not (yet) been called by
  (their) name(s, and their) destinies had not
  (yet) been fixed,
(At that time) were the gods created within
  them.
[And a related myth goes on to explain:]
  A holy house, a house of the gods in a holy
  place, had not been made;
  A reed had not come forth, a tree had not
  been created;
  A brick had not been laid, a brick mold had
  not been built;

A house had not been made, a city had not
  been built;
A city had not been made, a living creature
  had not been placed (therein);
Nippur had not been made, Ekur had not
  been built;
Uruk had not been made, Eanna had not been
  built;
The *Apsû* had not been made, Eridu had not
  been built;
A holy house, a house of the gods, its
  dwelling, had not been made;
All the lands were sea;
The spring which is in the sea was a water
  pipe;
Then Eridu was made, Esagila (temple) was
  built.

After reading this selection, consider these
questions:
  1. What did the *Enuma Elish* consider
     essential before creation could begin?
  2. What can you learn about
     Mesopotamian architecture from these
     poems?
  3. Why was naming things a part of the
     creative process?

Alexander Heidel, *The Babylonian Genesis: The Story of Creation*,
2nd ed. (Chicago: University of Chicago Press, 1963), pp. 18, 62.

SELECTION 3:

The Epic of Gilgamesh

T*he epic of Gilgamesh, discussed by Frankfort in selection 1, examines
human mortality in one of the most popular myths of ancient Mesopotamia. The tale, possibly Sumerian or Akkadian in origin, was translated into several other languages of the ancient world: Hittite, Hurrian, and
Babylonian. The written composition dates from between 2000 and 1000
B.C., but its oral form is centuries older.*

  *Gilgamesh, a Mesopotamian king (who really did exist in the third mil-
lennium B.C.), had in the epic a wonderful friend whose death caused him
much grief. For this reason he set off to find the source of immortality from
Utnapishtim, the survivor of the flood that once destroyed much of human
life. The following selection tells of the failure of Gilgamesh to reach his*

goal and of his carelessness, which allowed the serpent to become immortal rather than humans. Utnapishtim narrates.

"Gilgamesh, I shall reveal a secret thing, it is a mystery of the gods that I am telling you. There is a plant that grows under the water, it has a prickle like a thorn, like a rose; it will wound your hands, but if you succeed in taking it, then your hands will hold that which restores his lost youth to a man."

When Gilgamesh heard this he opened the sluices [obstructions to stop the flow of water] so that a sweet-water current might carry him out to the deepest channel; he tied heavy stones to his feet and they dragged him down to the water-bed. There he saw the plant growing; although it pricked him he took it in his hands; then he cut the heavy stones from his feet, and the sea carried him and threw him on to the shore. Gilgamesh said to Urshanabi the ferryman, "Come here, and see this marvelous plant. By its virtue a man may win back all his former strength. I will take it to Uruk of the strong walls; there I will give it to the old men to eat. Its name shall be *The Old Men Are Young Again;* and at last I shall eat it myself and have back all my lost youth." So Gilgamesh returned by the gate through which he had come, Gilgamesh

and Urshanabi went together. They traveled their twenty leagues and then they broke their fast; after thirty leagues they stopped for the night.

Gilgamesh saw a well of cool water and he went down and bathed; but deep in the pool there was lying a serpent, and the serpent sensed the sweetness of the flower. It rose out of the water and snatched it away, and immediately it sloughed its skin and returned to the well. Then Gilgamesh sat down and wept, the tears ran down his face, and he took the hand of Urshanabi; "O Urshanabi, was it for this that I toiled with my hands, is it for this I have wrung out my heart's blood? For myself I have gained nothing; not I, but the beast of the earth has joy of it now. Already the stream has carried it twenty leagues back to the channels where I found it. I found a sign and now I have lost it. Let us leave the boat on the bank and go."

After reading this selection, consider these questions:

1. Where did Gilgamesh go in search of the plant that would give immortality?
2. Why did Gilgamesh want to bring back the plant to Uruk?
3. Does Gilgamesh seem angry or resigned about the loss of the plant? Why might ancient people attribute immortality to the serpent?

N.K. Sandars, ed., *The Epic of Gilgamesh* (London: Penguin Books, 1971), pp. 116–17.

SELECTION 4:

Creation in the Book of Genesis

The beginnings of humanity were of great interest to people in the ancient world. Both Mesopotamians and Egyptians had creation stories, but none can match the account portrayed in the Hebrew Scriptures, telling of

Adam and Eve. Probably written down in the eighth century B.C., the Adam and Even story was part of earlier oral traditions. There are two creation accounts in the Bible's first book, Genesis. The first account portrays God effortlessly making the world in six days, then resting on the seventh. The author calls God Yahweh, so Scripture scholars call this the Yahwist version. The second author, known as the Elohist because he uses the name "Lord God" (Elohim) for the Creator, tells of Adam (in Hebrew the word for man) and Eve (life) as well as explains how evil came into the world.

When the Lord God made earth and heaven, there was neither shrub nor plant growing wild upon the earth, because the Lord God had sent no rain on the earth; nor was there any man to till the ground. A flood used to rise out of the earth and water all the surface of the ground. Then the Lord God formed a man from the dust of the ground and breathed into his nostrils the breath of life. Thus the man became a living creature. Then the Lord God planted a garden in Eden away to the east, and there he put the man whom he had formed. The Lord God made trees spring from the ground, all trees pleasant to look at and good for food; and in the middle of the garden he set the tree of life and the tree of the knowledge of good and evil.

There was a river flowing from Eden to water the garden, and when it left the garden it branched into four streams. The name of the first is Pishon; that is the river which encircles all the land of Havilah, where the gold is. The gold of that land is good; bdellium and cornelians are also to be found there. The name of the second river is Gihon; this is the one which encircles all the land of Cush. The name of the third is Tigris; this is the river which runs east of Asshur. The fourth river is the Euphrates.

The Lord God took the man and put him in the garden of Eden to till it and care for it. He told the man, "You may eat from every tree in the garden, but not from the tree of the knowledge of good and evil; for on the day that you eat from it, you will certainly die." Then the Lord God said, "It is not good for the man to be alone. I will provide a partner for him." So God formed out of the ground all the wild animals and all the birds of heaven. He brought them to the man to see what he would call them, and whatever the man called each living creature, that was its name. Thus the man gave names to all cattle, to the birds of heaven, and to every wild animal; but for the man himself no partner had yet been found. And so the Lord God put the man into a trance, and while he slept, he took one of his ribs and closed the flesh over the place. The Lord God then built up the rib, which he had taken out of the man, into a woman. He brought her to the man, and the man said:

> Now this, at last—
> bone from my bones,
> flesh from my flesh!—
> this shall be called woman,
> for from man was this taken.

That is why a man leaves his father and mother and is united to his wife, and the two become one flesh. Now they were both naked, the man and his wife, but they had no feeling of shame towards one another.

The serpent was more crafty than any wild creature that the Lord God had made. He said to the woman, "Is it true that God has forbidden you to eat from any tree in the garden?" The woman answered the serpent, "We may eat the fruit of any tree in the garden, except for the tree in the middle of the garden; God has forbidden us either to eat or to touch the fruit of that; if we do, we shall die." The serpent said, "Of course you will not die. God knows that as soon as you eat it, your eyes will be opened and you will be like gods knowing both good and evil." When the woman saw that the fruit of the tree was good to eat, and that it was pleasing to the eye and tempting to

Genesis 2:5–3:7, The New English Bible with the Apocrypha (Oxford and Cambridge: University Press, 1970), pp. 2–4.

contemplate, she took some and ate it. She also gave her husband some and he ate it. Then the eyes of both of them were opened and they discovered that they were naked; so they stitched fig-leaves together and made themselves loincloths.

After reading this selection, consider these questions:

1. What does the Elohist creation account have in common with those of Mesopotamia? What is unique?
2. Why would Adam and Eve desire the knowledge of good and evil?
3. How does the role of the woman figure in this creation account?

SELECTION 5:

A Modern Commentary on Genesis

A *modern author, Jack Miles, describes his understanding of this portrait of human origins in the Book of Genesis:*

The second account of creation—which, in a continuous reading, is, of course, the sequel rather than an alternative to the first account—shows a narrowing of the focus and a heightening of the tension between creator and human creature. Mankind is no longer situated on "the earth" as a gigantic natural paradise in which to be fertile and increase but only in "a garden in Eden, in the east," which God has planted and given to "the man" to till and tend. And the free mastery that mankind was to exercise as God's image is also restricted: "Of every tree of the garden you are free to eat; but as for the tree of knowledge of good and bad, you must not eat of it; for as soon as you eat of it, you shall die."

In the first account of creation, something is commanded but nothing is forbidden. Now, for the first time, there is a prohibition. It seems to be imposed in man's interest, but we wonder: If the man is to master the earth (recalling the first account of creation), why may he not be allowed the knowledge of good and evil? The man is of-

fered no motive for his obedience other than one that makes no sense. And the Lord God in this second creation story seems noticeably more anxious in confrontation with his creature than God seemed in the first.

The air of anxiety grows more acute when the Lord God creates woman. In context, this second account of that event reads like the story of what really happened on the sixth day, an explanation of why God, in the first account, did not "see that they were good." The Lord God, unlike God, does not see the man as good even by inclusion. No, something is wrong with the man, and of the flaw the Lord God can only say: "It is not good for man to be alone; I will make a fitting helper for him." But all the Lord God's efforts to come up with an adequate helper fail. He brings to the man "all the wild beasts and all the birds of the sky," an extraordinary parade, and allows the man the power-laden privilege of naming them, but "no fitting helper [is] found." By clear implication, the man rejects the whole of God's labors in creating other living creatures: They may be "good," but they are not good for him. The Lord

Jack Miles, *God: A Biography* (New York: Knopf, 1995), pp. 30–32.

God, now genuinely laboring, driven to an extreme expedient, creates a woman from one of the man's ribs.

The man, in the first words in the Bible spoken by a human being, acclaims her with joy but without expressing any gratitude or otherwise acknowledging the Lord God. . . .

In the first account of creation, the male and the female also say nothing in response to the God who has created them, but for his part God seems to expect nothing. His only expectation is that they should be, fruitfully, themselves, subduing the earth and serving, thereby, as his image. The first creation story thus contains no story whatsoever of human transgression.

How very different the expanded second account. . . .

When the serpent tells the woman that, contrary to what the Lord God said, she will not die if she eats of the tree of the knowledge of good and evil, the serpent is telling the truth. She and the man do not die when they break the Lord God's command; certainly, they do not die, as the Lord God had warned, "as soon as you eat of it." Is the serpent's ability to foil the Lord God's plan a reflection of the Lord God's power? Is the serpent his rival? Or is the entire temptation episode, as we might put it, a setup? Is the serpent the Lord God's secret or unwitting agent?

One may escape all these difficulties and preserve the serpent's role as a deceiver by arguing that the couple did indeed die at once but that theirs was a spiritual rather than a physical death. This is the classic theological interpretation of "the fall of man," the "original sin." However, as we shall see again and again, the narrative we are reading is not much given to spiritualized or purely symbolic meanings but is extremely fond of deception stories of all kinds. Rather than eliminate the conflict by spiritualizing the threatened death or rationalizing the apparent deceit, we may trace the conflict back to the Lord God, a cause of both weal and woe in the lives of his creatures because good and evil impulses conflict within his character.

After reading this selection, consider these questions:

1. Why does tension enter into the Elohist creation account?
2. How does Miles understand the role of the serpent?
3. What justification might there be for considering the Elohist creation story the basis for the Christian belief in original sin?

SELECTION 6:

Laws from Hammurabi's Code

*O*nce the city-states of Mesopotamia took shape in the third millennium B.C., a political organization followed. At first it appears that a city assembly held power, but as constant conflicts over land and water rights became the norm, so too did the emergence of a single ruler, probably the commander of the army. Among his other tasks was the need to settle disputes and prescribe laws for the good order of the state. Because society was now more stratified and private property more common, the law required more detail.

One of the oldest codes, and surely the most famous, is that composed by Hammurabi, a Babylonian ruler of the 1700s B.C. The code was writ-

ten on a large black stele, or monument, now kept in the Louvre in Paris, France. Its second law specified a trial by water, thought to be a pure substance; an accused who floated (i.e., was rejected) when thrown into the water was presumed guilty. This form of water trial lasted until A.D. 1700 in European society. The original English translation of this text uses the word seignior, *a person in the upper or middle class, which is translated as* person *in the document below.*

1. If a [person] accuses a(nother) [person] and brings a charge of murder against him, but has not proved it, his accuser shall be put to death.

2. If a [person] brings a charge of sorcery against a(nother) [person], but has not proved it, the one against whom the charge of sorcery was brought, upon going to the river, shall throw himself into the river, and if the river has then overpowered him, his accuser shall take over his estate. If the river has shown that [person] to be innocent and he has accordingly come forth safe, the one who brought the charge of sorcery against him shall be put to death, while the one who threw himself into the river shall take over the estate of his accuser.

3. If a [person] comes forward with false testimony in a case, and has not proved the word which he spoke, if that case was a case involving life, that [person] shall be put to death.

4. If he came forward with (false) testimony concerning grain or money, he shall bear the penalty of that case.

5. If a judge gave a judgment, rendered a decision, deposited a sealed document, but later has altered his judgment, and others shall prove that that judge altered the judgment which he gave, then he shall pay twelvefold the claim which holds in that case. Furthermore, they shall expel him in the assembly from his seat of judgment and he shall never again sit with the judges in a case.

6. If a [person] steals the property of the temple or state, that [person] shall be put to death; also the one who received the stolen goods from his hand shall be put to death.

7. If a [person] has purchased or he received for safekeeping either silver or gold or a male slave or a female slave or an ox or a sheep or an ass or any sort of thing from the hand of another [person's] son or slave without witnesses and contracts, since that [person] is a thief, he shall be put to death.

8. If a [person] steals either an ox or a sheep or an ass or a pig or a boat, if it belonged to the temple (or) if it belonged to the state, he shall make thirtyfold restitution. If it belonged to a private citizen, he shall make good tenfold. If the thief does not have sufficient to make restitution, he shall be put to death. . . .

14. If a [person] has stolen the young son of a(nother) [person], he shall be put to death.

15. If a [person] has helped either a male slave of the state or a female slave of the state or a male slave of a private citizen or a female slave of a private citizen to escape through the city-gate, he shall be put to death. . . .

20. If the slave has escaped from the hand of his captor, that [person] shall (so) affirm by god to the owner of the slave and he shall then go free.

21. If a [person] has made a breach in a house, they shall put him to death in front of that breach and wall him in.

22. If a [person] committed robbery and has been caught, that [person] shall be put to death. . . .

128. If a [person] acquired a wife, but did not draw up the contracts for her, that woman is no wife.

129. If the wife of a [person] has been caught while lying with another man, they shall bind them and throw them into the water. If the husband of the woman wishes to spare his wife, then the king in turn may spare his subject.

Theophile J. Meek, "The Code of Hammurabi," in James B. Pritchard, ed., *Ancient Near Eastern Texts Relating to the Old Testament* (Princeton: Princeton University Press, 1955), vol. 1, pp. 166–167, 171.

After reading this selection, consider these questions:

1. Do you think these penalties are too severe? Can you explain why they are severe?
2. Which law do you think is most just?

Which do you think is most unfair?
3. How does crime and punishment in the modern world differ from ancient Mesopotamian practice?

CHAPTER 3
Egypt: How Did the Pharaohs Rule?

Chronologically, Egypt was the second of the world's great civilizations. More than five thousand years ago, the people who lived along the Nile were able, through much hard work, to clear the brush and drain the marshes along the riverbanks. The effort was worthwhile, for underneath the reeds and water lay extremely fertile black soil, washed down from the hills of eastern Africa. Moreover, the annual flood of the Nile deposited almost an inch of new topsoil on the fields near the river.

Villages appeared, then small towns, but never large cities. An entire range of social classes evolved; over time the larger and stronger village chiefs absorbed their neighbors' lands. Eventually, around 3200 B.C., there were only two rulers, one governing Upper Egypt (south of the Delta as far as the first cataract at Aswan) and one governing Lower Egypt (the Delta region). Even two proved to be too many; ultimately one dominated, under the title of pharaoh, which translates as "great house."

Over the decades the pharaoh became a divine figure, a god sent to rule the land of Egypt. Horus, the falcon god, had bestowed on him all power on earth. Without the ceremonies that he performed, Egyptians were sure that the world they knew would collapse in chaos.

How did the pharaohs rule, and why did the Egyptians accept their authority?

SELECTION 1:

The Life of a Pharaoh

The following selection, by a modern scholar, describes the pharaoh's surprisingly strenuous daily life.

The childhood of Pharaoh was happy and carefree. The ancient Egyptians loved children and allowed them great latitude. As a small boy the crown prince ran about naked in the sunshine with his small brothers and sisters, like the offspring of the humblest peasant. The child sported pretty ornaments and his head was shaven except for a single long side lock or Horus lock. As soon as he was old enough he was put in charge of a tutor, whose business it was to teach him reading, writing and the elements of arithmetic, architecture, astronomy and other arts and sciences with which he would later need a measure of acquaintance. Lessons were long and thorough.

Once the years of childhood were behind him the boy became rapidly aware of the onerous duties awaiting him when he grew up. During his adolescence he served an apprenticeship as an army officer, in company with the sons of noblemen and young foreign princes sent to Egypt to be educated. Under the Middle and New Kingdoms he took part in his father's campaigns or undertook campaigns of his own. He made frequent hunting expeditions, for male royalty set great store by regular massacres of animals and game. Forays were made into the desert to track down the rarer sorts of beast, which were dispatched with spear or bow, on foot or from a chariot. Regular military tournaments were held at which royal princes were expected to display exceptional skill with weapons and as charioteers.

The future Pharaoh was married in childhood to the most suitable of his small sisters, half-

sisters or cousins. When he was a man he was permitted to take as many additional wives and mistresses as he desired, but it was essential that his immediate heir should possess the strongest possible strain of royal blood. The spiritual potency of the king, on which the well-being of his subjects depended, was enhanced by the purity of his breeding. Theoretically the actual blood of the sun god had been transmitted by Horus into the royal veins. The priesthood took this conception very seriously. It frowned upon any watering down of the divine ichor in the Pharaonic bloodvessels by marriages outside the royal family. To safeguard the purity of the succession it was advisable that the king should procreate as many children as possible within what is called the forbidden degree. To this end he not infrequently married his own daughters. . . .

His word was literally law. Justice was defined as "what Pharaoh loves," wrongdoing as "what Pharaoh hates." The king's slightest word was oracular, his most trivial pronouncement was *ex cathedra* [had the force of law]. His rôle as secular ruler was inseparably combined with his rôle as god. He kept his people in good order by means of divine utterance: his statements were statutes in themselves. In theory he directed every phase of secular and religious activity. He was at the same time high priest and chief justice. Whoever acted as priest or official throughout the land acted as his deputy. The Pharaohs were as a general rule very hard workers, and in the world of Oriental plot and counterplot in which they lived a sense of affairs came easily to them.

Although he was held to be "the divine man," in contrast to "the mortal man" or vizier, the king usually contrived to transact a vast amount of

J.E. Manchip White, *Ancient Egypt* (New York: Thomas Y. Crowell Company, 1970), pp. 14–17.

mortal business in a lifetime largely employed in elaborate ceremonial. Kings of weak character sometimes became complete prisoners of ceremonial, and indeed many of them appear to have succumbed to it. To survive the number of religious services the king was required to celebrate in the course of a single day called for a stout frame and a buoyant spirit.

It was the actual performance by the king of the daily liturgy that rendered efficacious the liturgies celebrated elsewhere in Egypt. In his legal capacity, the king was supposed to be accessible to all his subjects. He constituted a final court of appeal. The privilege of appeal to Pharaoh indicates his supremacy in the field of law, although it is doubtful whether many persons were possessed of sufficient temerity to bring their cases to his notice. Pharaoh remained a remote personage even in the comradely circumstances of a foreign campaign. The contemplation of this lonely and magnificent figure, burdened by the weight of his divine destiny, filled his subjects with dread. Approach to him was difficult. Perhaps no monarch in world history was so hemmed in by "the divinity that doth hedge a king." As crown prince he doubtless contrived to lead a reasonably entertaining existence, but once his brows were encircled by the sacred diadems, once he became a Horus upon his coronation day, he was a being dedicated and apart.

After reading this selection, consider these questions:

1. Why was it important for the pharaoh to marry his relatives?
2. What role did ceremony play in the life of the pharaoh? Why?
3. What made the life of the pharaoh a lonely one?

SELECTION 2:

Thutmose III's Hymn of Victory

Invariably, pharaohs were the victors in the many inscriptions left in Egypt's temples. Along with a hieroglyphic narrative, a carving depicting the pharaoh defeating his enemies gave the illiterate a visual image of their ruler's greatness as commander of the army.

Thutmose III, who reigned from about 1490 to 1436 B.C., earned a reputation as an empire builder, extending Egypt's borders to include Palestine and Syria all the way to the Euphrates River. At Karnak, near ancient Thebes, he ordered the following hymn carved on the walls as a testament to his exploits. The setting of the hymn is the pharaoh's approach to the temple of Amon-Re, the patron deity of Thebes. The image of Amon-Re is brought before Thutmose, who then greets the god, adores his image, and tells the god how his fame has been enhanced, thanks to Thutmose's victories. Menkheperre was the pharaoh's official name.

J.H. Breasted, ed., *Ancient Records of Egypt,* 5 vols. (New York: Russell & Russell, 1906), vol. 2, pp. 263–64.

Utterance of Amon-Re, lord of Thebes:
Thou comest to me, thou exultest, seeing my beauty,

O my son, my avenger, Menkheperre, living forever.
I shine for love of you,
My heart is glad at your beautiful coming into my temple;
[My] two hands furnish your limbs with protection and life.
How pleasing is your pleasantness toward my body.
I have established you in my dwelling,
I have worked a marvel for you;
I have given to you might and victory against all countries,
I have set your fame, [even] the fear of you, in all lands.
Your terror as far as the four pillars of heaven;
I have magnified the dread of you in all bodies,
I have put the roaring of your majesty among the Nine Bows.
The chiefs of all countries are gathered in your grasp,
I myself have stretched out my two hands,
I have bound them for you.
I have bound together the Nubian Troglodytes by tens of thousands and thousands,
The Northerners by hundreds of thousands as captives.
I have felled your enemies beneath your sandals,
You have smitten the hordes of rebels according as I commanded you.
The earth in its length and breadth, Westerners and Easterners are subject to you,
You trample all countries, your heart glad;
None presents himself before your majesty,
While I am your leader, so that you may reach them.
You have crossed the water of the Great Bend of Naharin with victory, with might.

I have decreed for you that they hear your roarings and enter into caves;
I have deprived their nostrils of the breath of life.
I have set the terrors of your majesty in their hearts,
My serpent-diadem upon your brow, it consumes them,
It makes captive by the hair the Kode-folk,
It devours those who are in their marshes with its flame.

Cut down are the heads of the Asiatics, there is not a remnant of them;
Fallen are the children of their mighty ones.
I have caused your victories to circulate among all lands,
My serpent-diadem gives light to your dominion.
There is no rebel of yours as far as the circuit of heaven;
They come, bearing tribute upon their backs,
Bowing down to your majesty according to my command.
I have made powerless the invaders who came before you;
Their hearts burned, their limbs trembling.
I have come, causing you to smite the princes of Zahi;
I have hurled them beneath your feet among their highlands.
I have caused them to see your majesty as lord of radiance,
So that you have shone in their faces like my image.
I have come, causing you to smite the Asiatics,
You have made captive the heads of the Asiatics of Retenu.
I have caused them to see your majesty equipped with your adornment,
When you take the weapons of war in the chariot.
I have come, causing you to smite the eastern land,
You have trampled those who are in the districts of God's-Land.
I have caused them to see your majesty like a circling star,
When it scatters its flame in fire, and gives forth its dew.

After reading this selection, consider these questions:
1. What do you suppose compelled the pharaoh to boast of his victories?
2. Why does the pharaoh identify his victories with those of the god?
3. From studying this hymn, how would you characterize the style of pharaonic speech?

SELECTION 3:
The Great Pyramid

There is hardly anyone who, when thinking of Egypt, does not recall the pyramids. The great age of pyramid building occurred during the Old Kingdom, the first period of recorded Egyptian history, and the most impressive pyramids, those of Giza, date from about 2680 to 2350 B.C. To this day they remain the largest stone structures ever built on the earth. In the selection below, John A. Wilson, a leading American authority on ancient Egypt, explains how they were built.

In particular, the Great Pyramid, near the beginning of the Fourth Dynasty, is a tremendous mass of stone finished with the most delicate precision. Here were six and a quarter million tons of stone, with casing blocks averaging as much as two and a half tons each; yet those casing blocks were dressed and fitted with a joint of one-fiftieth of an inch—a scrupulous nicety worthy of the jeweler's craft. Here the margin of error in the squareness of the north and south sides was 0.09 per cent and of the east and west sides, 0.03 per cent. This mighty mass of stone was set upon a dressed-rock pavement which, from opposite corners, had a deviation from a true plane of only 0.004 per cent. The craftsman's conscience could not humanly have done better. Such cold statistics reveal to us an almost superhuman fidelity and devotion to the physical task at hand. Certainly, such exactness and conscientiousness were not characteristics of Egyptian builders in later times, who were frequently guilty of hasty, showy, but insecure construction.

The earliest dynasties constituted ancient Egypt's trial of strength and were the one period in which her physical achievements were marked by the greatest honesty and care. The several pyramids of the Third and Fourth Dynasties far surpass later pyramids in technical craftsman-

ship. Viewed as the supreme efforts of the state, they show that earliest historical Egypt was once capable of scrupulous intellectual honesty. For a short time she was activated by what we call the "scientific spirit," experimental and conscientious. After she had thus discovered her powers and the forms which suited her, the spirit was limited to conservative repetition, subject to change only within known and tested forms.

We of the age which glorifies progress to ever better forms and conditions may deplore such a slackening of spirit. But we must understand the ancient mythmaking mind, which sought security in arresting time by clinging to the divinely set origins and thus ignoring the future and which did not inquire too closely into the unknown because that belonged to gods rather than men. In that setting we should give all credit to Egypt's earliest achievements and to her success in working out forms which lasted for long centuries. After all, stability was what she desired, and she effected a culture which gave her satisfaction for some fifteen hundred years. . . .

A significant factor in the building of the pyramids was the lack of any such machines as we should consider essential for the movement of huge masses of stone. The missing element was the wheel, in a vehicle for the delivery of stone, in a pulley, or in a crane. Without wheeled carriages, pulleys, or cranes, how could they deliver heavy blocks into precise place at high elevations? They used sloping ramps of brick and

John A. Wilson, *The Culture of Ancient Egypt* (Chicago: University of Chicago Press, 1951), pp. 54–55, 70–71.

earth, ramps which could later be destroyed. For the maneuvering of blocks, they had ropes, sledges, levers, and cradles, and they used a mortar of sand and gypsum as a lubricating medium, a slippery surface for the sliding of blocks into precise place. They enjoyed all the manpower which could be employed within any one space for any one operation. Above all, they took the needed time to do each little job with their "primitive" means: the calculation of a particular operation, the cutting and rebuilding of the ramp to deliver a five- or ten-ton block exactly, and the delicate measuring and cutting of stone for the most refined fitting. We moderns could duplicate their result with their methods, if we thought it worth while to use such limited resources and if we had the patience to undertake the task in terms of a lifetime.

The ancient engineer faced other unprecedented problems of stress. The pyramid form was ideal in overcoming some of the difficulties of great weight, built up to 480 feet and thus crushing downward with brutal mass. Burial chambers within a pyramid were successfully protected against the downward thrust of the mountain of stone. There was also consolidation inside the pyramid by "accretion faces," that is, solid retaining walls constructed in the form of a stepped pyramid and holding different segments of the structure in place.

Calculations were made in units of measurement originally of the simplest nature but formalized by this time into officially accepted standards, the royal cubit or forearm of 20.6 inches, subdividing into 7 palms or 28 fingers. In the Great Pyramid this unit provides us with good round numbers for major elements: 280 cubits for the height, 440 for a side of the base, 90 for the longest inner passage, and a burial chamber of $20 \times 10 \times 11$. What has been said about construction methods applies also to the mathematics with which the engineers made their calculations. There were two awkward factors. They added and subtracted as we do, but their multiplication and division used a process of doubling and doubling again as long as necessary, and then adding those pairs of numbers which came closest to the required factors.

After reading this selection, consider these questions:
1. Why were the architects of the pyramids so precise in their construction?
2. What skills were demonstrated by the pyramid builders?
3. What effect would the building of the pyramids have on the Egyptian population?

SELECTION 4:

A Father Advises His Son

*T*he pharaoh required a large corps of civil servants to run the country. Scribes were as important to the machinery of government as computers are in today's world. Any man employed in this position hoped his son would succeed him, for the many advantages of this occupation over most other employment were obvious.

In this text from the Middle Kingdom of Egypt, a civil servant who works as a scribe gives advice to his son as he begins his arduous training.

Beginning of the teaching
made by the man of Sile,
called Duaf's son Khety
for his son called Pepy,
while journeying south to the Residence [the
    palace school]
to place him in the scribal school,
in the midst of the children of the officials and
    the foremost of the Residence. . . .

"As for a scribe in any position in the Residence
he shall not be wretched in it."

He fills another's need; shall he not end up
    content?
I cannot see another trade like it,
of which those verses could be said.
I shall make you love writing more than your
    mother;
I shall present its beauties to you.
Now, it is greater than any trade.
There is not its like in the land.
When he was a child, he began to flourish;
he will be consulted, will be sent to do missions,
when he is not yet arrived at (the age to) wear a
    kilt.

I cannot see a sculptor on a mission,
nor a goldsmith being sent.
I have seen the metal-worker at his labour
at the mouth of his furnace,
his fingers like the stuff of a crocodile;
he stinks more than fish-roe.

And the barber is (still) shaving at evening's end.
To the town he takes himself;
to his corner he takes himself;
from street to street he takes himself
to search for people to shave.
He is vigorous with his arms to fill his belly,
like a bee which can eat (only) as it has worked.

And the gardener is bringing a yoke,
each of his shoulders weighted with age,

R.B. Parkinson, *Voices from Ancient Egypt: An Anthology of Middle Kingdom Writings.* Oklahoma Series in Classical Civilization (Norman: University of Oklahoma Press, 1991), pp. 73–76.

and with a great swelling on his neck,
which is festering;
he spends the morning watering the corianders,
and his supper is by the *Shaut*-plants,
having spent the midday in the orchard.
Because of his produce, it happens that he sinks
    down dying,
more so than (with) any other trade.

And the farmer laments more than the guinea
    fowl,
his voice louder than the raven's (?),
with his fingers made swollen
and with an excessive stink.
He is weary, having been assigned to the Delta,
and then he is in rags.

And the washerman washes on the shore,
and nearby is the crocodile.
"Father, I shall leave the flowing (?) water,"
say his son and daughter,
"for a trade that one can be content in,
more so than any other trade,"
while his food is mixed with shit.
There is no part of him clean,
while he puts himself amongst the skirts of a
    woman who is in her period (?);
he weeps, spending the day at the washing
    board.
He is told: "Dirty clothes!
Bring yourself over here," and the (river)-edge
    overflows with them.

The fowl-catcher, he is very wearied, gazing at
    the birds.
If the flocks of birds pass over him, then he
    says, "If only I had a net!"
God does not let this happen to him,
so that he is wearied by his state.

I will likewise tell you of the fisherman.
He is more wearied than (a man of) any other
    trade:
he who is a labourer in the river,
a consorter with crocodiles.
Even if the total of his reckoned (catch) comes
    to him,
then he is in woe:

doesn't he (then) say, "The crocodile's waiting!",
blinded by fear?
If he comes out of the flowing (?) water,
then he's as if smitten by god's might.
Look, no trade is free from a director,
except the scribe's: the director is him.

But if you know writings, it shall be well for
    you,
more than these trades I have shown you.
Look at them, at their wretchedness: none says
    to him
"A farmer, and a man". Take heed!
Look at what I have done in coming south to the
    Residence,
look, I do it for your sake!
A day in the school-room is excellent for you;
it is for eternity, its works are (like) stone.

The workmen I have shown you hurry by,
risen early and rebellious. . . .

Thank god for your father and your mother,
who put you on the path of life.
Look at these (maxims) I have put before you
and the children of your children.

After reading this selection, consider these
questions:
1. What made the scribe so important in
   Egyptian society?
2. How did the life of a scribe bring with
   it special privileges?
3. If you lived in ancient Egypt, would
   the father's advice convince you to
   follow the scribe's vocation?

SELECTION 5:

Egyptian Women

*Historians today are paying more attention to the position of women in
past societies. In ancient Egypt, evidence suggests that women enjoyed a
more favorable position than did their counterparts in other ancient societies. This selection, a brief essay by the Egyptologist and historian Peter
A. Piccione from the University of Charleston, South Carolina, presents
some tentative conclusions based on recent reexaminations of the available evidence.*

In general, the work of the upper and middle
class woman was limited to the home and the
family. This was not due to an inferior legal status, but was probably a consequence of her customary role as mother and bearer of children, as
well as the public role of the Egyptian husbands
and sons who functioned as the executors of the

mortuary cults of their deceased parents. It was
the traditional role of the good son to bury his
parents, support their funerary cult, to bring offerings regularly to the tombs, and to recite the
offering formula. Because women are not regularly depicted doing this in Egyptian art, they
probably did not often assume this role. When a
man died without a surviving son to preserve his
name and present offerings, then it was his brother who was often depicted in the art doing so.
Perhaps because it was the males who were regularly entrusted with this important religious task,

Peter A. Piccione, "The Status of Women in Ancient Egyptian Society," 1995. On-line. Internet. Available at www.library.nwu.edu/
class/history/B94/B94women.html.

that they held the primary position in public life.

As far as occupations go, in the textual sources upper class woman are occasionally described as holding an office, and thus they might have executed real jobs. Clearly, though, this phenomenon was more prevalent in the Old Kingdom than in later periods (perhaps due to the lower population at that time). In Edward Wente's publication of Egyptian letters, he notes that of 353 letters known from Egypt, only 13 provide evidence of women functioning with varying degrees of administrative authority.

One of the most exalted administrative titles of any woman who was not a queen was held by a non-royal woman named Nebet during the Sixth Dynasty, who was entitled, "Vizier, Judge and Magistrate." She was the wife of the nomarch of Abydos and grandmother of King Pepi II. However, it is possible that the title was merely honorific and granted to her posthumously. Through the length of Egyptian history, we see many titles of women which seem to reflect real administrative authority, including one woman entitled, "Second Prophet (i.e., High Priest) of Amun" at the temple of Karnak, which was, otherwise, a male office. Women could and did hold male administrative positions in Egypt. However, such cases are few, and thus appear to be the exceptions to tradition. Given the relative scarcity of such, they might reflect extraordinary individuals in unusual circumstances.

Women functioned as leaders, e.g., kings, dowager queens and regents, even as usurpers of rightful heirs, who were either their step-sons or nephews. We find women as nobility and landed gentry managing both large and small estates, e.g., the woman Tchat who started as overseer of a nomarch's household with a son of middling status; married the nomarch; was elevated, and her son was also raised in status. Women functioned as middle class housekeepers, servants, fieldhands, and all manner of skilled workers inside the household and in estate-workshops.

Women could also be national heroines in Egypt. Extraordinary cases include Queen Ahhotep of the early Eighteenth Dynasty. She was renowned for saving Egypt during the wars of liberation against the Hyksos, and she was praised for rallying the Egyptian troops and crushing rebellion in Upper Egypt at a critical juncture of Egyptian history. In doing so, she received Egypt's highest military decoration at least three times, the Order of the Fly. Queen Hatshepsut, as a ruling king, was actually described as going on military campaign in Nubia. Eyewitness reports actually placed her on the battlefield weighing booty and receiving the homage of defeated rebels.

The position of women in Egyptian society was unique in the ancient world. The Egyptian female enjoyed much of the same legal and economic rights as the Egyptian male—within the same social class. However, how their legal freedoms related to their status as defined by custom and folk tradition is more difficult to ascertain. In general, social position in Egypt was based, not on gender, but on social rank. On the other hand, the ability to move through the social classes did exist for the Egyptians. Ideally, the same would have been true for women. However, one private letter of the New Kingdom from a husband to his wife shows us that while a man could take his wife with him, as he moved up in rank, it would not have been unusual for such a man to divorce her and take a new wife more in keeping with his new and higher social status. Still, self-made women certainly did exist in Egypt, and there are cases of women growing rich on their own resources through land speculation and the like.

After reading this selection, consider these questions:

1. Do you think that there was a connection between ancient Egypt's prosperity and women's social position there? If so, what might this connection be?

2. To what extent does the evidence suggest that it was upper-class—and not ordinary—women whose position was relatively favorable in ancient Egypt?

3. What evidence suggests that ancient Egypt was still a male-dominated society, despite the accomplishments of individual women?

SELECTION 6:

Archaeological Discoveries in Sudan

The history of sub-Saharan Africa begins in the region of the Sudan, with a kingdom known as Kush, or (an alternative name) Nubia. Like Egypt, Kush had the Nile to water its land, and because rain fell in this part of Africa, forests also existed, something unknown in Egypt.

In ancient times, therefore, Kush made very important contributions to Egyptian life. Trade between the two regions was brisk, for Nubian gold, hides, and recruits for the pharaoh's armies were much in demand. The Egyptians built forts in Nubia to control access to the Nile and were, during the New Kingdom, able to spread the Egyptian language south of Aswan. In the eighth century B.C., kings of Kush were sufficiently strong to invade Egypt and for several generations held control of the country. Unfortunately, much of the history of Kush remains unknown, for archaeologists are still uncovering the remains of these early African peoples. In the following selection, a modern archaeologist describes the excavations in the Sudan, at Napata, one of the centers of Kushite life in 663 B.C. after the Assyrians (conquerors from northern Mesopotamia) expelled the Kushites from Egypt.

Unfortunately the town of Napata has not been identified and though temples have been found on both sides of the river, there is no trace of domestic occupation. Remains of what may have been a palace and of store rooms suggest that the royal residence and the town of Napata may have been on the left bank, and that the area around Gebel Barkal on the other side of the river may have been reserved for the service of the gods. The presence of a great temple, and others discovered more recently by an Italian expedition, strongly suggests that this was so. A recent discovery, by an expedition from the Museum of Fine Arts in Boston led by Dr T. Kendall, has shown that the famous hill of Gebel Barkal, below which lies the Amun temple, had a semi-

detached pinnacle previously thought to have been a colossal statue but now known not to be. This pinnacle contains a small shrine cut into the rock which may have contained a statue of Taharqa and above it was found evidence that inscriptions with the name of Taharqa, and of King Nastasen (who lived three hundred years later), were carved in the rock and that a metal sheet, which the finder considers must have been of gold, was fixed there. Dr Kendall also suggests that the very noticeable pinnacle was regarded as a gigantic representation of the Uraeus, the cobra-head symbol of Egyptian royalty which was adopted by the rulers of Kush.

The development of a strong Egyptian influence in the culture of the Napatans is seen most clearly in the royal burial customs. Starting with a typically Nubian burial style the early rulers were buried under mounds with the bodies laid on a bed, similar to the *angareeb*, the standard

P.L. Shinnie, *Ancient Nubia* (London: Kegan Paul, 1996), pp. 100–102.

bed of the Sudan today, made of a wooden framework and a mattress of rope. The next stage was the use of mastabas to cover the burials, and then the kings were buried under pyramids which are, in their size and sharply pointed angle, certainly derived from those in use by private persons in the New Kingdom, as seen at Deir el Median at Thebes and, in Nubia, at Aniba. At these places they were not used for royal burials but for those of important non-royal personages.

The first king to be buried under a pyramid was probably Piankhy, though the destruction of the superstructure of his burial place makes it difficult to be certain that it was a pyramid and not a mastaba. A pyramid is likely and the later kings certainly seem to have been placed in tombs cut into rock under small pyramids. From this time on, at various places, all Napatan and subsequently all Meroitic royal burials were under pyramids and the bed burials of earlier times were replaced by the use of wooden coffins and in some cases of stone sarcophagi.

Other examples of Egyptian influence can be seen in the use of the Egyptian language, written in hieroglyphs, for royal inscriptions, though it is unlikely that Egyptian was the spoken tongue. Temples closely followed the patterns of Egyptian ones and were used for the worship of Egyptian gods, of whom Amun was the most important. A range of objects of Egyptian design have been found in the tombs. These may have been imported from Egypt or made locally either by groups of expatriate Egyptians or by local craftsmen trained to copy Egyptian styles. Since the earlier burials at Kurru are of Nubian style and it is only from the time of Piankhy that Egyptian ones begin to dominate, it can be supposed that it

was the close connection with Egypt arising after Piankhy's invasion that was responsible for the change. . . .

After Taharqa, the Napatan kings never set foot in Egypt, but maintained a fiction of Egyptian kingship by using the titulary of the pharaohs. Of these kings some have left details of their activities in inscriptions written in Egyptian hieroglyphs. . . .

The history of Nubia during the time of the Napatan kings is based almost entirely on a study of royal burials and temples, and there is very little other archaeological material to give a more complete picture of the life of the time. Settlements have not been found and the only place where it is possible to see some of the indigenous material of the time is in the cemetery at Sanam. Here the burials fall into three different groups: the first being that in which the bodies were mummified and Egyptian or Egyptian-style objects were placed in brick-built chamber graves; the second contained extended burials in rectangular pits with Egyptian types of pottery; the third had contracted burials and contained, along with Egyptian pottery, vessels reminiscent of those of C-Group and Kerma times [earlier pottery traditions].

After reading this selection, consider these questions:
1. What was the relation between Egypt and Kush?
2. How did the Kushite kings prepare for their burials?
3. Why was the example of Egyptian kingship so strong in Kush?

CHAPTER 4
Ancient India: How Did Aryan Conquerors Transform the Subcontinent?

The subcontinent of India produced the first civilization outside Southwest Asia and Egypt. Historians call it either the Indus Valley civilization (named for the river that provided its water) or the Harappan civilization (after its most prominent city, whose ruins are in present-day Pakistan). Exactly how this civilization arose is still uncertain, although many historians believe that the initial stimulus was the arrival of traders from Mesopotamia. We do not even know what these ancient Indians called themselves, or what language they spoke, for their writing, carved on seals, has not yet been deciphered.

Growing out of villages that date back to the third millennium B.C., the Indus Valley (or Harappan) civilization flourished for almost a thousand years, between about 2500 and 1500 B.C., until India was invaded by tribes speaking an Indo-European language or languages. (Indo-European is the language group to which most of the languages of modern Europe, the Caucasus, Iran, Afghanistan, and much of northern India and Pakistan belong.) These invaders were the Aryans. Their migration out of their original homeland, between the Black Sea and the Caspian Sea in present-day southern Russia, was a widespread dispersal over most of Europe, Iran, and India. In India, the Aryan conquerors possibly destroyed the Indus Valley civilization and imposed certain cultural values, including the caste system, that have been basic to the Indian way of life ever since. As you read this chapter, ask yourself what evidence remains of the early Aryans' impact on Indian society and culture.

Despite flourishing for almost a thousand years, Harappa was in decline during the centuries before the Aryans overwhelmed it, for reasons unclear. Climate change may have been involved, causing deforestation, drought, and floods. When the Aryans charged into India from Iran, they reduced Harappa and the other Indus Valley cities to rubble.

SELECTION 1:

India's First Civilization

This selection, written by a modern archaeologist, takes us back to the ancient city of Harappa before the Aryan invasions. In several ways the Indus Valley civilization was unique. It extended over the largest area of all the very ancient civilizations: More than 150 widely dispersed sites of villages and towns have been identified. The Indus Valley people were great traders, sailing more than 800 miles down the Indus River and across the Persian Gulf to reach Mesopotamia. Its political chiefs were the first to plan cities, and its architects invented indoor plumbing. Its religious beliefs, after undergoing many later transformations, probably helped forge Hinduism, the dominant religion of modern India.

Based on the most recent work at the site, we know that the first settlers at Harappa established a small agricultural village on the edge of an oxbow lake near the ancient Ravi River around 3300 B.C. This location was ideal for agriculture as well as for access to rich hunting and fishing grounds. The earliest village occupation was characterized by small mud-brick buildings. Skilled artisans practiced a wide range of crafts: pottery making, copper and bronze working, and the making of exquisite ornaments from semi-precious stone and marine shell. As the settlement became more established, it also gained importance as a crossroads for trade between the highlands to the west and north and the vast alluvial plains to the east and south. Gradually, the village grew into a town, and eventually the town became one of the four largest cities of the Indus Valley civilization. . . .

The large urban centers of this civilization consisted of administrative, ritual, and residential buildings made primarily of baked brick and equipped with elaborate drainage facilities for removal of wastewater and rainwater. The people living in the cities developed extensive trade networks for obtaining raw materials and distributing foodstuffs and finished goods. Specialized technologies of metalworking, lapidary, and ceramics were perfected to make elaborate ornaments and specialized tools that were used locally or traded to distant lands. A highly standardized system of stone weights was developed for trade and possibly taxation. These weights were used in all the settlements of the Indus Valley, and many have been found at sites in Oman and even in Mesopotamia.

Texts from Mesopotamian cities state that "onions," cotton, hardwoods, pearls, carnelian, peacocks, and monkeys were imported from the land of Meluhha, which can be identified as the Indus Valley. The Indus cities in return obtained a range of goods that included raw materials, copper, gold, woolen items, and perfumes.

The ruling elites of the Indus cities developed a distinctive form of writing that was used on seals, trade goods, pottery, and even personal objects. This writing remains a mystery, even though careful archaeological studies are helping to develop a new understanding of how writing was used in the Indus Valley. However, because the writing has not yet been deciphered, it is extremely difficult to reconstruct accurately the economic, religious, or political systems of the Indus cities.

Most scholars agree that the Indus cities were

Jonathan Mark Kenoyer, "The Ancient City of Harappa," *Asian Art and Architecture*, vol. 9, no.1 (Winter 1996), pp. 86–89.

organized under some form of government that ruled over a vast hinterland through a combination of religious and economic control. There is little evidence of an extensive military establishment, and it is important to note that there are no representations in the archaeological record of people at war with each other. Surely there was conflict, and most of the cities were surrounded by massive mud-brick or stone walls for defense, but clearly the depiction of conflict was not something that was necessary to legitimize and augment the power of a ruler, as was the case in so many other societies.

The only context in which physical aggression is depicted is on seals or tablets that show a man fighting a wild animal, usually a bull or water buffalo. Several seals show a deity grappling with two tigers, while others depict a bull trampling a human. The depiction of struggle between people and wild animals is a theme that may stand as a metaphor of conflict between good and evil, or between civilized and wild.

Without written texts it is not possible to make specific interpretations of these narrative scenes or of the various other symbols used by the Indus people. However, there are strong connections between the art and technology of the Indus Valley civilization and the subsequent cultures of the Indian subcontinent. The concept of yoga is depicted on many Indus seals along with specific symbols that later are used in the iconography of Buddhist and Hindu ritual art: fish designs, swastikas, the stepped cross, and the pipal leaf design. Many of the technologies, such as bead making, shell working, glazed faience and terracotta ceramic production, metallurgy, and even architectural forms continue on into the later cultures of the subcontinent. The standardized system of weights established in the Indus cities reemerges during the subsequent Early Historic Period around 300 B.C. and continues to be used in traditional trading even today.

These strong continuities provide general models for interpreting the Indus culture, but the excavated cities of Mohenjo-daro and Harappa, and numerous other sites, remain the sole source of information for reconstructing this ancient society.

After reading this selection, consider these questions:

1. Why was the long-range trade of Harappa important for understanding the Indus Valley civilization's history?
2. What kind of historical evidence has been discovered at Harappa that cannot be properly interpreted until the ancient language of the Indus Valley is deciphered?
3. What elements of the civilization of the Indus Valley have been passed on to later Indian civilization?

SELECTION 2:

The Aryans Enter India

The Aryans who invaded India around 1500 B.C. were warriors whose highest value was martial prowess. Conquerors and destroyers, they left little record of their way of life except for their great epic poetry, which was kept alive for centuries by oral tradition before it was written down. These epics, and commentaries on them, constitute a foundation for all later Indian culture. In the following selection, a modern historian summarizes what we know about the early Aryans' conquest of India.

The story has been repeated for millennia, sung in temples, chanted in halls, told by words and actions of how a warrior people came out of the vastness of inner Asia through the passes of the northwest to fall upon the fortified cities of India and to conquer: riding horse-drawn chariots, driving herds of cattle, sheep, and goats, worshipping cosmic deities like Indra of the thunder and Agni of the fire, sacrificing, quarreling, gambling, drinking, singing, dancing—the Rig-Veda account of the Aryan tribes is one of the oldest epics in the world. It is part of an oral tradition which lies at the heart of Hinduism.

The Aryans were a pastoral people moving along routes already ages old, a people already affected by the sedentary world with which they were in contact even before arriving in India. They were organized into a rough class system headed by warrior chiefs whose rank was retained partially by accumulated wealth counted by herds and partially by prowess in battle. They spoke an Indo-European language and both by speech and cosmology were one with that group of pastoral nomads who inhabited the heart of the Eurasian continent in the early second millennium B.C. and whose later migrations so profoundly affected the ancient world.

After their conquest of the Punjab plain and the middle Ganges Valley, tradition has it that the settling-in process by which Aryan and non-Aryan people were integrated included the development and the change of the Aryan religious forms to more universal significance. The Brahmans explained the meaning and form of Vedic ritual, while the Upanishads philosophized and speculated upon them. It would seem that these later treatises were aimed at reinforcing the Vedic beliefs and rituals, which time and new environments were changing, and also at converting non-Aryan and presumably indigenous people.

The Mahabharata records a split between these kingdoms of the Aryans and an internecine strife that was climaxed in an epic battle in the central Ganges Valley in which the gods and men of many lands fought to the death. Afterward the victors seem to have settled in, with the broad reaches of the peninsula and the lower Ganges Valley yet before them. The Ramayana, in turn, tells of the kidnapping of Rama's wife Sita by Ravanna, a demonic king of Lanka (Ceylon), and her eventual rescue by Rama, aided by his ally Hanuman, the monkey king.

These two epics illustrate the spread of an essentially Indian tradition to south and east. As with the previous diffusion of traits from the west—hand axes, microliths, pastoralism, agriculture, bronze, etc.—the initiating ethos was now Indianized, that is, while still related generically to its origin, given peculiar character and suitability by its Indian environment. . . .

[The author then takes exception to this literary account, found in the four Vedas, the first records of the Aryans. The Doab is the region between the Ganges and the Yamuna Rivers in northern India.]

Yet the Aryan invasion is a literary account. It was probably not an invasion of hordes of Central Asian nomads who in great and overwhelming waves swept from the steppes to the Doab. It is more likely that Indo-European-speaking pastoral tribes of a variety of traditions and probably of a diversity of ethnic backgrounds gradually infiltrated the fertile plain from Peshawar to the Punjab. This pattern of movement is more characteristic of pastoral peoples than the great migrations historians are prone to dramatize. As pastoralists they may have established traditional seasonal routes but at least initially were unlikely to settle in large permanent sedentary settlements. Thus their traces archaeologically are less likely to be in terms of habitation and more likely to be necropoli or even isolated monuments. In the thickly settled Punjab of today traces of old campgrounds probably have long since disappeared, and it is only the more permanent settlements of a later stage which will be found.

After reading this selection, consider these questions:
1. What were the values held by the Aryan invaders of India?
2. What is the connection between

Walter A. Fairservis Jr., *The Roots of Ancient India* (New York: Macmillan, 1971), pp. 345–46, 358.

Aryan literature and the movement of people in India?

3. Why does the author argue that the Vedas are not always accurate?

SELECTION 3:

A Hymn to Indra and a Hymn to Agni

Selections A and B below are songs to Indra and Agni, the two most popular deities during the earliest period of the Aryan invasion. They were chanted by the Brahman priests to gain divine favor over their Dravidian enemies, the indigenous people of the country who may have been related ethnically to the Harappans. The first song portrays the battles as a cosmic struggle, a fight between Indra and Vritra, the primeval dragon. The second recognizes the need for Agni's help.

To Indra

I will declare the manly deeds of Indra, the
   first that he achieved, the thunder-wielder.
He slew the dragon, then disclosed the waters,
   and cleft the channels of the mountain torrent.
He slew the dragon lying on the mountain: his
   heavenly bolt of thunder Tvashtar fashioned.
Like lowing kine [cattle] in rapid flow descend-
   ing the waters glided downward to the ocean.
Impetuous as a bull, he chose the Soma, and in
   three sacred beakers drank the juices.
The Bounteous One grasped the thunder for his
   weapon, and smote to death this firstborn of
   the dragons.
When, Indra, you had slain the dragon's firstborn, and overcome the charms of the
   enchanters,
Then, giving life to sun and dawn and heaven,
   you found not one foe to stand against you.
Indra with his own great and deadly thunder
   smote into pieces Vritra, worst of Vritras.

As trunks of trees, what time the axe has felled
   them, low on the earth so lies the prostrate
   dragon.
He, like a mad weak warrior, challenged Indra,
   the great impetuous many-slaying hero.
He, brooking not the clashing of the weapons,
   crushed—Indra's foe—the shattered forts in
   falling.
Footless and handless still he challenged Indra,
   who smote him with his bolt between the
   shoulders.
Emasculated yet claiming manly vigor, thus
   Vritra lay with scattered limbs dissevered.
There as he lies like a bank-bursting river, the
   waters taking courage flow above him.
The dragon lies beneath the feet of torrents which
   Vritra with his greatness had encompassed.

To Agni

Produce your stream of flames like a broad onslaught. Go forth impetuous like a king with his
elephant; . . . after your greedy onslaught. You are
an archer; shoot the sorcerers with your hottest
arrows.

   Your whirls fly quickly. Fiercely flaming

Ralph T.H. Griffith, F. Max Müller, and Herman Oldenberg, trans., *Rig-Veda, The Sacred Books of the East* (1897) quoted in Allie M. Frazier, ed., *Hinduism*, vol. 1 of *Readings in Eastern Religious Thought* (Philadelphia: Westminster Press, 1969), pp. 75–76, 83–84.

touch them. O Agni, send forth with the ladle your heat, your winged flames; send forth unfettered your firebrands all around.

Being the quickest, send forth your spies against all evil-doers. Be an undeceivable guardian of this clan. He who attacks us with evil spells, far or near, may no such foe defy your track.

Rise up, O Agni! Spread out against all foes! Burn down the foes, O god with the sharp weapon! When kindled, O Agni, burn down like dry brushwood, the man who exercises malice against us.

Stand upright, strike the foes away from us! Make manifest your divine powers, O Agni! Unbend the strong bows of those who incite demons against us. Crush all enemies, be they relations or strangers.

He knows your favor, O youngest one, who makes a way for a sacred speech like this. May you beam forth to his doors all auspicious days and the wealth and the splendor of the niggard.

May he be fortunate and blessed with good rain, who longs to gladden you with constant offerings and hymns through his life in his house. May such longing ever bring auspicious days to him, O Agni.

I praise your favor; it resounded here. May this song which is like a favorite wife, awaken for you. Let us brighten you, being rich in horses and chariots. May you maintain our knightly power day by day.

May the worshipper here frequently of his own accord approach you, O god who shines in darkness, resplendent day by day. Let us worship you sporting and joyous, surpassing the splendor of other people.

Whoever, rich in horses and rich in gold, approaches you, O Agni, with his chariot full of wealth. You are the protector and the friend of him who always delights in showing you hospitality.

After reading this selection, consider these questions:

1. What images does the hymn use to describe the struggle between Indra and the dragon?
2. Can you find a comparison between the hymn to Agni and that of the Egyptian hymn to Amon-Re (chapter 3, selection 2)?
3. Why would these hymns have been composed?

SELECTION 4:

Caste in Ancient India

Essential to any understanding of the ancient Aryan society, as well as all of later Indian society to the present, is the notion of caste. (The word itself is Portuguese and means "race.") Caste defines a person's status in life, the occupation he or she must follow, and whom one may marry. In the following article the idea of caste is explored by Indian historian Romila Thapar. Dasas was the name the Aryans gave to the indigenous people of India against whom they fought.

When the Aryans first came to India they were divided into three social classes, the warriors or aristocracy, the priests, and the common people. There was no consciousness of caste, as is clear from remarks such as "a bard am I, my father is a leech and my mother grinds corn." Professions were not hereditary, nor were there any rules limiting marriages within these classes, or taboos on whom one could eat with. The three divisions merely facilitated social and economic organization.

The first step in the direction of caste (as distinct from class) was taken when the Aryans treated the Dasas as beyond the social pale, probably owing to a fear of the Dasas and the even greater fear that assimilation with them would lead to a loss of Aryan identity. Ostensibly the distinction was largely that of color, the Dasas being darker and of an alien culture. The Sanskrit word for caste, *varna*, actually means color. The color element of caste was emphasized, throughout the period, and was eventually to become deep-rooted in north-Indian Aryan culture. Initially, therefore, the division was between the Aryans and the non-Aryans. The Aryans were the *dvija* or twice-born castes (the first being physical birth and the second the initiation into caste status), consisting of the *kshatriyas* (warriors and aristocracy), the *brahmans* (priests), and the *vaishyas* (cultivators); the fourth caste, the *shudras*, were the Dasas and those of mixed Aryan-Dasas origin.

The actual mechanism of caste was not a formal division of society into four broad groups. The first three castes were probably a theoretical framework evolved by the brahmans, into which they systematically arranged various professions. Combinations and permutations within the latter were inevitable and were explained as originating in the inter-mixing of castes. The fourth caste, however, appears to have been based both on race as well as occupation (as was also the case later with the emergence of the out-castes, whose position was so low that in later centuries even their

Romila Thapar, *A History of India* (Baltimore: Penguin Books, 1966), vol. 1, pp. 37–40.

touch was held to be polluting).

The caste status of an occupation could change over a long period. Gradually the Aryan *vaishyas* became traders and landowners and the *shudras* moved up the scale to become the cultivators (though not in the condition of serfs). Aryan ascendancy over the Dasas was now complete. But although the *shudras* were permitted to cultivate the land, they were still excluded from *dvija* status, and were to remain so, an exclusion which prevented them from participating in Vedic ritual and led them to worship their own gods. This vertical division of society made it easier in later centuries to accept new ethnic groups. Each new group to arrive in India took on the characteristics of a separate sub-caste and was thereby assimilated into the larger caste structure. The position of the new sub-caste in the hierarchy was dependent on its occupation and, on occasion, on its social origins.

The establishment of caste was no doubt promoted by other factors as well, and the process by which the *shudras* became cultivators is inherent in these factors. With the transition from nomadic pastoralism to a settled agrarian economy, specialization of labor gradually became a marked feature of Aryan society. The clearing of the forests and the existence of new settlements led to the emergence of a trading community engaged in the supply and exchange of goods. There was thus a natural separation between the agriculturists, those who cleared and colonized the land, and the traders, those who established the economic links between the settlements, the latter coming from the class of wealthier landowners who could afford economic speculation.

The priests were in any case a group by themselves. The warriors, led by the king, believed their function to be solely that of protection, on which function the entire well-being of each community depended. The king emerged as the dominant power, and the warriors (*kshatriyas*) were therefore of the first rank in caste. The priests (brahmans) came next, followed by the more prosperous landowners and traders (*vaishyas*), and finally the cultivators (*shudras*).

The priests were not slow to realize the significance of such a division of society and the supreme authority which could be invested in the highest caste. They not only managed to usurp the first position by claiming that they alone could bestow divinity on the king (which was by now essential to kingship) but they also gave religious sanction to caste divisions. A late hymn of the *Rig-Veda* provides a mythical origin of the castes:

> When the gods made a sacrifice with the
> Man as their victim, . . .
> When they divided the Man, into how
> many parts did they divide him?
> What was his mouth, what were his
> arms, what were his thighs and his
> feet called?
> The brahman was his mouth, of his arms
> were made the warrior.
> His thighs became the vaishya, of his
> feet the shudra was born.
> With Sacrifice the gods sacrificed the
> Sacrifice, these were the first of the
> sacred laws.
> These mighty beings reached the sky,
> where are the eternal spirits, the gods.

The continuance of caste was secured by its being made hereditary: the primitive taboo on commensality (eating together) became a caste law, and this in turn made it necessary to define marriage limits, leading to elaborate rules of endogamy and exogamy. The basis and continuance of the caste system depended not on the four-fold division but on the vast network of sub-castes, which was intimately connected with occupation.

Eventually, the sub-caste (*jati*, literally "birth") came to have more relevance for the day-to-day working of Hindu society than the main caste (*varna*), since the functioning of society was dependent on sub-caste relationships and adjustments, the *varna* remaining an over-all theoretical framework. Sub-caste relationships were based on specialization of work and economic interdependence. With caste becoming hereditary, and the close connection between occupation and sub-caste, there was an automatic check on individuals moving up in the hierarchy of castes. Vertical mobility was possible to the sub-caste as a whole and depended upon the entire group acting as one and changing both its location and its work. An individual could express his protest only by joining a sect which disavowed caste, such as were to evolve from the sixth century B.C. onwards.

After reading this selection, consider these questions:

1. What does the author say about the origins of class and caste?
2. What enabled the brahmans to rise to the position of the primary class?
3. What were some of the regulations that kept castes from mixing?

SELECTION 5:

The Bhagavad-Gita

The longest poem in world literature and one of the earliest Aryan literary works is the Mahabharata. It tells of a battle between two noble families reflecting the constant warfare that marked the period of the Aryan invasion into India. One part of the Mahabharata is known as the Bhagavad-Gita, the Lord's song, which professes to explain one of the fundamental ideas of the Brahman religion: reincarnation. Arjuna, commander of one army, is reminded of this when Lord Krishna, disguised as his charioteer, carries on this conversation. Lord Krishna was one of the incarna-

tions of Vishnu. Arjuna must not be frightened of fighting his relatives and killing them, for this is not the end of their existence.

Our bodies are known to end,
but the embodied self is enduring,
indestructible, and immeasurable;
therefore, Arjuna, fight the battle!

He who thinks this self a killer
and he who thinks it killed,
both fail to understand;
it does not kill, nor is it killed.

It is not born,
it does not die;
having been,
it will never not be;
unborn, enduring,
constant, and primordial,
it is not killed
when the body is killed.

Arjuna, when a man knows the self
to be indestructible, enduring, unborn,
unchanging, how does he kill
or cause anyone to kill?

As a man discards
worn-out clothes
to put on new

and different ones,
so the embodied self
discards
its worn-out bodies
to take on other new ones.

Weapons do not cut it,
fire does not burn it,
waters do not wet it,
wind does not wither it.

It cannot be cut or burned;
it cannot be wet or withered;
it is enduring, all-pervasive,
fixed, immovable, and timeless.

It is called unmanifest,
inconceivable, and immutable;
since you know that to be so,
you should not grieve!

After reading this selection, consider these questions:
1. What qualities does Lord Krishna attribute to the self?
2. How does Krishna's statement encourage Arjuna to fight and, if necessary, kill his enemies?
3. Does Krishna's teaching have any relation to the caste system?

Bhagavad-Gita, Barbara Stoler Miller, trans. (New York: Bantam Books, 1986), pp. 129–30.

SELECTION 6:

What Is Reality?

Beginning about 600 B.C., a number of Aryan philosophers probed more deeply into the meaning of reality. Enlisting disciples who sat near them so as to be able to hear, they held forth on the essential nature of the visible universe. Their writings are known as Upanishads, the Sanskrit word that means "sitting near." (Sanskrit is the ancient Indo-European language of Aryan India.) This Upanishad is told in the form of a story about *a young man named Svetaketu who, returning from his studies convinced that he knows it all, meets his father. His father questions what he thinks his education has taught him.*

"Fetch me from thence a fruit of the Nyagrodha tree."

"Here is one, Sir."

"Break it."

"It is broken, Sir."

"What do you see there?"

"These seeds, almost infinitesimal."

"Break one of them."

"It is broken, Sir."

"What do you see there?"

"Not anything, Sir."

The father said: "My son, that subtle essence which you do not perceive there, of that very essence this great Nyagrodha tree exists.

"Believe it, my son. That which is the subtle essence, in it all that exists has its self. It is the True. It is the Self, and That Thou Art, O Svetaketu."

"Place this salt in water, and then wait on me in the morning."

The son did as he was commanded.

The father said to him: "Bring me the salt, which you placed in the water last night."

The son having looked for it, found it not, for, of course, it was melted.

The father said: "Taste it from the surface of the water. How is it?"

The son replied: "It is salt."

"Taste it from the middle. How is it?"

The son replied: "It is salt."

"Taste it from the bottom. How is it?"

The son replied: "It is salt."

The father said: "Throw it away and then wait on me."

He did so; but salt exists for ever.

Then the father said: "Here also, in this body, forsooth, you do not perceive the True, my son; but there indeed it is there.

"That which is the subtle essence, in it all that exists has its self. It is the True. It is the Self, and That Thou Art."

After reading this selection, consider these questions:

1. How does this conversation relate to the passage between Lord Krishna and Arjuna (chapter 4, selection 5)?

2. What does this selection tell you about the brahman view of reality?

3. How do you think this attitude toward reality might affect Indian society?

F. Max Müller, trans., *Upanishads: The Sacred Books of the East* (1879), quoted in Allie M. Frazier, ed., *Hinduism,* vol. 1 of *Readings in Eastern Religious Thought* (Philadelphia: Westminster Press, 1969), pp. 135–36.

CHAPTER 5
India's Classical Age: What Were Buddhist Values?

As India passed through the age of the Vedas, in which brahmans controlled society's religious and much of its political life, some individuals began to criticize the values espoused by Brahmanism. In the sixth century B.C. a dissenter emerged who is considered one of the greatest thinkers and religious prophets of world history: Siddhārtha Gautama (ca. 568–488 B.C.).

Rejecting Brahmanism, Gautama sought many paths to understand reality before he succeeded, thereby becoming the Buddha—the "Enlightened One." As the Buddha, he urged people to find a way to avoid suffering and pain. His goal was not to found a religion, but this in fact is what happened as his teaching developed. The selections in this chapter all focus on the Buddhist "way" and the values that it bequeathed to India. As you read, try to identify distinctively Buddhist beliefs and look for ways in which they influenced Indian society.

SELECTION 1:

The Buddha Explains His Teachings

In this selection, Siddhārtha himself explains his teachings. Certain features should be noted. The first is the belief that the atman, *the innermost essence of every human being, experiences constant reincarnation. (Thus Buddhism accepts the older idea of reincarnation; compare the Bhagavad-Gita in chapter 4 selection 5.) A second tenet is that eventually, if a person acquires sufficient karma,* he or she may at last reach a state known as nirvana, in which reincarnation ceases and the soul blissfully dissolves into nothingness, freed from pain and suffering.*

Known as the Buddha, Gautama began teaching his doctrine throughout India. His teaching did not endorse Brahman sacrifices and said nothing about caste; thus, it proved very popular among those at the bottom of the social ladder. What the Buddha taught was open to all, men and women alike, regardless of caste, once one understood the Four Noble Truths and followed the path to enlightenment. In selection 1, in which Gautama speaks of the asavas, he refers to desires—for sexual pleasure and for physical existence—and to our willingness to tolerate ignorance.

Thus with mind concentrated, purified, cleansed, spotless, with the defilements gone, supple, dexterous, firm, and impassable, I directed my mind to the knowledge of the remembrance of my former existences. I remembered many former existences, such as, one birth, two births, three, four, five, ten, twenty, thirty, forty, fifty, a hundred, a thousand, a hundred thousand births; many cycles of dissolution of the universe, many cycles of its evolution, many of its dissolution and evolution; there I was of such and such a name, clan, color, livelihood, such pleasure and pain did I suffer, and such was the end of my life.

Passing away thence I was born elsewhere. There too I was of such and such a name, clan, color, livelihood, such pleasure and pain did I suffer, and such was the end of my life. Passing away thence I was reborn here. Thus do I remember my many former existences with their special modes and details. This was the first knowledge that I gained in the first watch of the night. Ignorance was dispelled, knowledge arose. Darkness was dispelled, light arose. So is it with him who abides vigilant, strenuous and resolute.

Thus with mind concentrated, purified, cleansed, spotless, with the defilements gone, supple, dexterous, firm and impassable, I directed my mind to the passing away and rebirth of beings. With divine, purified, superhuman vision I saw beings passing away and being reborn, low and high, of good and bad color, in happy or miserable existences according to their karma. Those beings

---

*Karma is a subtle and important concept in Buddhist thought but is difficult to define in a few words. Essentially, it refers to the sum total of the consequences of one's actions, thoughts, and attitudes, which accumulate during a lifetime but also through an endless series of reincarnations. Karma is the life force that sustains and directs our physical existence.

Edward J. Thomas, *The Life of Buddha as Legend and History* 3rd ed. (London: Routledge and Kegan Paul, 1949), pp. 67–68.

who lead evil lives in deed, word, or thought, who speak evil of the noble ones, of false views, who acquire karma through their false views, at the dissolution of the body after death are reborn in a state of misery and suffering in hell. But those beings who lead good lives in deed, word, and thought, who speak no evil of the noble ones, of right views, who acquire karma through their right views, at the dissolution of the body after death are reborn in a happy state in the world of heaven. . . . This was the second knowledge that I gained in the second watch of the night. . . .

Thus with mind concentrated, purified, cleansed, spotless, with the defilements gone, supple, dexterous, firm, and impassable, I directed my mind to the knowledge of the destruction of the āsavas. I duly realized (the truth) 'this is pain,' I duly realized (the truth) 'this is the cause of pain,' and I duly realized (the truth) 'this is the way that leads to the destruction of pain.' I duly realized 'these are the āsavas'. . .'this is the cause of the āsavas'. . .'this is the destruction of the āsavas.' As I thus knew and thus perceived, my mind was emancipated from the āsava of sensual desire, from the āsava of desire for existence, and from the āsava of ignorance.

And in me emancipated arose the knowledge of my emancipation. I realized that destroyed is rebirth, the religious life has been led, done is what was to be done, there is nought (for me) beyond this world. This was the third knowledge that I gained in the last watch of the night. Ignorance was dispelled, knowledge arose. Darkness was dispelled, light arose. So is it with him who abides vigilant, strenuous, and resolute.

After reading this selection, consider these questions:

1. What are the teachings of the Buddha about present life?
2. What does Buddhism say about karma?
3. What is the purpose of life for a disciple of the Buddha? How does this differ from the prevailing modern American point of view?

SELECTION 2:

The Role of Buddhism

Although Buddhism soon developed into a religion, a present-day American Buddhist publication argues that that is not what the Buddha himself intended.

Buddhism is not a religion because, first, the Buddha is not a "supernatural being power." The Buddha is simply a person who has reached Complete Understanding of the reality of life and the universe. Life refers to us and universe refers to our living environment. The Buddha taught that all beings possess the same ability within to reach Complete Understanding of themselves and their environment and to free themselves from all sufferings, thus attaining utmost happiness. All beings can become Buddhas and all beings and the Buddha are equal in nature. The Buddha is not a God, but a teacher, who teaches us the way to restore Wisdom and Understanding by conquering the greed, anger and ignorance which blind us at the present moment. Buddha is a Sanskrit word meaning, "Wisdom, Awareness/Understanding." We call the founder of

Chin Kung, *A Path to True Happiness*, Triratnani Disciples, trans. (Richardson, TX: Dallas Buddhist Association, 1994), pp. 2–5.

Buddhism, Buddha Shakyamuni, the "Original Teacher." He has attained Complete Understanding and Wisdom of life and the universe. Buddhism is his education to us; it is his teaching that shines the way to Buddhahood.

Second, Buddhism is not a religion because "belief" in the Buddha's teachings is not blind belief, blind faith and far from superstition. Buddha Shakyamuni taught us not to blindly believe what he told us, he wants us to try the teachings and prove them for ourselves. The Buddha wants us to know not merely believe. The Buddha's teachings flow from his own experience of the way to understand the true reality of life and the universe, and show us a path of our own to experience the truth for ourselves. This is much like a good friend telling us of his trip to Europe, the sights he has seen, and the way to go there to see for ourselves. The Buddha uses a perfectly scientific way of showing us reality in its true form.

Third, Buddhism is not a religion because all the "rites and celebrations" are not centered on a supernatural being, but rather on the people attending the assemblies. The ceremonies and celebrations in Buddhism all serve an educational purpose, a reminder of the Buddha's teachings and encouragement to all students who practice them.

After reading this selection, consider these questions:

1. According to the authors, why is Buddhism not a religion?
2. What do the authors contend that Buddhism wants its followers to know?
3. What function does Buddhist worship serve?

SELECTION 3:

A Story from Ancient India

In the classical Indian world a major form of entertainment was storytelling. An accomplished narrator was highly honored in the Indian village. In his or her stories, heroes and heroines fighting the forces of evil abounded.

The storyteller also had an opportunity to reinforce society's values. As you read the following selection, keep in mind what these values were for the men, women, and children of India twenty-five-hundred years ago. This passage comes from a collection of Indian tales known as the Panchatantra. *The story takes place in southern India, in the kingdom of Madras.*

Ashvapati, the virtuous king of Madras, grew old without offspring to continue his royal family. Desiring a son, Ashvapati took rigid vows and observed long fasts to accumulate merit. It is said that he offered 10,000 oblations to the goddess Savatri in hopes of having a son. After eighteen years of constant devotion, Ashvapati was granted his wish for an offspring even though the baby born was a girl.

The king rejoiced at his good fortune and named the child Savatri in honor of the goddess who gave him this joy to brighten his elder years.

Savatri was both a beautiful and an intelligent

Roy C. Amore and Larry D. Shinn, *Lustful Maidens and Ascetic Kings: Buddhist and Hindu Stories of Life* (New York: Oxford University Press, 1981), pp. 28–30, 32–33.

child. She was her father's delight and grew in wisdom and beauty as the years passed. As the age approached for Savatri to be given in marriage as custom demanded, no suitor came forward to ask her father for her hand—so awed were all the princes by the beauty and intellect of this unusual maiden. Her father became concerned lest he not fulfill his duty as a father and incur disgrace for his failure to provide a suitable husband for his daughter. At last, he instructed Savatri herself to lead a procession throughout the surrounding kingdoms and handpick a man suitable for her.

Savatri returned from her search and told her father that she had found the perfect man. Though he was poor and an ascetic of the woods, he was handsome, well educated, and of kind temperament. His name was Satyavan and he was actually a prince whose blind father had been displaced by an evil king. Ashvapati asked the venerable sage Narada whether Satyavan would be a suitable spouse for Savatri. Narada responded that there was no one in the world more worthy than Satyavan. However, Narada continued, Satyavan had one unavoidable flaw. He was fated to live a short life and would die exactly one year from that very day. Ashvapati then tried to dissuade Savatri from marrying Satyavan by telling her of the impending death of her loved one. Savatri held firm to her choice, and the king and Narada both gave their blessings to this seemingly ill-fated bond.

After the marriage procession had retreated from the forest hermitage of Savatri's new father-in-law, Dyumatsena, the bride removed her wedding sari and donned the ocher robe and bark garments of her ascetic family. As the days and weeks passed, Savatri busied herself by waiting upon the every need of her new family. She served her husband, Satyavan, cheerfully and skillfully. Satyavan responded with an even-tempered love which enhanced the bond of devotion between Savatri and himself. Yet the dark cloud of Narada's prophecy cast a shadow over this otherwise blissful life.

When the fateful time approached, Savatri began a fast to strengthen her wifely resolve as she kept nightly vigils while her husband slept.

The day marked for the death of Satyavan began as any other day at the hermitage. Satyavan shouldered his axe and was about to set off to cut wood for the day's fires when Savatri stopped him to ask if she could go along saying, "I cannot bear to be separated from you today." Satyavan responded, "You've never come into the forest before and the paths are rough and the way very difficult. Besides, you've been fasting and are surely weak." Savatri persisted, and Satyavan finally agreed to take her along. Savatri went to her parents-in-law to get their permission saying she wanted to see the spring blossoms which now covered the forest. They too expressed concern over her health but finally relented out of consideration for her long period of gracious service to them.

Together Satyavan and Savatri entered the tangled woods enjoying the beauty of the flowers and animals which betoken spring in the forest. Coming to a fallen tree, Satyavan began chopping firewood. As he worked, he began to perspire heavily and to grow weak. Finally, he had to stop and lie down telling Savatri to wake him after a short nap. With dread in her heart, Savatri took Satyavan's head in her lap and kept a vigil knowing Satyavan's condition to be more serious than rest could assuage. In a short time, Savatri saw approaching a huge figure clad in red and carrying a small noose. Placing Satyavan's head upon the ground, Savatri arose and asked the stranger of his mission. The lord of death replied, "I am Yama and your husband's days are finished. I speak to you, a mortal, only because of your extreme merit. I have come personally instead of sending my emissaries because of your husband's righteous life."

Without a further word, Yama then pulled Satyavan's soul out of his body with the small noose he was carrying. The lord of death then set off immediately for the realm of the dead in the south. Grief stricken and yet filled with wifely devotion, Savatri followed Yama at a distance. Hours passed yet hunger and weariness could not slow Savatri's footsteps. She persisted through thorny paths and rocky slopes to follow Yama and his precious burden. As Yama walked south he thought he heard a woman's anklets tinkling on the path behind him. He turned around to see Savatri in the distance following without pause. He called out to her to return to Satyavan's body and to perform her wifely duties of cremating the dead. Savatri approached Yama and responded, "It is said that those who walk seven steps together are friends. Certainly we have traveled farther than that together. Why should I return to a dead body when you possess the soul of my husband?"

Yama was impressed by the courage and wisdom of this beautiful young woman. He replied, "Please stop following me. Your wise words and persistent devotion for your husband deserve a boon. Ask of me anything except that your husband's life be restored, and I will grant it." Savatri asked that her blind father-in-law be granted new sight. Yama said that her wish would be granted, and then he turned to leave only to find that Savatri was about to continue following. Yama again praised her devotion and offered a second, and then a third boon. Savatri told Yama of the misfortune of her father-in-law's lost kingdom and asked that Yama assist in ousting the evil king from Dyumatsena's throne. Yama agreed. Then Savatri utilized her third boon to ask that her own father be given one hundred sons to protect his royal line, and that too was granted by Yama.

Yama then set off in a southerly direction only to discover after a short while that Savatri still relentlessly followed him. Yama was amazed at the thoroughly self-giving attitude displayed by Savatri and agreed to grant one last boon if Savatri would promise to return home. Yama again stipulated that the bereaved wife could not ask for her husband's soul. Savatri agreed to the two conditions and said, "I only ask for myself one thing, and that is that I may be granted one hundred sons to continue Satyavan's royal family." Yama agreed only to realize, upon prompting from Savatri, that the only way Satyavan's line could be continued would be for him to be restored to life. Although he had been tricked by the wise and thoughtful Savatri, Yama laughed heartily and said, "So be it! Auspicious and chaste lady, your husband's soul is freed by me." Loosening his noose Yama permitted the soul of Satyavan to return to its earthly abode and Savatri ran without stopping back to the place where Satyavan had fallen asleep. Just as Savatri arrived at the place where her husband lay, he awoke saying, "Oh, I have slept into the night, why did you not waken me?"

After reading this selection, consider these questions:

1. How does the storyteller point out the virtues of Savatri? What are these virtues?
2. How does the god of death capture the soul of Satyavan?
3. How might the audience listening to this story have reacted to Savatri's quest to have her husband brought back to life?

SELECTION 4:

The Religion of Asoka

Buddhism scored a great success when it won over Asoka (ca. 274–ca. 236 B.C.), an emperor of the Mauryan dynasty. In the fourth century B.C. the Mauryans formed the first great empire of India, with its capital at Pataliputra, now Patna. Asoka, after conquering many neighboring peoples, had a change in heart that can only be understood as a conversion to Buddhism. In this selection, a modern historian assesses Asoka's understanding of Buddhism and his attempt to apply it to the governance of an empire.

Although Asoka unquestionably was familiar with a body of sacred Buddhist literature . . . the teaching of the edicts gives the impression of being different from that of most Buddhist works. We find no distinct reference to the doctrine of *karma*, or transmitted merit and demerit, nor is any allusion made to *nirvâna*, as the goal to be obtained by the good man. No doubt the emperor believed in *karma*, although he does not plainly say so, and very probably he may have looked forward to *nirvâna*, although he does not express the hope. His precepts . . . are purely practical and intended to lead men into the right way of living, not into correct philosophical positions.

Many passages in the edicts indicate that he believed firmly in the "other world" or "future life." He tells us . . . that all his exertions were directed to the end that he might discharge his debt to animate beings, make some of them happy in this world, and also enable them in the other world to gain heaven. . . .

Still more emphatic is the declaration . . . that only the things concerning the other world are regarded by His Majesty as bearing much fruit, and he concludes by adjuring his descendants to place all their joy in efforts which avail for both this world and the next. . . .

While Asoka took infinite pains to issue and enforce "pious regulations," he put his trust in the "superior effect of reflection" as the chief agent in the promotion of "the growth of piety among men and the more complete abstention from killing animate beings, and from sacrificial slaughter of living creatures." Nor did he rely solely upon the combined effect of reflection and pious regulations for the success of his propaganda. He continually extolled the merit of almsgiving, and attached much importance to practical works of benevolence, in the execution of which he set a good example.

After reading this selection, consider these questions:
1. Why does the author think that Asoka did not have access to all Buddhist teaching?
2. Does Asoka's idea of Buddhism conform to orthodox Buddhism?
3. Asoka placed great emphasis on generosity. Why is this such a high value for Buddhists?

Vincent A. Smith, *Asoka* (3rd rev. ed., Oxford: Clarendon Press, 1964), pp. 63–65.

Selection 5:
Edict XIII of Asoka

All over the Mauryan empire Asoka erected pillars with his edicts carved upon them. The document that forms this selection, Rock Edict XIII, is the most emphatic in showing his conversion to Buddhist principles. In this ancient text his coronation name, Devanampiya Piyadasi, is used.

Eight years after his coronation King Devanampiya Piyadasi conquered the Kalingas. In that (conquest) one hundred and fifty thousand people were deported (as prisoners), one hundred thousand were killed (or maimed) and many times that number died. Thereafter, with the conquest of Kalinga, King Devanampiya Piyadasi (adopted) the practice of morality, love of morality and inculcation of morality. For there arose in King Devanampiya Piyadasi remorse for the conquest of Kalinga. For when an unsubdued country is conquered there occur such things as slaughter, death and deportation of people and these are regarded as very painful and serious by King Devanampiya Piyadasi.

Brahmans and ascetics live everywhere, as well as votaries of other sects and householders who practice such virtues as support of mother and father, service of elders, proper treatment of friends, relatives, acquaintances and kinsmen and slaves and servants and steadfastness in devotion to duties. They too suffer injury (separation from loved ones), slaughter and deportation of loved ones. And for those whose love is undiminished, their friends, acquaintances, relatives and kinsmen suffer calamity. And that is injury to them. This plight of men is regarded as serious by King Devanampiya Piyadasi. Outside of the territory of the Greeks there is no land where communities such as those of Brahmans and ascetics are not to be found. Nor is there any land where men do not have faith (religion) of one sect or another.

Hence, whatever the number of men then killed (or wounded) and died and were deported at the annexation of Kalinga, a hundredth or a thousandth part (thereof) even is regarded as serious by King Devanampiya Piyadasi. Furthermore, if anyone does wrong (to him) the person should be suffered or pardoned. To the forest folk, who live in the royal dominions of King Devanampiya Piyadasi, it may be pointed out that the king, remorseful as he is, has the strength to punish the wrongdoers who do not repent. For King Devanampiya desires that all beings should be safe, self-restrained, tranquil in thought and gentle. . . .

Whatever has been gained by this victory of morality, that has been pleasant. This happiness has been secured through victory of morality but even that is not as great for the King Devanampiya as the gain of the next world. For this purpose this rescript on morality has been written that my sons and great grandsons should cease to think of new conquests and in all the victories they may gain they should be content with forbearance and slight punishment. For them the true conquest should be that of morality; all their delight should be delight in morality for benefit in this world and the next.

After reading this selection, consider these questions:

1. Why does Asoka regret his conquests?
2. What does Asoka think of the Greeks?
3. Why would Asoka have his edicts carved on stone pillars?

B.G. Gokhale, *Asoka Maurya* in *Twayne's Rulers and Statesmen of the World Series* (New York: Twayne, 1966), pp. 157–58.

SELECTION 6:

The Taming of Elephants

*S*trabo *(ca. 60 B.C.–ca. A.D. 21), a famous ancient Greek geographer, traveled widely and gathered lore from those who had gone even farther afield. The taming of elephants was a subject of great interest to Greeks*

and Romans, a few of whom visited India. Strabo borrowed his informa-
tion from an earlier Greek historian, Megasthenes.

The passage in this selection shows that contact between India and the
Mediterranean world was abundant. Each found things to admire and
things to avoid. Mediterranean people's knowledge of elephants was lim-
ited to a few spectacular instances of the use of imported animals in war
(especially the Carthaginian general Hannibal's invasion of Italy in the
second century B.C.) *or in great public shows of exotic wonders. Since Eu-*
ropeans, in their colder climate, had no opportunity to learn how ele-
phants were tamed, they would have found this selection very entertaining.

The manner of hunting the elephant is as follows. Round a bare piece of ground is dug a deep ditch about five or six stadia in extent, and over this a very narrow bridge is thrown at the place of entrance. Into the enclosure three or four of the tamest female elephants are then driven. The men themselves lie in wait in concealed huts. The wild elephants do not approach this trap by day, but they enter it by night in single file. When all have passed the entrance, the men secretly close it. They then introduce the strongest of the tame combatants, the drivers of which fight with the wild animals, and also subdue them by hunger. When the latter are at length overcome with fatigue, the boldest of the drivers dismount unobserved, and each of them creeps under his own elephant, and from this position creeps under the belly of the wild elephant and ties his legs together. When this has been done they incite the tame elephants to beat those which are tied by the legs till they fall to the ground. Thereupon they bind the wild and tame elephants together by the neck with thongs of raw ox-hide, and to prevent them shaking themselves in order to shake off those who attempt to mount them, they make cuts round their neck, and then put thongs of leather into the incisions, so that the animals are forced by pain to submit to their bonds and remain quiet.

From the number taken, such as are too old or too young to be serviceable are rejected and the rest are led away to the stables. Here they tie their feet one to another, and their necks to a pillar firmly fixed in the ground, and tame them by hunger. Their strength they restore afterwards with green reeds and grass. In the next place they teach them to obey, effecting this by soothing them, some by words, and others by song and the music of the drum. Few of them are difficult to be tamed, for they are naturally of a mild and gentle disposition, so as to approximate to rational beings. Some of them have taken up their drivers who have fallen in battle and carried them off in safety from the field. Others have fought in defence of their masters who had sought refuge by creeping between their forelegs, and have thus saved their lives. If in a fit of anger they kill either the man who feeds them or the man who trains them, they are so overpowered with regret that they refuse food, and sometimes die of hunger.

After reading this selection, consider these questions:

1. What methods did Indian elephant trainers use to entice wild elephants into their enclosure?
2. Why do you suppose Mediterranean people would have been interested in elephants?
3. The taming of wild elephants in this passage sounds cruel. What does this tell us about ancient values?

John W. McCrindle, *Ancient India as Described in Classical Literature*. 1901. Reprinted (Amsterdam: Philo Press, 1975), pp. 49–50.

CHAPTER 6
Ancient China:
What Shaped Its Outlook?

Chinese civilization begins in the second millennium B.C. with the expansion of agricultural villages in the Yellow River valley in the northern part of the country. Geographically isolated by distance from the other early centers of civilization (Mesopotamia, Egypt, and the Indus Valley), Chinese society developed a distinctive style. Millet, the grain that became the staple of early Chinese life, grew so easily in the Yellow River valley's rich soil that it did not need additional fertilizer. Population thus spurted upward, and toward the end of the second millennium those characteristics emerged that signify civilization: the creation of governments, the development of a religious tradition, the use of metals, and the erection of public buildings. Because wood rather than stone or mud brick was the preferred building material, far fewer architectural monuments of early China survive than in India or the Near East. The first Chinese dynasty, the Xia, appeared about 2200 B.C., but historians have little reliable information about it. Likewise, the Shang dynasty (1780–1050 B.C.), which followed the Xia, is understood more on the basis of archaeological finds than of written documentation.

Yet it was during the Shang period that many Chinese inventions first appeared. During this period, rulers called themselves Sons of Heaven—a rank above that of mere mortals—thus establishing one of the enduring traditions of Chinese government. Equally significant was the development during the Shang period of the distinctive Chinese system of writing, which was originally used by shamans (healers claiming magical powers) to record inscriptions on bones that they used to predict the future.

China knew no peace after the Shang dynasty collapsed. During the centuries of turmoil that followed, China was engulfed in almost constant warfare. By the time of the powerless Eastern Zhou emperors, who nominally ruled after 771 B.C. but could not settle internal disputes, warlords used iron weapons in battles over land and prestige. During this Warring States period the great Chinese thinker Confucius (551–479 B.C.) lived, whose teaching is the subject of selections 1 and 2. It was also during this time that another classic of Chinese thought, the *Dao De Qing* (selections 3 and 4) was compiled. In many ways the doctrines of Confucius and of the *Dao De Qing* oppose one another, but together they have become fundamental to the Chinese way of thinking. One way of understanding how seemingly contradictory views about life can be reconciled in Chinese thought is to grasp the concept of yin and yang—the perpetual interaction of opposites. Although the yin/yang concept comes from the most ancient period of Chinese history, it received its classical statement about two thousand years ago (selection 5).

The Warring States period ended in 221 B.C. with the reestablishment of a strong central government under the Qin dynasty, which conquered all its rivals (selection 6). The Qin did not last long, but under the Han dynasty that succeeded it—and which is the subject of chapter 7—a balance of Confucian and Daoist philosophies was achieved that ever after shaped Chinese public and private life. As you read the selections in chapter 6, ask yourself why the Chinese of the Warring States period longed for order and consider the different ways in which they hoped to overcome chaos and fear. Remember, too, that for many Chinese, Confucianism is a philosophy that regulates public and family life, whereas Daoism is a philosophy of the individual's inner life.

SELECTION 1:

The Legacy of Confucius

In the following selection, an eminent American historian of China, the late John K. Fairbank, assesses the unsettling world in which Confucius lived— a world of petty states constantly fighting among themselves and looking for ways to strengthen their grip on the territory and people they ruled.

The early Chinese philosophers, in any case, were first of all practical politicians. They were part of the new class of bureaucrats, produced by the spread of literacy and the needs of an increasingly complex political system. Such men often wandered from state to state, offering their services where they would be most appreciated. Great thinkers among them, whether successful or not as practical politicians, attracted followers and thus became teachers. Their disciples gradually formed into schools of philosophy, and from these schools the sayings of the original masters, as reworked and supplemented by many later hands, eventually emerged as the philosophical books of Zhou times.

Although the philosophers were often daring innovators, many of them looked to supposedly golden ages of the past for their inspiration, as have many other thinkers elsewhere in the world. In a civilization particularly concerned with the problems of society, it was natural that history, as

John K. Fairbank et al., *East Asia: Tradition and Transformation*, rev. ed. (Boston: Houghton Mifflin, 1989), pp. 41, 44.

the repository of human experience, should become the special focus of attention. This interest in the past, together with the peculiar Chinese respect for the written word, produced a tremendous veneration for the writings of earlier times. This, of course, has been a common trait throughout the world, but it seems to have been particularly strong among the Chinese. Confucius and other ancient Chinese philosophers looked upon the writings of earlier ages as classics from which they drew their own teachings, and this idea persisted in East Asia until recent times. For over two thousand years Chinese scholars, when faced with new problems, tried to wring the answers from reinterpretations of the classics.

To the Chinese, with their love of order and classification, "the Classics" is not just a vague term for ancient literature in general but means a clearly specified set of books associated with the dominant Confucian tradition. These works, together with the vast body of commentaries that has grown up around them, constitute the first of the traditional four divisions of Chinese literature. . . .

Confucius was a native of the tradition-bound central state of Lu. He aspired to high political office and wandered in vain from state to state in search of appointment. Thus, in his chosen role as a practical politician, he was a failure; in his incidental occupation as a teacher, however, time proved him an unparalleled success. At first glance the concepts Confucius taught seem unexciting and flat. He showed the bias of his day in his paramount interest in political problems. While he fully recognized the spirits and Heaven (Tien), sometimes showing a sense of mission derived from the latter, he was obviously not much interested in the suprahuman realm. To an inquiry about death, he replied, "Not yet understanding life, how can you understand death?" Even in the political sphere, he merely claimed to be a devoted student of antiquity and transmitter of the wisdom of the past. The disorder of his

own day, he felt, could be corrected if men would return to the political and social order supposedly created by the founders of the Zhou dynasty, King Wen and the Duke of Zhou.

To return to the ancient Way, Confucius felt, men must play their assigned roles in a fixed society of authority. The idea is succinctly expressed in the statement: "Let the ruler be a ruler and the subject a subject; let the father be a father and the son a son." Later this concept was expressed by the term "the rectification of names" (*jeng ming*), by which Confucians really meant that society should be made to conform with theory.

All this sounds ultraconservative, but Confucius was in fact a great, though probably unconscious, innovator in his basic concept that good government was fundamentally a matter of ethics. He did not question the hereditary right of the lords to rule, but he insisted that their first duty was to set a proper example of sound ethical conduct. In a day when might was right, he argued that the ruler's virtue and the contentment of the people, rather than power, should be the true measures of political success. Chinese thought before Confucius might be characterized as premoral; it centered on auguries and sacrifices. Confucius was China's first great moralist, the founder of a great ethical tradition in a civilization which above all others came to concentrate on ethical values.

After reading this selection, consider these questions:

1. Why did Chinese philosophers find a golden past attractive?
2. What gave the teaching of Confucius so much influence over Chinese society?
3. Does your idea of good government agree with the views of Confucius? Why or why not?

SELECTION 2:

Confucian Wisdom

Confucius never achieved the political leadership that he sought, but instead made his mark as a teacher of young men who wanted to make careers in public life. This selection, which consists of extracts from his Analects, *gives some idea of how and what he taught.*

The Master said, 'The determined scholar and the man of virtue will not seek to live at the expense of injuring their virtue. They will even sacrifice their lives to preserve their virtue complete.'

Tsze-kung asked about the practice of virtue. The Master said, 'The mechanic, who wishes to do his work well, must first sharpen his tools. When you are living in any state, take service with the most worthy among its great officers, and make friends of the most virtuous among its scholars.' . . .

The Master said, 'If a man take no thought about what is distant, he will find sorrow near at hand.'

The Master said, 'It is all over! I have not seen one who loves virtue as he loves beauty.'

The Master said, 'He who requires much from himself and little from others, will keep himself from *being the object of* resentment.'

The Master said, 'When a man is not *in the habit of* saying—"What shall I think of this? What shall I think of this?" I can indeed do nothing with him!'

The Master said, 'When a number of people are together, for a whole day, without their conversation turning on righteousness, and when they are fond of carrying out *the suggestions of* a small shrewdness;—theirs is indeed a hard case.'

The Master said, 'The superior man *in everything* considers righteousness to be essential. He performs it according to the rules of propriety. He brings it forth in humility. He completes it with sincerity. This is indeed a superior man.'

The Master said, 'The superior man is distressed by his want of ability. He is not distressed by men's not knowing him.'

The Master said, 'What the superior man seeks, is in himself. What the mean man seeks, is in others.'

The Master said, 'The superior man is dignified, but does not wrangle. He is sociable, but not a partisan.'

The Master said, 'The superior man does not promote a man *simply* on account of his words, nor does he put aside *good* words because of the man.'

Tsze-kung asked, saying, 'Is there one word which may serve as a rule of practice for all one's life?' The Master said, 'Is not RECIPROCITY such a word? What you do not want done to yourself, do not do to others.'

The Master said, 'In my dealings with men, whose evil do I blame, whose goodness do I praise, beyond what is proper? If I do sometimes exceed in praise, there must be ground for it in my examination *of the individual*.'

The Master said, 'The object of the superior man is truth. Food is not his object. . . . So with learning;—emolument may be found in it. The superior man is anxious lest he should not get truth; he is not anxious lest poverty should come upon him.

Confucian *Analects*, 15 and 16 in *The Chinese Classics*, James Legge, trans., 3rd ed., 5 vols. (Hong Kong: Hong Kong University Press, 1960), vol. 1, pp. 297–301, 303.

After reading this selection, consider these questions:

1. In what area does Confucius find virtue for the individual?
2. What instruction does Confucius give for human relationships?
3. Which of the maxims of Confucius do you still find valid for people in the modern world?

SELECTION 3:

Searching for the Dao

While Confucius and his followers were formulating their strong beliefs in active participation in government, a countertrend arose among many young men who favored an attitude of withdrawal and contentment within a self-contained world. Taking nature as a guide, those who subscribed to this philosophy became known as Daoists. The Dao is a subtle concept best translated as "the Way," and it implied conforming to the natural course of things rather than fighting for change. This means avoiding the life of stress that a political career so frequently brought.

Historian C.P. Fitzgerald here takes a careful look at Daoism. (Fitzgerald, and several other writers excerpted in this book, uses the older Wade-Giles system of transcribing Chinese words into English, according to which Dao and Daoism are romanized as Tao and Taoism, and the Dao De Qing *is romanized as* Tao Te Ching.*)*

The Taoists denied the value of any active participation in the affairs of mankind. Non-action was preferable to benevolent activity, which was itself a sign of the corruption of the times. With many pointed illustrations the *Tao Tê Ching* emphasized the principle of non-activity. The value of a bowl is not the utensil itself, but in the empty space it encloses. Again, the utility of a wheel depends, not on the rim or the spokes, but on the empty spaces within the hub. This theory of government advocated simplicity and denied the value of instruction for the mass of the people. . . .

Taoism was thus a mystical creed, of which the appeal was necessarily limited to men of philosophical temperament free from the pressing cares of the world. The scholar or the noble-man might renounce the cares of state or family and retire to a mountain, but the mass of the Chinese people, incessantly occupied with the need to earn their livelihood, could not find much guidance in a rule of life which denied the value of any earthly activity. No state could be organized on Taoist lines, for Taoism condemned the organization of society as a folly. Inevitably Taoism was rejected by the statesmen and the rulers who were recasting the destiny of the Chinese people.

Yet Taoism, for all its unpractical idealism, or perhaps on that account, continued to find a certain support, for its roots were in one of the outstanding qualities of the Chinese character, the capacity for patient endurance. It has always appealed to the Chinese dislike of meticulous regulation, and to the attitude of contemplative detachment with which the Chinese are wont to regard affairs which do not immediately concern

C.P. Fitzgerald, *China: A Short Cultural History* (Boulder: Westview Press, 1985), pp. 84, 87–88.

them. If there is truth in the view that a nation emphasizes the importance of those moral qualities which are not naturally strong in the national character, then the appeal of Taoism lies in the reaction from the Confucian insistence on virtues and qualities which are antipathetic to the genius of the race.

The desire for a system of morality which denied the value of family ties and public duties, and which emphasized contemplation and non-participation persisted after Taoism had long ceased to be a school of philosophy and had sunk to the level of a popular religion. Buddhism owed much of its success to the fact that the doctrine of renunciation of the world was already established in China, and met an abiding need of the Chinese mind.

After reading this selection, consider these questions:
1. Contrast Confucianism and Daoism.
2. Why was the appeal of Daoism limited to a part of the population?
3. What qualities of Daoism caused it to become a religious belief?

SELECTION 4:

Advice from the Dao De Qing

The following selection is extracted from the Dao De Qing *(The Classic of the Way of Virtue), illustrates the philosophical foundation of Daoism. Traditionally, the author of the* Dao De Qing *was considered to be Laozi (or, to use the older English spelling, Lao Tsu), a contemporary of Confucius, but there is no certainty that such a person ever existed. More likely the* Dao De Qing *is an ancient anthology of the writings of many thinkers.*

The meaning of the Dao De Qing *has been discussed ever since its brief, cryptic words were first written thousands of years ago. Many scholars today believe that it, like Confucius's* Analects, *was addressed to rulers and to the men who advised them. It is helpful to remember that* Dao *was an ancient Chinese concept meaning "the Way" the universe is ordered, to which rulers ought to conform.*

Do you think you can take over the universe and improve it?
I do not believe it can be done.

The universe is sacred.
You cannot improve it.
If you try to change it, you will ruin it.
If you try to hold it, you will lose it.

So sometimes things are ahead and sometimes they are behind;
Sometimes breathing is hard, sometimes it comes easily;
Sometimes there is strength and sometimes weakness;
Sometimes one is up and sometimes down.

Therefore the sage avoids extremes, excesses, and complacency.
Whenever you advise a ruler in the way of Tao,

Lao Tsu, *Tao Te Ching*, Gia-Fu Feng and Jane English, trans. (London: Wildwood House, 1973), pp. 29, 30.

Counsel him not to use force to conquer the
  universe.
For this would only cause resistance.
Thorn bushes spring up wherever the army has
  passed.
Lean years follow in the wake of a great war.
Just do what needs to be done.
Never take advantage of power.
Achieve results,
But never glory in them.

Achieve results,
But never boast.
Achieve results,
But never be proud.
Achieve results,

Because this is the natural way.
Achieve results,
But not through violence.

Force is followed by loss of strength.
This is not the way of Tao.
That which goes against the Tao
  comes to an early end.

After reading this selection, consider these
questions:

1. Why is passivity a feature of Daoism?
2. How might Daoism relate to the
   movement to protect the environment?
3. What advice does Daoism have for
   rulers? Is it valid?

SELECTION 5:

Yin and Yang

Traditional Chinese culture cannot be understood without appreciating the concept of yin and yang. The following selection is a document written by an unknown author in the Han period (second century B.C.–second century A.D.). In this ancient writing a mythical figure, the Yellow Emperor, explains the perpetual interaction of the two opposing natural forces, yin and yang, throughout the universe as well as in the human body. In our bodies, according to this concept, the balance of yin and yang determines our moods and explains the diseases that afflict us. The yin/yang concept also helps Chinese thinkers to reconcile seemingly opposing philosophies, such as Confucianism and Daoism.

The Yellow Emperor said: "The principle of Yin and Yang is the foundation of the entire universe. It underlies everything in creation. It brings about the development of parenthood; it is the root and source of life and death; it is found within the temples of the gods. In order to treat and cure diseases one must search for their origins.

"Heaven was created by the concentration of Yang, the force of light; Earth was created by the concentration of Yin, the force of darkness. Yang stands for peace and serenity; Yin stands for confusion and turmoil. Yang stands for destruction; Yin stands for conservation. Yang brings about disintegration; Yin gives shape to things. . . .

"The pure and lucid element of light is manifested in the upper orifices, and the turbid element of darkness is manifested in the lower orifices. Yang, the element of light, originates in the

"The Interaction of Yin and Yang," Mark Coyle, trans., in Patricia Buckley Ebrey, ed., *Chinese Civilization and Society: A Source Book* (New York: Macmillan, 1981), pp. 36–37.

pores. Yin, the element of darkness, moves within the five viscera. Yang, the lucid force of light, truly is represented by the four extremities; and Yin, the turbid force of darkness, stores the power of the six treasures of nature.

"Water is an embodiment of Yin, as fire is an embodiment of Yang. Yang creates the air, while Yin creates the senses, which belong to the physical body. When the physical body dies, the spirit is restored to the air, its natural environment. The spirit receives its nourishment through the air, and the body receives its nourishment through the senses. . . .

"If Yang is overly powerful, then Yin may be too weak. If Yin is particularly strong, then Yang is apt to be defective. If the male force is overwhelming, then there will be excessive heat. If the female force is overwhelming, then there will be excessive cold. Exposure to repeated and severe cold will lead to fever. Exposure to repeated and severe heat will induce chills. Cold injures the body while heat injures the spirit. When the spirit is hurt, severe pain will ensue. When the body is hurt, there will be swelling. Thus, when severe pain occurs first and swelling comes on later, one may infer that a disharmony in the spirit has done harm to the body. Likewise, when swelling appears first and severe pain is felt later on, one can say that a dysfunction in the body has injured the spirit. . . .

"Nature has four seasons and five elements. To grant long life, these seasons and elements must store up the power of creation in cold, heat, dryness, moisture, and wind. Man has five viscera in which these five climates are transformed into joy, anger, sympathy, grief, and fear. The emotions of joy and anger are injurious to the spirit just as cold and heat are injurious to the body. Violent anger depletes Yin; violent joy depletes Yang. When rebellious emotions rise to Heaven, the pulse expires and leaves the body. When joy and anger are without moderation, then cold and heat exceed all measure, and life is no longer secure. Yin and Yang should be respected to an equal extent." . . .

The Yellow Emperor asked, "Is there any alternative to the law of Yin and Yang?"

Ch'i Po answered: "When Yang is the stronger, the body is hot, the pores are closed, and people begin to pant; they become boisterous and coarse and do not perspire. They become feverish, their mouths are dry and sore, their stomachs feel tight, and they die of constipation. When Yang is the stronger, people can endure winter but not summer. When Yin is the stronger, the body is cold and covered with perspiration. People realize they are ill; they tremble and feel chilly. When they feel chilled, their spirits become rebellious. Their stomachs can no longer digest food and they die. When Yin is the stronger, people can endure summer but not winter. Thus Yin and Yang alternate. Their ebbs and surges vary, and so does the character of their diseases."

After reading this selection, consider these questions:

1. What can you learn from the concepts of yin and yang?
2. What does this selection say about the Chinese approach to illness?
3. How does a search for balance explain much about life?

SELECTION 6:

China's First Emperor

In 221 B.C. a ruler named Qin Shi Huangdi conquered all the petty states of China and established a centralized empire. Determined to uproot the old political order, he ordered the destruction of most philosophical books, including those of Confucius—all of which he associated with the chaos of the Warring States period. In 1974 Shi Huangdi's tomb was discovered, and archaeologists were astonished to discover in it more than seventy-five hundred life-size clay soldiers that had been buried with him.

What kind of ruler was this mighty despot, the "First Emperor"? In this selection, two modern historians comment on his reign. They use the Wade-Giles system of romanizing his names, Prince Cheng and Shih Huang-ti. They also refer to his dynasty as the Ch'in rather than the modern, or pinyin, Qin.

By 221 BC all resistance had ended and Prince Cheng was able to proclaim himself Shih Huang-ti, 'the First Emperor'. Although the Ch'in dynasty was of short duration, such was the energy and determination of its founder that this period represents a turning point in the history of Chinese civilization. In place of the old feudal system of government belonging to the Classical Age a centralized monarchy was established. The bureaucratic type of government that had developed in Ch'in became the model for future Chinese political organization, lasting until the twentieth century. The significance of the revolutionary change that Ch'in Shih Huang-ti began and Liu Pang, the founder of the following purely Chinese dynasty, the Han, completed cannot be underestimated. The early civilization of China *was* the working out of the possibilities offered by imperial unification.

The ruthless determination that had directed the 'Tiger of Ch'in' in his defeat of the Warring States soon became evident in the organization of the Ch'in Empire. In order to unify China he was obliged to become one of the great destroyers of history. Lacking any degree of economic integration, the Ch'in Empire was insecure in two main directions—the east and the north. The deposed aristocracy of the old feudal states posed an internal political threat, especially in the lower valley of the Yellow River, whilst in the north there was danger from the Hsiung Nu nomads, probably the Huns who invaded the Roman Empire in the fourth century. Military control seemed the

quickest and most efficient way of bringing stability. Therefore, Ch'in Shih Huang-ti abolished feudal holdings; compelled the nobles to reside at the capital, Hsienyang, where isolated from their supporters they remained without influence; awarded the *nung* greater rights over their land, but made them liable for taxes; and divided the Empire into new administrative areas under the control of military governors and civil administrators. Everything was reduced 'in a uniform manner': there was standardization of weights and measures, written language, and even vehicle axles, which ended the transfer and reweighing of goods at borders because of differences in ruts made by cartwheels from one state to another. The freer interchange of people and commodities fostered a wider national consciousness, though Ch'in Shih Huang-ti was careful to restrict the benefits that the *shang* derived from the growth of commerce.

The location of the imperial capital in the Wei valley was militarily sound. From Hsienyang, protected on three sides by mountain or desert, Ch'in Shih Huang-ti could sweep down the valley of the Yellow River into the lowlands and retire into an almost impregnable stronghold whenever the forces of the eastern provinces were organized. A network of tree-lined roads radiating from the capital was begun so that imperial orders and troops could be rapidly conveyed to the farthest outposts. Resentment was felt over the geographical location of the imperial capital, tucked away in the north-western corner of the Empire, but the same strategic and economic reasons were to prejudice the Former Han rulers in favour of the Wei valley. The refusal of Ch'in Shih Huang-ti to countenance any survival of

Yong Yap and Arthur Cotterell, *The Early Civilization of China* (New York: G.P. Putnam's Sons, 1975), pp. 74, 77.

feudalism—he would not grant fiefs to his own sons or relatives, lest the old rivalries of the Warring States period return—alienated the more traditional *shih* and caused Li Ssu, the chief minister, to recommend the 'Burning of the Books'. What this statesman feared was an alliance between the old aristocracy and Confucian scholars. Although Confucius had not condemned the Empire, he was unaware of such a possibility, so that his followers during the Ch'in dynasty were opposed to the end of feudalism. By imperial edict all schools of philosophy were required to close, with the exception of the Legalists, and all books were to be destroyed, except the imperial archives and works on medicine, divination and agriculture. This sweeping measure effectively destroyed feudalism; it caused a definite break in consciousness. When, in Han times, the ancient texts were painfully reconstructed from memory and the badly tattered copies that had been hidden at great personal risk, the feudal world seemed historically remote. Education rather than birth appeared as the important social qualification. If Li Ssu broke the power of the nobles, he had weakened the Ch'in dynasty too. The *shih* were united in hatred against the imperial house; the official class of Ch'in alone remained loyal.

After reading this selection, consider these questions:

1. Why did Qin Shi Huangdi (Ch'in Shih Huang-ti) feel compelled to destroy so much of ancient Chinese culture? Do you think he was justified?
2. In what ways were Qin Shi Huangdi's policies dictated by China's geography?
3. Why was the location of the capital important for Qin Shi Huangdi?

CHAPTER 7
The Han Empire:
Why Was It Crucial for China's History?

The borders of the Han Empire somewhat resemble those of modern China. The Han dynasty, which began in 202 B.C. when a rebel named Liu Bang overthrew the Qin rulers and seized their throne, lasted four hundred years. But by resurrecting the ancient Chinese philosophical classics and establishing their ideas as the fundamentals on which the government of imperial China rested, the Han dynasty left an indelible mark on the Chinese people and their culture. For example, the Chinese ever since have called themselves "the Han."

The Han period was one of great prosperity. Trade in silk, wax, and cloth helped raise living standards to new highs. Efficient agricultural production allowed Han China to feed the world's largest population.

To govern the state, the Han emperors selected men who had passed a series of examinations in order to qualify for the civil service. Rather than depend on unreliable aristocrats, the Han wanted the most talented people to fill their bureaucracy. Begun in 124 B.C., this examination system lasted until the early twentieth century. The writings of Confucius and of Confucian scholars were among the most important subjects tested in these examinations.

In reading the selections that follow, focus your attention on the ways in which the Han emperors sought and maintained power, on who assisted them in governing, and on the political ideas on which they based their authority. Ask yourself: What were the forces that made Han China a stable society? What factors undermined its stability? And was this a just society?

SELECTION 1:

The Gao Zu Emperor's Wars

This selection is taken from an account by the most important ancient Chinese historian, Sima Quan, who became the court historian in 108 B.C. His dynastic histories provided a model for all later Chinese historians' writings about their nation's past. He opens his story with the revolution against the Qin that brought Liu Bang to power. On becoming the ruler, Liu Bang adopted the name of "the Gao Zu emperor." After quoting from Liu Bang's exhortation to his supporters, Sima Quan then details the many wars that the new emperor fought to consolidate his position.

"The world has long suffered beneath Qin. Now, though you men of Pei should guard the city for the sake of the magistrate, the other nobles who have risen in rebellion will join in massacring the inhabitants of the city. If you will unite and do away with the magistrate, select from among your sons a worthy man to be your leader, and declare yourselves with the other nobles, then your homes and families shall all be spared. But if you do not, you will all be massacred without further ado!"

The elders then led the young men and together they murdered the magistrate of Pei, opened the city gates, and welcomed Gao Zu. They wished to make him magistrate, but Gao Zu announced, "The world today is in chaos with the nobles rising up everywhere. If you do not make a wise choice of a leader now, you will be cut down in one stroke and your blood will drench the earth. It is not that I care for my own safety, but only that I fear my abilities are not sufficient to insure your welfare. This is a most serious business. I beg you to consult once more among yourselves and select someone who is truly worthy."

Xiao He, Cao Can, and the other civil officials were concerned for their own safety and, fearful that if they assumed leadership and the undertak-

ing proved unsuccessful, Qin would exterminate their families, they all yielded in favor of Gao Zu. Then all the elders announced, "For a long time we have heard of the strange and wonderful happenings and the predictions of greatness concerning Liu Ji. Moreover, when we divine by the tortoise and milfoil, we find that no one receives such responses as Liu Ji!"

With this, Gao Zu declined several times but, since no one else dared to accept the position, he allowed himself to be made governor of Pei. He then performed sacrifices to the Yellow Emperor and to the ancient warrior Chi Yu in the district office of Pei and anointed his drums with the blood of the sacrifice. All his flags and banners he had made of red. Because the old woman had said that it was the son of the Red Emperor who had killed the snake, the son of the White Emperor, he decided to honor the color red in this fashion.

The young men and distinguished officials such as Xiao He, Cao Can, Fan Kuai, and others gathered together for him a band of two or three thousand men of Pei and attacked Hu-ling and Fang-yü. They then returned and guarded the city of Feng.

In the second year of the Second Emperor [208 B.C.] Chen She's general Zhou Wen marched west with his army as far as Xi and then returned. Yan, Ahou, Qi, and Wei all set up their own kings and Xiang Liang and Xiang Yu began their uprising in Wu.

Records of the Grand Historian of China: The Shih Chi of Ssu-ma Ch'ien, Burton Watson, trans., 3 vols. (New York: Columbia University Press, 1961), vol. 1, pp. 82–83.

Qin's overseer in the province of Su River, a man named Ping, led a force of troops and surrounded Feng for two days. The governor of Pei marched out of the city and fought and defeated him. Then, ordering Yong Chi to guard Feng, he led his troops to Xi. The magistrate of Su River, Zhuang, was defeated at Xi and fled to Qi where the governor Pei's marshal of the left captured and killed him. The governor of Pei returned and camped in the district of Gang, proceeding as far as Fang-yu. Zhou Shi had arrived to attack Fang-yu, but had not yet engaged in battle. (Zhou Shi was a man of Wei who had been sent by Chen She to seize the area.)

After reading this selection, consider these questions:

1. How did the Gao Zu emperor assume the leadership of the rebellion against the Qin?
2. What are the dangers of calling for a revolution?
3. Why were so many wars required for the Gao Zu emperor to come to power?

SELECTION 2:

Staffing the Civil Service

Ruling China required a civil service with sufficient knowledge to accomplish all the tasks that the emperor expected of its members. The system followed a strict and elaborate hierarchy, for the Chinese were very sensitive to status. The imperial examination system was meant to provide the best qualified men for appointment to office. Two modern historians explain how it worked.

The position of the official class is illustrated in the Chinese histories. From these writings a picture of a highly complex civil service emerges; one in which grade and privilege were protected and revered. The structure of government provided for the steady promotion of the official from a junior to senior post, and with their gradual rise through the hierarchy they duly incurred further privileges, benefits and dignity. The official view of the official is described thus in an edict of 144 B.C.: "Now the officials are the teachers of the people. It is proper that their carriages and quadriges [chariots drawn by four horses], their clothes and robes should correspond to their dignity."

The edict then goes on to describe at length precisely how the carriages of officials of each grade should be painted. For example: "We order that on carriages of important officials ranked at two thousand piculs [a variable weight measure, usually about 133 lb, which represented the annual stipend, in grain, of the officials] both side screens should be painted vermilion; and on those of officials whose positions are ranked from one thousand to six hundred piculs the left screen only should be vermilion." This same edict goes on to say that any official who "departs into the hamlets" not garbed according to his rank should be reported to the Lieutenant Chancellor who "shall beg the throne to order him to be punished."

One of the major problems facing Gao Zu was finding enough officials to operate the ever-expanding government machine. In 196 B.C., he issued an edict to senior officials of the states and

Edmund Capon and William Macquitty, *Princes of Jade* (London: Sphere Books, 1973), pp. 64–66.

commanderies throughout the kingdom requesting that they should send likely candidates to the capital for examination. The *Han Shu* records:

> Now I, by the spiritual power of heaven, and by my capable gentlemen and high officials have subjugated and possess the Empire and made it into one family. I wish it to be enduring so that generation after generation should worship at my ancestral temple. Capable persons have already shared with me in its pacification. Should it be that any capable persons are not to share together with me in its comfort and its benefits? If there are any capable gentlemen or sirs who are willing to follow and be friends with me, I can make them honorable and illustrious.

This was also a useful way for the Emperor to gain widespread loyalties by drawing upon people from all regions to staff his government.

These, in broad terms, were the principles of government instituted by the first Emperor of Han. The system derived substantially from the preceding Qin, and was to change very little for the next two thousand years. Its two principal characteristics became permanent features of Chinese society. First, there was the status of the officials, that favored elite, educated in the *Classics*, virtuous, worthy and held in the highest regard as the representatives of the Emperor. The officials formed a hierarchy quite distinct from the aristocracy, men like Prince Liu Sheing, who ruled the enfeoffed states and kingdoms, which were the hereditary possessions of privileged lines. In the Late Zhou period the *Chün-tzu* had been an inherited position, which no doubt caused the irreconcilably reactionary attitudes adopted by them at that time. But the Han continued in the Qin tradition of appointment and promotion through examination.

In spite of Gao Zu's initial dislike of Confucianism he instituted a system of government through professional scholars of which Confucius himself would have heartily approved. As the Han government and institutions became established an official class developed and with it, certain benefits accrued to official families. For example, opportunities arose for the advancement of their sons into an official government position which would not be so easily available to the commoner.

As the general wealth of the Han Empire increased so there emerged a social class new to China, the merchants, traders and businessmen. However they were by no means accorded the status and dignity of the scholar-official—a sure sign of the impact of the Confucian ideal. The position of the merchant in Early Han society is made clear in an Imperial edict of 199 B.C. during the reign of Gao Zu. It reads: "Merchants are not to be permitted to wear brocade, embroidery, flowered silk, crepe linen, sackcloth or wool, carry weapons, or ride a quadrige or a horse.". . .

With Gao Zu's tough, uncompromising and yet realistic rule the foundations of the Han were laid. It was an auspicious beginning, although the best was yet to come. The reign of the Emperor Wu Di from 141 to 87 B.C. is generally and justifiably considered as the apogee of Han power. He ascended the throne at the tender age of fifteen and a half, and yet seems to have been in no way overawed by his predicament. He was a man of tremendous energy and adopted an increasingly autocratic position.

Gao Zu had established an elaborate machinery for the management of the Han Empire, in which the officials played a vital part. His immediate successors developed and refined this system—until Wu Di. The unwritten law of China located the emperor at the summit of the political and social structure, but left the running of the country to his highly placed bureaucrats. Wu Di overthrew this traditional hierarchy and increasingly took on the duties of government, acting more as a prime minister than as a head of state or monarch. His actions set a precedent, for subsequent governments tended to alternate between eras of personal administration by dynamic emperors and eras of government by the bureaucrats. Traditionally the Emperor was beyond reproach and could do no wrong.

Periods of imperial rule, such as Wu Di's, tended therefore to end in disaster because no check, criticism or reformation of his decisions and actions could be made. This forms a contrast to the less decisive, but generally more flexible and stable, rule under the bureaucrats.

After reading this selection, consider these questions:

1. What were the privileges of a Chinese official?
2. Is an examination system a good way to recruit civil servants?
3. Why did the merchant class fail to enjoy high social status?

SELECTION 3:

Chinese Buddhism

During the Han dynasty, one change of enormous importance for future Chinese history and civilization occurred. Beginning in the first century B.C., Buddhism reached China from India, carried at first by monks traveling along the trade routes that stretched north into Central Asia and then eastward into the heart of China. Ideas or religions that originate outside China have, historically, been resisted by the Chinese, but Buddhism proved to be a great exception. The spread of Buddhism in China (and still later to Japan) is comparable in historical importance to the later conversions of the Roman world to Christianity and of Southwest Asia and North Africa to Islam. In the following selection, a modern Western historian assesses the gradual integration of Buddhism into the Chinese worldview, complementing (but not displacing) Confucianism and Daoism, and what this meant for Chinese civilization.

On the surface no culture could seem more alien to China than the Indian culture from which Buddhism emerged. The languages are poles apart, for Sanskrit is alphabetic, highly inflected, polysyllabic, and has a very complicated grammatical system; while Chinese is written in ideograms, is basically monosyllabic and uninflected, and has an extremely economical grammatical system. Chinese literature, despite Daoism, is comparatively earthbound, while Indian takes off in flights of imagination; China was this-worldly, while the Indian tradition pursued other-worldly goals; China dealt with historical timespans, India with cosmic eons; and China was concerned with family ethics, while India

Raymond Dawson, *The Chinese Experience* (New York: Charles Scribner's Sons, 1978), pp. 117–18.

was devoted to universal salvation. How was this great gulf to be crossed?

The initial success is partly explained by the fact that the Chinese who first became interested in Buddhism regarded it not as a foreign religion so much as an offshoot of Daoism; and the religion's domestication was further assisted by the fact that Daoist terms had to be used to translate the key concepts of Buddhism. At the same time Buddhism at this early stage appealed to the general human desire for salvation and the protection of powerful gods, instead of attempting to propagate very specific Indian ideas.

The Neo-Daoist influence was very effective in preparing the way for Buddhism in the Chinese-held south; but in the north . . . the barbarian rulers preferred to lend an ear to foreign proponents of a foreign religion rather than become too dependent on Chinese advisers. Buddhist monks also (like eunuchs at the imperial palace or clerics at European courts) had the attraction of having no family attachments to provide another focus of loyalty, and so they seemed likely to prove trustworthy servants. Consequently these proponents of an unworldly religion were soon drawn into politics, which they were glad to embrace for the opportunity it gave them of securing patronage for their faith.

The credulous barbarian chieftains were not, of course, won for Buddhism by the exposition of metaphysical subtleties, but by the monks' apparently magical powers. The performance of miracles persuaded the superstitious rulers not only of the efficacy of their Buddhist counselors but also of the power of the Buddhist deities to protect the state, which remained the important reason for imperial patronage of Buddhism even in the more sophisticated era of the Tang. Magical practices were also a feature of Buddhism in its Indian birthplace; and great pilgrims, scholars, and translators did not abide permanently on the higher plane of doctrine, but descended to perform their various party tricks.

The famous monk and translator Kumarajiva, for example, was an adept at swallowing needles, a skill he often displayed before hosts of awed spectators. And when the pilgrim Xuan Zang went to India he saved himself from being killed by pirates by concentrating his thought on Maitreya in the Tushita Heaven, with the miraculous consequence that a great wind arose, and the waters of the Ganges mounted and capsized the pirates' ships, which made them repent and become lay members of the Buddhist community. Performances of magic were featured among the entertainments at the great Buddhist festivals, and this interest in magic stemmed naturally from the fact that Buddhist philosophy considered the world to be an illusion.

After reading this selection, consider these questions:

1. How did Buddhism enter China, and why did many Chinese convert to Buddhism?
2. What was the connection between Buddhism and Daoism?
3. Confucianism was a set of beliefs and practices dealing with how China should be governed and how Chinese family life should be conducted. How might Confucian teachings be reconciled with Buddhism?

SELECTION 4:

The Han Dynasty Assessed

A *modern European historian of ancient China assesses the successes and the failures of Han rule in this selection. Note in particular the Han emperors' constant need to defend China's northern borders against threats from hostile barbarian tribes. (In this, as in other respects, Han China and the Roman Empire faced similar problems.) Note also the important innovations in military technology and organization that the Chinese achieved. It may help to remember that the famous Great Wall, which still stretches along China's traditional northern border, had been begun under the Han dynasty's predecessor, the Qin.*

Han power, as exercised during the reign of Wudi against the "barbarians," was partly due to the regime's capacity for organization. Having got into its stride, the governmental machine could enlist conscripts not only to go on campaign, but also to secure fresh supplies and construct roads; similarly, the system of lines of defense, which we call the Great Wall, was well maintained and was extended at this period.

China had another crucial advantage over her enemies. She could rely on her agricultural economy and to an even greater degree on the products of her industry and craftsmanship—iron and steel weapons, luxury articles like silk—which the surrounding peoples wished to buy. These products of state-controlled factories (after 119 B.C.) constituted a means of exerting pressure, a trading asset, a major trump card in the game of Chinese diplomacy, the economic basis on which the system of tribute was to be founded. The government also kept strict control of the export of goods (weapons, iron tools and domestic animals) that might strengthen the military power or increase the economic resources of the barbarians.

Another cause of success was the fact that Chinese fighting methods had changed radically since the beginning of the century, having adapted to those of her enemies. The use of the chariot in battle was virtually abandoned. In their encounters with the Xiongnu the Han showed a technical virtuosity and a mobility that they had learnt from the nomads. The commonest tactic on both sides consisted in rapid raids employing few men, mostly horsemen, designed to dislodge the enemy, seize his cattle and horses, and induce his chiefs to surrender. Clearly such a form of battle did not result in decisive victory for either camp; Wudi never finally defeated the Xiongnu. Fighting methods were very different in Central Asia; they required troops who were less highly trained but could endure long marches and lay siege to towns.

Conscripts—mounted bowmen of the northern and north-western provinces, crossbowmen on foot and other infantrymen of the central and

eastern provinces—made up but a small part of the army at the end of the second century; the core of the troops consisted of mercenaries, true professionals, and convicts.

A further source of Han superiority was its weaponry, which was increasingly made of iron and steel, especially in the case of the long swords used by the cavalry; instead of leather armor, armor made of iron plaques was improved as the plaques became smaller and were used in conjunction with scale-like plates. This coat of mail now also covered a larger area of the chest and shoulders. The crossbow, which had been invented during the Period of the Warring States and had a bronze mechanism of extraordinary precision which the Han kept secret—remained one of the weapons that China's neighbors feared most. Improved models like the repeating crossbow may have come into common use at this time.

Yet another cause of the Han victories, especially those of the years 129 to 119, lay in the valor of their generals, who included Wei Qing and Huo Qubing (died 117, aged twenty-four), Li Guangli and Li Guang. Not all received equal reward for their merits. Li Guang, who was an extraordinary bowman, committed suicide when he was over sixty rather than suffer sentence for having lost his way in the desert with his men; Li Ling, his grandson and another ill-starred officer, surrendered to the Xiongnu in 99 B.C. after defeat in unequal combat.

It should be remembered that a Chinese general returning after a setback risked beheading and that an officer who surrendered to the Xiongnu and was taken prisoner endangered his whole family. Li Ling's mother, wife and son were executed when the government heard of his defection. Sima Qian, the historian, who had defended him before the emperor, was accused of wishing to deceive the latter and was sentenced to castration. Thus the last campaigns of Wudi's reign cost China many brave officers, including Li Guangli, who went over to the enemy in 90, and Li Ling, who died among the Xiongnu in 74.

Every Han victory depended not only on good organization, on the bravery and endurance of the men and on rapid conveyance of provisions, but also on an adequate supply of horses. Wudi's

Michele Pirazzoli-t'Serstevens, *The Han Dynasty*, Janet Seligman, trans. (New York: Rizzoli, 1982), pp. 90–91.

wars emptied all the stud-farms of the empire; the campaigns of 119 B.C. alone resulted in the loss of 100,000 horses. We touch here on a vital point and one of the major difficulties encountered by the Han: an insufficient supply of fresh horses. In 118 the government fixed the price of a stallion at 200,000 cash (or 20 gold *jin*). In this way it encouraged the breeding of horses. Moreover, the introduction of new breeds from the western lands, the planting of lucerne from seeds brought back by Zhang Qian, had enabled the government to reconstitute a cavalry. The fact remains that Wudi's campaigns were extremely expensive in horses, equipment and above all in human lives. To cite a single example: Li Guangli returned from the Fergahan campaign with 10,000 of the 60,000 soldiers with whom he had set out.

These wars were also costly in terms of the defensive systems involved, the need to maintain garrisons and provide them with grain. Yet in the long term the implementation of the government's policy of colonization proved an asset. Conquered commanderies, especially those of the north-west, were occupied immediately by Chinese colonists, dispatched (usually forcibly) to develop the new territories. The main transfers of population took place in 127 (100,000 persons in Shuofang commandery), 120 (725,000 persons), 118, 111, 100, 99 and 92 B.C. It has been calculated that over two million persons were directed to the northern frontiers in this way during Wudi's reign.

After reading this selection, consider these questions:

1. What prompted the Han emperors' campaign to expand China's borders?
2. What happened to a Han general who was defeated?
3. How do horses figure into the Han victories?

SELECTION 5:

A Chinese Woman Among the Barbarians

The Han were acutely aware of the cultural and social differences between themselves and the "barbarian" peoples beyond the Great Wall. This sense of cultural distance should be clearly apparent after reading this extract from a poem written by a Chinese woman, Tsai Yen, who was captured by barbarians and eventually became the wife of a chief of the Tatars. Note in particular Tsai Yen's opening complaint that "the mandate of Heaven / Was withdrawn from the Han Dynasty." The concept of "the mandate of Heaven" is important in the Chinese tradition: It means that an imperial dynasty is legitimate only as long as it protects the Chinese people and rules justly; when a dynasty no longer fulfills this condition, it loses "the mandate of Heaven" and deserves its downfall.

I was born in a time of peace,
But later the mandate of Heaven
Was withdrawn from the Han Dynasty.

Heaven was pitiless.
It sent down confusion and separation.
Earth was pitiless.
It brought me to birth in such a time.
War was everywhere. Every road was dangerous.
Soldiers and civilians everywhere
Fleeing death and suffering.
Smoke and dust clouds obscured the land
Overrun by the ruthless Tatar bands.
Our people lost their will power and integrity.
I can never learn the ways of the barbarians.
I am daily subject to violence and insult.
I sing one stanza to my lute and a Tatar horn.
But no one knows my agony and grief.

II

A Tatar chief forced me to become his wife,
And took me far away to Heaven's edge.
Ten thousand clouds and mountains
Bar my road home,
And whirlwinds of dust and sand
Blow for a thousand miles.
Men here are as savage as giant vipers,
And strut about in armor, snapping their bows.
As I sing the second stanza I almost break the
    lutestrings.
Will broken, heart broken, I sing to myself.

VII

The sun sets. The wind moans.
The noise of the Tatar camp rises all around me.
The sorrow of my heart is beyond expression,
But who could I tell it to anyway?
Far across the desert plains,
The beacon fires of the Tatar garrisons
Gleam for ten thousand miles.
It is the custom here to kill the old and weak
And adore the young and vigorous.
They wander seeking new pasture,
And camp for a while behind earth walls.

Cattle and sheep cover the prairie,
Swarming like bees or ants.
When the grass and water are used up,
They mount their horses and drive on their cattle.
The seventh stanza sings of my wandering.
How I hate to live this way!

XI

I have no desire to live, but I am afraid of death.
I cannot kill my body, for my heart still has
    hope
That I can live long enough
To obtain one and only desire—
That someday I can see again
The mulberry and catalpa trees of home.
If I had consented to death,
My bones would have been buried long ago.
Days and months pile up in the Tatar camp.
My Tatar husband loved me. I bore him two sons.
I reared and nurtured them unashamed,
Sorry only that they grew up in a desert outpost.
The eleventh stanza—sorrow for my sons
At the first notes pierces my heart's core.

XIII

I never believed that in my broken life
The day would come when
Suddenly I could return home.
I embrace and caress my Tatar sons.
Tears wet our clothes.
An envoy from the Han Court
Has come to bring me back,
With four stallions that can run without stopping.
Who can measure the grief of my sons?
They thought I would live and die with them.
Now it is I who must depart.
Sorrow for my boys dims the sun for me.
If we had wings we could fly away together.
I cannot move my feet,
For each step is a step away from them.
My soul is overwhelmed.
As their figures vanish in the distance
Only my love remains.
The thirteenth stanza—
I pick the strings rapidly
But the melody is sad.
No one can know
The sorrow which tears my bowels.

The Orchid Boat: Women Poets of China, Kenneth Rexroth and Ling Chung, trans. (New York: McGraw-Hill, 1972), pp. 4–7.

XVII

The seventeenth stanza. My heart aches, my
   tears fall.
Mountain passes rise before us, the way is hard.
Before I missed my homeland
So much my heart was disordered.
Now I think again and again, over and over,
Of the sons I have lost.
The yellow sagebrush of the border,
The bare branches and dry leaves,
Desert battlefields, white bones
Scarred with swords and arrows,
Wind, frost, piercing cold,
Cold springs and summers
Men and horses hungry and exhausted, worn

out—
I will never know them again
Once I have entered Chang An.
I try to strangle my sobs
But my tears stream down my face.

   After reading this selection, consider these
questions:
   1. Based on Tsai Yen's verses, describe
      Tatar life.
   2. What aspects of Tatar life does Tsai
      Yen find intolerable from the Chinese
      point of view?
   3. Why does Tsai Yen have ambiguous
      feelings about returning to Han
      China?

SELECTION 6:

Han China and Rome Compared

As has already been pointed out, Han China and imperial Rome faced similar problems, including fending off barbarian threats and maintaining a sprawling empire that embraced most of the civilized world as known to Chinese or Romans. Both empires eventually collapsed, although their legacies to their respective civilizations were enormous. In selection 6, modern historian S.A.M. Adshead perceptively compares the Han and imperial Roman experiences.

The Roman empire was laid out like an amphitheater around the arena of the Mediterranean. Rome itself was the imperial box, the older coastal provinces were the stalls, the new inland *limes* [borderland] provinces were the heavily buttressed upper circles. The internal differentiation was between, on the one hand, upper and lower, *limes* and city, and on the other, sun and shade, the old urbanization of the east, the new urbanization of the west.

   The Han empire, *per contra* [on the other hand], was laid out like a wheel. The region of the two imperial capitals, Ch'ang-an and Lo-yang, formed the hub; the converging valleys of the Wei, the Fen, the Ching, the Lo, the Han and the Huang-ho [all Chinese rivers] formed the spokes. The internal differentiation was between center and circumference, capital and provinces. Both

S.A.M. Adshead, *China in World History* (New York: St. Martin's Press, 1988), pp. 15–18.

empires in antiquity were centrally planned, but Rome in a series of concentric circles, China in a series of radiating lines. The Roman empire was the work of a city state which sought to stabilize its dominion by universalizing cities, city life, institutions and values. It tended therefore to homogenization, a general rise in the level of urbanization, a Conrad Hilton civilization of everywhere-similar fora, basilicas, theaters, baths, circuses and insulae. The Chinese empire, on the other hand, was the work of a bureaucratic territorial state which sought to stabilize its dominion by monopolizing for the court capital resources, amenities, protection and prestige. It tended therefore to heterogenization, to a fall in the general level of urbanization following the unification of the empire and a growing disparity between the lifestyles of court and country. Both empires lived by and for cultural glamour and conspicuous consumption but in the one case they were diffused, in the other concentrated.

A comparison of the extent and character of the communications systems of the two areas suggests that Han China was less integrated than the Roman empire. According to [American historian Joseph] Needham, the Roman empire under Hadrian [early second century A.D.] covered 1,763,000 square miles and had 48,500 miles of road, an average of 27.5 miles of road per 1,000 square miles of territory. Han China, on the other hand, covered 1,532,000 square miles and had 22,000 miles of road, an average of only 14.35 miles of road per 1,000 square miles of territory. Moreover, while for Han China, roads were the essence of the communications system, for Rome they were only an adjunct to the Mediterranean whose sea lanes will have at least doubled the total length of routes. Needham suggests that the greater use of rivers and canals for transportation in China as compared to Europe counterbalanced the advantage of the Mediterranean. This may be true for the later periods of Chinese history, the Tang and the Sung [both later Chinese dynasties], for example, when the Grand Canal has been completed, but it is doubtful for the Han. Neither the Yellow River nor its tributaries, in whose valleys Chinese civilization was then centered, are good for navigation and most

Han hydraulic activity was for irrigation, not communication. Like the Achaemenid [Persian] empire, Han China was a road state on a plateau, and this in itself ensured inferiority in spatial integration to a Mediterranean empire, since in premodern conditions land transport was twenty to forty times more expensive that water transport. Moreover, the loess limited the utility of the roads by its vertical cleavage, crevassing and occlusion of adjacent valleys. Teilhard de Chardin [a French scholar in northern China in the twentieth century] vividly describes this terrain: "an unbelievable network of fissures with vertical walls, in the midst of which one feels as lost and paralyzed as in the middle of the trees of a forest or the waves of the sea." Needham seems to imply that Han China and Rome were not dissimilar in spatial relations; to me, the evidence suggests that they were strikingly different.

Even allowing for accidents of survival, it is difficult not to conclude from the archaeological remains that Han China was a less splendid society than Imperial Rome. The Great Wall no doubt is a stupendous monument, though most of its imposing appearance dates from Ming [fifteenth–seventeenth centuries] rather than Han times, but it stands by itself, and though Chinese cities had impressive walls, they did not contain the monumental public buildings of the Classical West—the amphitheaters, aqueducts, arches, basilicas, baths, circuses, theaters and temples. Rome was a federation of city states, Han China was a swollen court; but in addition, the difference between their towns was rooted in different options for building materials and different conceptions of what a house was for.

The fundamental options of Rome and, following her, Europe generally, were for stone, diffusion of heat by hypocausts or multiple fireplaces, and durability. A house was a capital investment, perhaps the prototype of all fixed capital investment, an assertion of culture in the face of nature. The fundamental Chinese options, on the other hand, were for wood, concentration of heat at the *kang* or heated divan, and reparability. A house was a charge on income, an extension of consumer non-durables, an adaptation of culture to nature. In the West, buildings were in principle winter palaces, exclusions of weather, permanent embodiments of hearth and family. In China, buildings were in principle summer houses, modifications of weather, makeshift additions to the real home which was the loess cave or the family tomb. The one option produced monumentality and splendor, the other convenience and harmony. . . .

The body politic of the Han was healthier than that of the Roman empire. With its superior physical technology in arable farming and metallurgy and its lower degree of urbanization, intercommunication and luxury building, the Han world did not suffer from irremediable contradictions between superstructure and base, state and society. Frictions there were, no doubt, but they were adjustable without cataclysm.

In the Roman body politic, on the other hand, with its more primitive physical technology yet more grandiose and more parasitic sociology, there were such contradictions, especially after

the Illyrian emperors, in response to the military mutinies and barbarian invasions of the mid-third century, doubled the army and multiplied fortifications without sufficient provisions for increased agricultural productivity behind the front. The huge carapace of the Roman *limes* imposed a burden on the organism it shielded that was far heavier than the Han protectorate garrisons in Central Asia. The Great Wall is impressive, but with Han Wu Di's forward policy, it ceased to be a frontier and Han China was not a *limes* society with its attendant costs and dangers.

After reading this selection, consider these questions:
1. Why did the Roman federation of city-states not develop in Han China?
2. How did Roman and Chinese construction methods differ?
3. Why did the Great Wall lose its importance after Wu Di's reign?

UNIT 2

The Early European Experience

CONTENTS

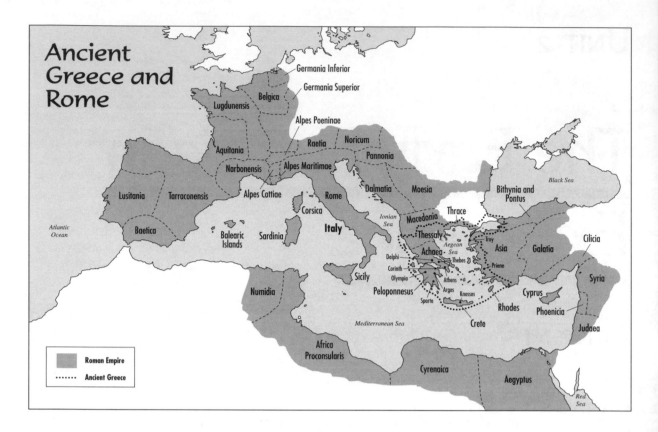

Ancient Greece and Rome

Germania Inferior
Germania Superior
Belgica
Lugdunensis
Alpes Poeninae
Raetia
Noricum
Aquitania
Pannonia
Narbonensis
Alpes Maritimae
Alpes Cottiae
Dalmatia
Moesia
Black Sea
Lusitania
Tarraconensis
Rome
Bithynia and Pontus
Corsica
Thrace
Ionian Sea
Macedonia
Atlantic Ocean
Baetica
Balearic Islands
Italy
Thessaly
Troy
Asia
Galatia
Cilicia
Sardinia
Sardinia
Aegean Sea
Achaea
Delphi
Priene
Sicily
Corinth
Thebes
Syria
Olympia
Athens
Numidia
Peloponnesus
Argos
Knossos
Cyprus
Sparta
Phoenicia
Rhodes
Crete
Judaea
Mediterranean Sea
Africa Proconsularis
Cyrenaica
Aegyptus
Red Sea

Roman Empire
.... Ancient Greece

Europe and the Byzantine Empire, About 1000

Kingdom of Norway
Kingdom of Sweden
Kingdom of Scotland
Kingdom of the Volga Bulgars
Irish Kingdoms
Kingdom of Denmark
Russia
Kingdom of England
Kingdom of Germany
Duchy of Poland
HOLY ROMAN EMPIRE
Kdm. of Hungary
Principality of Tmutarakan
Atlantic Ocean
Kingdom of France
Kingdom of Navarre
Kdm. of Croatia
Kingdom of the Asturias and Leon
Kingdom of Burgundy
Kdm. of Serbia
Black Sea
Kdm. of Georgia
Co. of Barcelona
Kingdom of Italy
Adriatic Sea
Kdm. of Bulgaria
Principality of Transylvania
Caliphate of Cordova
Tyrrhenian Sea
BYZANTINE EMPIRE
Maghreb
Idrisids
Mediterranean Sea
Ionian Sea
Hamdanids
Zeirids
Mediterranean Sea
Fatimite Caliphate

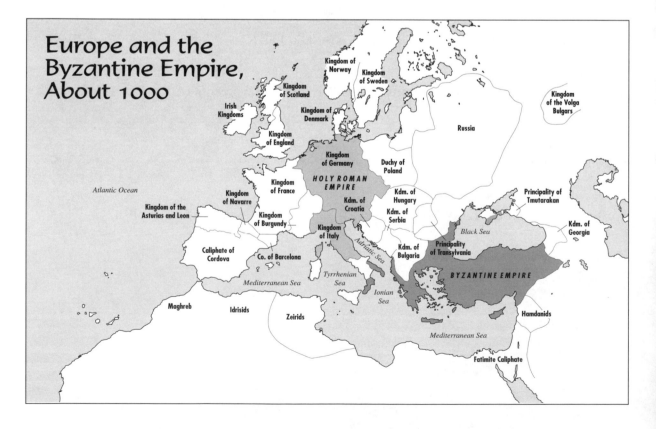

UNIT 2
The Early European Experience

European civilization first began on the small islands of the Aegean Sea and on Crete. From there the cultivation of wheat, grapes, and olives that supported their economies passed to the mainland. Here the Indo-European peoples whom we know as Greeks took what they learned and adapted it to their own circumstances.

One city, Athens, was especially adept at seizing opportunities to build an empire through seaborne trade in wine and oil. Even more importantly, Athenians introduced a form of government as yet unknown in the ancient world, whereby a majority of citizens, rather than a single ruler and his advisers, decided policy. The Athenians called their constitution a democracy, a word that we use today to describe our own political system. Athenian democracy and social organization was not perfect; some of its weaknesses are demonstrated in the selections that follow.

Rome followed Athens at the center of the Mediterranean stage and held that position for six hundred years. Early Roman politicians spoke of their system of government as a republic and were as proud as any Athenian of the way it worked. The Romans could also point to their creation of an empire that encompassed the Mediterranean, a feat never before accomplished which provided their elites with a very comfortable way of life. Our selections speak of the building of the Republic, the causes of its expansion, and finally its breakdown, which led to the assumption of power by the Caesars.

Rome built an empire that encompassed most of the world known to Western people of the time, and which eventually adopted Christianity as its religion. In the Byzantine Empire, ancient Rome's direct heir, a synthesis of Mediterranean life emerged: Roman political institutions, the Christian religion, and Greek culture.

While Byzantium continued the classical tradition in eastern Europe, Germanic invaders destroyed much of its culture in the West. Charlemagne made the first attempt to link a Germanic kingdom to the earlier Mediterranean civilization.

In studying these selections, consider:

1. What were the differences and similarities between Athens and Rome?
2. What was the role of women in both societies?
3. Why did Christianity quickly develop a structure?
4. Contrast the culture of the Byzantine world with that of Charlemagne's Frankish kingdom.

CHAPTER 8
Ancient Greece: What Was the Ideal and the Reality of Democracy?

Compared with the great empires that we have been studying, ancient Greece was unique. Beginning about 750 B.C., when written records first appeared, the people of mainland Greece, the Greek islands, and the coast of Anatolia (modern Turkey) organized themselves not into large kingdoms, but rather into tiny self-governing cities, each jealously guarding its independence. The emergence of these city-states coincided with a great population and economic expansion in the Greek-speaking world. The city-states responded by building extensive trading networks and frequently dispatching their surplus population to colonies—new cities—that they established at many places along the shores of the Mediterranean.

Our English word *politics* comes from the ancient Greek word for city, *polis* (plural: *poleis*). Not only did the Greeks form the first cities on the European continent, they also made city life and its politics central to their way of life. How should cities be run? Who should be a citizen? How should public policy be determined? And who should rule? A king? A dictator? The local aristocrats? The richest men? Or all the people? The answers that the different Greek cities gave to these questions have added other words to our vocabulary: monarchy ("rule by one"), tyranny (dictatorial rule by an illegal usurper), oligarchy ("rule by the few"), ostracism (exiling from a city someone who was considered too dangerous to be allowed to remain), and, most important, democracy ("rule by the people [*demos*]").

It was in Athens, the largest and among the richest Greek cities, that the idea of self-government first occurred. By the early fifth century B.C., a democratic system of government was in place in Athens. For the next several centuries, any citizen could address the city assembly, might be chosen to serve on the city council, or could become a municipal administrator. Policy was decided by voting in the citizen assembly.

How well did Athenian democracy work, and was it a real democracy by modern standards? These are the questions you should keep in mind as you read the selections in this chapter.

SELECTION 1:

The Oration of Pericles

Pericles (ca. 490–431 B.C.), a leader of the Athenian city-state at the height of its wealth and power, had no doubt that Athenian democracy was a great success. In this selection he addresses the Athenian citizens early in a great war that Athens fought against its rival, Sparta. The occasion was the public funeral that was held for Athenian citizens killed in battle. At stake in this war was leadership of the entire Greek-speaking world, as well as Athens's economic dominance.

These were not Pericles' actual words; instead, they were written by the famous Athenian historian Thucydides (ca. 460–400 B.C.), whose Peloponnesian War *tells the dramatic and tragic story of how the ambition and arrogance of Athens eventually united most of Greece against it and led to its downfall. In putting these words into Pericles' mouth, Thucydides explains that he is providing the gist of what the orator had to say on this occasion. Whether or not Pericles actually said such things, Thucydides' version of his words is a classic call for citizens to take pride in governing themselves democratically. As such, it remains a key document of Western civilization.*

I shall begin with our ancestors: it is both just and proper that they should have the honour of the first mention on an occasion like the present. They dwelt in the country without break in the succession from generation to generation, and handed it down free to the present time by their valour. And if our more remote ancestors deserve praise, much more do our own fathers, who added to their inheritance the empire which we now possess, and spared no pains to be able to leave their acquisitions to us of the present generation. Lastly, there are few parts of our dominions that have not been augmented by those of us here, who are still more or less in the vigour of life; while the mother country has been furnished by us with everything that can enable her to depend on her own resources whether for war or for peace. That part of our history which tells of the military achievements which gave us our several

The Complete Writings of Thucydides: The Peloponnesian War (New York: Modern Library, 1951), pp. 103–105.

possessions, or of the ready valour with which either we or our fathers stemmed the tide of Hellenic or foreign aggression, is a theme too familiar to my hearers for me to dilate on, and I shall therefore pass it by. But what was the road by which we reached our position, what the form of government under which our greatness grew, what the national habits out of which it sprang; these are questions which I may try to solve before I proceed to my panegyric upon these men; since I think this to be a subject upon which on the present occasion a speaker may properly dwell, and to which the whole assemblage, whether citizens or foreigners, may listen with advantage.

Our constitution does not copy the laws of neighbouring states; we are rather a pattern to others than imitators ourselves. Its administration favours the many instead of the few; this is why it is called a democracy. If we look to the laws, they afford equal justice to all in their private differences; if to social standing, advancement in public life falls to reputation for capacity, class considerations not being allowed to interfere with merit; nor again does poverty bar the way, if a man is able to serve the state, he is not hindered by the obscurity of his condition. The freedom which we enjoy in our government extends also to our ordinary life. There, far from exercising a jealous surveillance over each other, we do not feel called upon to be angry with our neighbour for doing what he likes, or even to indulge in those injurious looks which cannot fail to be offensive, although they inflict no positive penalty. But all this ease in our private relations does not make us lawless as citizens. Against this fear is our chief safeguard, teaching us to obey the magistrates and the laws, particularly such as regard the protection of the injured, whether they are actually on the statute book, or belong to that code which, although unwritten, yet cannot be broken without acknowledged disgrace.

Further, we provide plenty of means for the mind to refresh itself from business. We celebrate games and sacrifices all the year round, and the elegance of our private establishments forms a daily source of pleasure and helps to banish the spleen; while the magnitude of our city draws the produce of the world into our harbour, so that to the Athenian the fruits of other countries are as familiar a luxury as those of his own.

If we turn to our military policy, there also we differ from our antagonists. We throw open our city to the world, and never by alien acts exclude foreigners from any opportunity of learning or observing, although the eyes of an enemy may occasionally profit by our liberality; trusting less in system and policy than to the native spirit of our citizens; while in education, where our rivals from their very cradles by a painful discipline seek after manliness, at Athens we live exactly as we please, and yet are just as ready to encounter every legitimate danger. . . .

Nor are these the only points in which our city is worthy of admiration. We cultivate refinement without extravagance and knowledge without effeminacy; wealth we employ more for use than for show, and place the real disgrace of poverty not in owning to the fact but in declining the struggle against it. Our public men have, besides politics, their private affairs to attend to, and our ordinary citizens, though occupied with the pursuits of industry, are still fair judges of public matters; for, unlike any other nation, regarding him who takes no part in these duties not as unambitious but as useless, we Athenians are able to judge at all events if we cannot originate, and instead of looking on discussion as a stumbling-block in the way of action, we think it an indispensable preliminary to any wise action at all.

After reading this selection, consider these questions:

1. What are the deeds of Athens that prompt Pericles to boast?
2. How does public opinion in Athens affect society, according to Pericles?
3. What kind of reception would this talk have received? Who was unlikely to support Pericles' views?

SELECTION 2:

Women in Athens

By modern American standards, Athenian democracy was flawed. Not everyone in the city participated. Athens was a slaveholding society, and slaves had no political rights. Foreigners, called metics, from other Greek city-states who lived in Athens were barred from citizenship. Women, even *if they were Athenian born, had no right to participate in politics. Indeed, the lives of most women (except for cultivated prostitutes, who entertained well-to-do men at dinner parties) were almost completely controlled by their husbands, fathers, or other male kinfolk. The following selection, written by a contemporary American historian, describes some aspects of women's life in democratic Athens.*

In 451/50 the Athenians passed a law about citizenship on the proposal of Perikles. It provided that a child should only have citizenship if both its parents were citizens. This law implied that women, as well as men, could be citizens. Attic Greek had two words for "citizen," *astos* (feminine *astē*) and *politēs* (feminine *politis*). Both are used of women. But proof of citizenship was not the same for men and for women. This is shown by the questions asked at the examination of men who had been chosen to the nine archonships [magistracies]. Each candidate was asked to state the name of his father, the deme [clan] of his father, the name of his father's father, the name of his mother, the name of his mother's father, and the deme of his mother's father. He was not asked to state the deme of his father's father, since it was the same as that of his father, membership in demes being hereditary in the male line. The candidate was not asked to state the deme of his mother, since women were not registered in demes. The lists kept by the demes attested the status of male citizens, but no such lists were kept to attest that of female citizens.

Before 451/50 there may have been no statute nor even any acknowledged rule governing the transmission of citizenship by descent. Certainly some male Athenians of earlier generations took foreign wives and their sons were citizens. In the fourth century the crucial step in recognizing a young man as a citizen came when he was in his eighteenth year and was presented to the assembly of his father's deme; the demesmen voted on oath whether to add him to their list. . . .

An Athenian woman did not marry; she was given in marriage. A law is quoted by Pseudo-Demosthenes [a minor political writer] to show

Raphael Sealey, *Women and Law in Classical Greece* (Chapel Hill: University of North Carolina Press, 1990), pp. 12–13, 25–26.

who has the right to give a woman in marriage:

> Whatever woman is pledged on just terms to be a wife by her father, or by her brother who has the same father, or by her paternal grandfather, the children born of her shall be legitimate (*gnēsioi*) children.

The word used here for wife is not *gynē*, the customary word of classical prose, but the archaic *damar*. The language of law could be conservative. The verb translated as "pledge" is *engyān*. It and its noun *engyēsis* are crucial for understanding classical marriage. It might equally be translated "entrust."

Engyēsis was an oral contract, made between the man who gave the woman into marriage and the bridegroom. The form of words is known. The man giving the woman said: "I pledge (such and such a woman) for the purpose of producing legitimate (*gnēsioi*) children." He uttered the verb *engyō* in the active. Uttering the same verb in the middle voice, the bridegroom replied: "I accept the pledge." The woman could be referred to in the passive participle. She was not a party to the contract but its passive object. The same verb was employed in the procedure for personal surety for repayment of a debt. The creditor "pledged" (active) the debtor (passive) to the person who offered himself as surety; the latter "accepted the pledge." The procedure of surety did not create a permanent relationship. It entrusted the debtor to a third person to ensure that the creditor could recover the loan. Marriage by *engyēsis* did not create a new community; it entrusted a woman to a man for the large but not unlimited purpose of bearing him heirs.

The man who gave the woman in marriage had been her *kyrios* (guardian, master) up to that point. When marriage was concluded, the husband became her *kyrios*. *Engyēsis* did not complete the conclusion of marriage; it needed to be followed by *ekdosis*, the transfer of the woman to the bridegroom's dwelling. *Engyēsis* could be revoked, as is illustrated by the contract between Euktemon and Demokrates. But *engyēsis* was more than a betrothal, since it was part of the procedure transferring *kyrieia* to the bridegroom.

The variable element in *engyēsis* was the dowry. In Athens dowry (*proix*) had a precise sense. It was a sum of money or valuables transferred from the woman's original family to the bridegroom for the woman's upkeep. If it was not a sum of money, it had to be assessed at a monetary value, so that the woman's original family could recover it if the marriage was dissolved. When property other than money was given as dowry, that property was sometimes said to be given "in lieu of dowry." The possibility of *engyēsis* without dowry is mentioned by a litigant hypothetically, but no actual occurrence is known. Since the dowry was intended for the support of the woman, the husband had to refund it if the marriage was dissolved. If he did not re-

fund it, the woman's relative(s) had an action against him and this action was called the *dikē sitou* or "action for grain." While the marriage lasted, the husband had full authority to administer the dowry. If, however, he fell into debt, his creditors might seize his property, but an attempt could at least be made to prevent them from seizing his wife's dowry. The dowry, administered by the husband, was distinct from the woman's paraphernalia, which were at her disposal. The stock phrase for her paraphernalia was "clothes and gold jewelry" (*himatia kai chrysia*), although their nature might vary.

After reading this selection, consider these questions:
1. How did marriage in ancient Athens take place?
2. What was meant by the term *kyrios*?
3. What was the role of the dowry for an Athenian wife?

SELECTION 3:

The Limits of Government

In Greek theater many strong women appear, demonstrating that their public life was not so limited as the law would make it. One of the most vivid female personalities appears in Sophocles' Antigone. Although the setting is Thebes, the play was produced in 441 B.C. before an Athenian audience. At this time the democracy was in the sure hands of Pericles and his followers. Antigone demonstrates that the state, as represented by King Creon, can be despotic and deserves to be resisted when it violates individual civil rights. Creon has denied burial to her brother Polyneices because of his attempt to overthrow him. However, according to Greek belief the unburied dead are not free to join loved ones in the Underworld and cannot rest, so Antigone has taken the matter into her own hands and buried Polyneices' corpse. The guard that Creon has placed over the body speaks.

GUARD: Someone left the corpse just now,
   burial all accomplished, thirsty dust
   strewn on the flesh, the ritual complete.
CREON: What are you saying? What man has
   dared to do it?
GUARD: I wouldn't know. There were no marks
   of picks,
   no grubbed-out earth. The ground was dry
   and hard,
   no trace of wheels. The doer left no sign.
   When the first fellow on the day-shift showed
   us,
   we were all sick with wonder.
   For he was hidden, not inside a tomb,
   light dust upon him, enough to turn the curse,
   no wild beast's track, nor track of any hound
   having been near, nor was the body torn. . . .
   [*Antigone is discovered, arrested, and
   brought before Creon.*]
CREON (*to Antigone*): You there, whose head is
   drooping to the ground,
   do you admit this, or deny you did it?
ANTIGONE: I say I did it and I don't deny it.
CREON (*to the guard*): Take yourself off wherever you wish to go
   free of a heavy charge.
CREON (*to Antigone*): You—tell me not at length
   but in a word.
   You knew the order not to do this thing?
ANTIGONE: I knew, of course I knew. The word
   was plain.

CREON: And still you dared to overstep these
   laws?
ANTIGONE: For me it was not Zeus who made
   that order.
   Nor did that Justice who lives with the gods
   below
   mark out such laws to hold among mankind.
   Nor did I think your orders were so strong
   that you, a mortal man, could over-run
   the gods' unwritten and unfailing laws.
   Not now, nor yesterday's, they always live,
   and no one knows their origin in time.
   So not through fear of any man's proud spirit
   would I be likely to neglect these laws,
   draw on myself the gods' sure punishment.
   I know that I must die; how could I not?
   even without your warning. If I die
   before my time, I say it is a gain.
   Who lives in sorrows many as are mine
   how shall he not be glad to gain his death?
   And so, for me to meet this fate, no grief.
   But if I left that corpse, my mother's son,
   dead and unburied I'd have cause to grieve
   as now I grieve not.
   And if you think my acts are foolishness
   the foolishness may be in a fool's eye.

After reading this selection, consider these
questions:
   1. What motivates Antigone to violate
      Creon's law?
   2. How does Antigone articulate the reli-
      gious views of ancient Athens?
   3. How might an Athenian audience
      react to this play?

Sophocles, *Antigone*, Elizabeth Wyckoff, trans., in *The Complete
Greek Tragedies*, David Grene and Richmond Lattimore, eds. (Chicago: University of Chicago Press, 1959), vol. 2, p. 167–168, 173–74.

SELECTION 4:

Greek Slaves

*The fact that democratic Athens—like the rest of ancient Greece—was a
slaveholding society has already been noted. In selection 4 the American*

historian M.I. Finley analyzes the slave population. Although Finley concludes that most of the slaves whose names are known were of non-Greek ("barbarian") origin, we also know that enslavement was the fate of many Greek citizens captured in wars with other city-states.

No modern historian would dispute the fact that the great majority of slaves were not of Greek origin. That is also suggested by a study of slave names. They include many names, more or less ethnic in origin, relating to the barbarian world: names of peoples (Thratta, Carion, Phrygios, Lydos, Syros), topographical names (Asia, Italia, Neilos), typically native names (Lydian Manes, Phrygian Midas, Paphlagonian Tibios), names of historical figures (Croesus, Amasis, Cleopatra). Furthermore, a slave of barbarian origin may very well have received a purely Greek name from his master, whereas the reverse is much less likely. A similar conclusion can be drawn from the rare lists of slaves which have been preserved and in which their origin is mentioned. Particularly striking is the fragmentary Athenian list of goods confiscated in 414 B.C. from those responsible for the sacreligious mutilation of the herms, on which 45 slaves appear, nearly all barbarians. The same is true of the slaves in the Attic silver mines, from the fourth century B.C. on, whose origins are known. Nor are there slaves in the comedies of Aristophanes to whom there is reason to attribute Greek origin.

However, as soon as one tries to extend this detailed research, in an attempt to estimate the relative proportion of Barbarians and Greeks in the whole stock of slaves, one is faced with all sorts of insuperable difficulties. In classical times, the slaves whose origin is indicated are very rare. Beyond the lists mentioned above, account can only be taken of, let us say, 20 or 30 cases—for example, the confidential agent of Pausanias, the regent of Sparta, an Argilian (from Argilos, neighbouring town of Amphipolis on the Thracian coast [modern northeastern Greece]), or the servants "coming from Dardanus" (on the east coast of the Hellespont [modern Turkey]) who were given to Xenophon during his stay at Scillus in the Peloponnese, or the miner Atotas, who on his gravestone in the Laurium district of Attica proclaims himself to be a Paphlagonian from the Black Sea Region. . . .

Now this enormous preponderance of Barbarians that one seems to be observing in the slave stock of Greek cities is difficult to understand if war had been the usual means of acquisition. Did the Greeks not in fact spend most of their time fighting each other rather than the Barbarians, which should have resulted in the reverse pattern? To which can be added the fact that their interventions in the barbarian world were too episodic and too dispersed to explain the regular supply of slaves originating from this or that remote area such as Paphlagonia, Phrygia [both in modern Turkey] or Syria; even if it is true that the Greeks on the periphery had to be particularly aggressive towards the Barbarians around them, such as the Thessalians on the margin of the Dacian Highlands [modern Romania] whom Aristophanes calls "insatiable slave dealers" (*Plutus* 521). The effect of such military operations could only have been to supply the market in periodic surges, in Greek cities as well as in a Hellenistic Kingdom such as Egypt.

There remains to be accounted for the apparent contrast between the frequent accounts of enslavement of Greeks as a consequence of war or piracy and the rarity of slaves of Greek origins. Apart from imagining that they were generally disposed of in Barbarian lands (which must have happened sometimes, to the great agitation of public opinion, but certainly was not systematic), one must therefore ask what became of them after their capture, at the moment when, put up for sale, they disappeared into the anonymous mass of slaves.

After reading this selection, consider these questions:

M.I. Finley, ed., *Classical Slavery* (London: Frank Cass, 1987), pp. 12–15.

1. Does the fact that the ancient Greeks practiced slavery on a large scale diminish your respect for Greek democracy? Why or why not?

2. The great Greek philosopher Aristotle justified slavery on the ground that people who had been enslaved were by definition inferior and thus deserved their fate. Why do you think he came to this conclusion?

3. Before the Civil War, defenders of slavery in the American South justified their region's "peculiar institution" by pointing to democratic Athens: slavery, they said, permitted slaveholders to enjoy the leisure and prosperity necessary to build a great civilization. Does the evidence that Finley presents support this argument?

SELECTION 5:

The Apology of Socrates

Although Sophocles' Antigone (selection 3) was a fictional character, Socrates (ca. 469–399 B.C.) was not. Ostensibly an ordinary Athenian citizen, he made himself famous by subtly questioning every conventional opinion of his fellow citizens. Unlike the professional educators of his day, called sophists, or teachers of wisdom, he wrote no books and accepted no fees. But he attracted a devoted circle of young followers, including some of the city's most prominent politicians.

Many Athenians did not care for Socrates' constant questioning of their politics and values. Depressed by their defeat in the Peloponnesian War and by the imposed rule of a pro-Spartan clique, these Athenians considered Socrates an unpatriotic nuisance—and after they restored democratic rule, they made him the scapegoat for all their troubles. He was tried on charges of corrupting the young men and denying the gods of Athens, found guilty, and condemned to choose between exile and death.

Plato, Socrates' disciple and the author of many dialogues that record his teaching, was present at the trial and later wrote down what his mentor said in his own defense. In reading Plato's version of Socrates' words, imagine the setting: Standing before a court of five hundred male citizens, the accused had to plead his own case without the benefit of a lawyer (although his friends might help him write his speech). To gain sympathy, defendants frequently brought forward their wives and children, looking as pitiful as possible. Socrates scorned such tricks.

It may be that some one of you, remembering his own case, will be annoyed that whereas he, in

standing his trial upon a less serious charge than this, made pitiful appeals to the jury with floods of tears, and had his infant children produced in court to excite the maximum of sympathy, and many of his relatives and friends as well, I on the

Plato, *The Apology*, in *The Last Days of Socrates*, Hugh Tredennick, trans. (New York: Penguin Books, 1969), pp. 67–69.

contrary intend to do nothing of the sort, and that although I am facing (as it might appear) the utmost danger. It may be that one of you, reflecting on these facts, will be prejudiced against me, and being irritated by his reflections, will give his vote in anger. If one of you is so disposed— I do not expect it, but there is the possibility—I think that I should be quite justified in saying to him, 'My dear sir, of course I have some relatives. To quote the very words of Homer, even I am not sprung 'from an oak or from a rock,' but from human parents, and consequently I have relatives; yes, and sons too, gentlemen, three of them, one almost grown up and the other two only children; but all the same I am not going to produce them here and beseech you to acquit me.'

Why do I not intend to do anything of this kind? Not out of perversity, gentlemen, nor out of contempt for you; whether I am brave or not in the face of death has nothing to do with it; the point is that for my own credit and yours and for the credit of the state as a whole, I do not think that it is right for me to use any of these methods at my age and with my reputation—which may be true or it may be false, but at any rate the view is held that Socrates is different from the common run of mankind. Now if those of you who are supposed to be distinguished for wisdom or courage or any other virtue are to behave in this way, it would be a disgrace.

I have often noticed that some people of this type, for all their high standing, go to extraordinary lengths when they come up for trial, which shows that they think it will be a dreadful thing to lose their lives; as though they would be immortal if you did not put them to death! In my opinion these people bring disgrace upon our city. Any of our visitors might be excused for thinking that the finest specimens of Athenian manhood, whom their fellow-citizens select on their merits to rule over them and hold other high positions, are no better than women. If you have even the smallest reputation, gentlemen, you ought not to descend to these methods; and if we do so, you must not give us license. On the contrary, you must make it clear that anyone who stages these pathetic scenes and so brings ridicule upon our city is far more likely to be condemned than if he kept perfectly quiet.

But apart from all question of appearances, gentlemen, I do not think that it is right for a man to appeal to the jury or to get himself acquitted by doing so; he ought to inform them of the facts and convince them by argument. The jury does not sit to dispense justice as a favor, but to decide where justice lies; and the oath which they have sworn is not to show favor at their own discretion, but to return a just and lawful verdict. It follows that we must not develop in you, nor you allow to grow in yourselves, the habit of perjury; that would be sinful for us both. Therefore you must not expect me, gentlemen, to behave towards you in a way which I consider neither reputable nor moral nor consistent with my religious duty; and above all you must not expect it when I stand charged with impiety by Meletus here.

Surely it is obvious that if I tried to persuade you and prevail upon you by my entreaties to go against your solemn oath, I should be teaching you contempt for religion; and by my very defense I should be virtually accusing myself of having no religious belief. But that is very far from the truth. I have a more sincere belief, gentlemen, than any of my accusers; and I leave it to you and to God to judge me as it shall be best for me and for yourselves.

After reading this selection, consider these questions:

1. Some historians believe that Socrates was flippant at his trial. Do you agree?
2. What are some differences between trials in the United States and those of ancient Greece?
3. Why does Socrates claim to have more religious belief than the members of the jury?
4. Does the fact that democratic Athens put Socrates on trial—and condemned him to death—diminish your respect for Athenian democracy? Why or why not?

SELECTION 6:

An Appraisal of Socrates

Socrates is remembered in Western civilization as a supreme example of a man of heroic integrity, who refused to compromise his right to be his society's truth-seeking "gadfly" even at the risk of his life, and who accepted death rather than be exiled from his native city. In the following selection, a prominent British historian of ancient Greece, John B. Bury, appraises Socrates' stand. Do you agree with Bury?

The ideas which we owe to Socrates are now so organically a part of the mind of civilized men that it is hard to appreciate the intellectual power which was required to originate them. Socrates was the first champion of the supremacy of the intellect as a court from which there is no appeal; he was the first to insist that a man must order his life by the guidance of his own intellect. Socrates was thus a rebel against authority as such; and he shrank from no consequences. He did not hesitate to show his companions that an old man has no title to respect because he is old, unless he is also wise; or that an ignorant parent has no claim to obedience on the mere account of the parental relation. Knowledge and veracity, the absolute sovereignty of the understanding, regardless of consequences, regardless of all prejudices connected with family or city—this was the ideal of Socrates, consistently and uncompromisingly followed. . . .

Though he was the child of democracy, born to a heritage of freedom in a city where the right of free discussion was unrestrained, the sacred name of democracy was not more sheltered than anything else from the criticism of Socrates. He railed, for instance, at the system of choosing magistrates by lot, one of the protections of democracy at Athens. He was unpopular with the mass, for he was an enemy of shams and ignorance and superstition. Honest democrats of the

type of Thrasybulus and Anytus, who did their duty, but had no desire to prove its foundations, regarded him as a dangerous freethinker who spent his life in diffusing ideas subversive of the social order.

They might point to the ablest of the young men who had kept company with him, and say: "Behold the fruits of his conversation! Look at Alcibiades, his favorite companion, who has done more than any other man to ruin his country. Look at Critias, who, next to Alcibiades, has wrought the deepest harm to Athens; who, brought up in the Socratic circle, first wrote a book against democracy, then visited Thessaly and stirred up the serfs against their masters, and finally, returning here, inaugurated the reign of terror.* Look, on the other hand, at Plato, an able young man, whom the taste for idle speculation, infused by Socrates, has seduced from the service of his country. Or look at Xenophon, who, instead of serving Athens, has gone to serve her enemies. Truly Socrates and his propaganda have done little good to the Athenian state."

However unjust any particular instance might seem, it is easy to understand how considerations of this kind would lead many practical unspeculative men to look upon Socrates and his ways with little favor. And from their point of view, they were perfectly right. His spirit, and the ideas that he made current, were an insidious menace

John B. Bury, *A History of Greece*, 3rd ed. (London: Macmillan, 1959), pp. 576, 579–80.

*Alcibiades and Critias, disciples of Socrates, were also Athenian politicians whose unwise policies helped ensure the city-state's defeat in the Peloponnesian war.

to the cohesion of the social fabric, in which there was not a stone or a joint that he did not question. In other words, he was the active apostle of individualism, which led in its further development to the subversion of that local patriotism which had inspired the cities of Greece in her days of greatness.

And this thinker, whose talk was shaking the Greek world in its foundations, though none guessed it, was singled out by the Delphic priesthood for a distinguished mark of approbation. In the truest oracle that was ever uttered from the Pythian tripod, it was declared that no one in the world was wiser than Socrates. We know not at what period of the philosopher's career this answer was given, but, if it was seriously meant, it showed a strange insight which we should hardly have looked for at the shrine of Delphi.

After reading this selection, consider these questions:

1. Why is Socrates held up as an example of heroism?
2. What does it mean to appeal to intellect as the final norm for right actions?
3. How would Confucius react to the speech of Socrates?

CHAPTER 9
Early Rome: What Explains the Republic's Rise and Fall?

O f all the cities in the ancient Mediterranean world, Rome was the most spectacularly successful. Founded according to tradition in 753 B.C., and at first simply one small town among many in central Italy, Rome expanded its power until, by 28 B.C., its rule extended from one end of the Mediterranean to the other.

How did Rome grow so mighty? For ancient Romans (and the few Greeks who admired them), the answer was simple: Rome was a republic, and self-government created virtuous, heroic citizens who could conquer the world. (The word *virtue* contains the Latin root *vir,* or "man"; originally meaning "manliness" and implying self-sacrificing courage and incorruptibility.) The problem with this self-congratulatory view was that, by the time Rome had conquered the Mediterranean, the Roman Republic itself had collapsed under corruption and civil war. Until then the wealth of conquered lands poured into the city, paying for imposing public buildings and lavish entertainment, including savage gladiatorial combats. Men and women of the upper classes enjoyed enormous wealth, much of it used to build luxurious country estates. These aristocrats dominated the ruling Senate and filled all the important offices, but they also fought each other in a century-long civil war. Eventually, in 27 B.C., Augustus Caesar (63 B.C.–A.D. 14) emerged as the victor. Although he claimed to be the republic's restorer, he in fact inaugurated the increasingly autocratic Roman Empire. As you read this chapter, keep in mind this outcome—and ask yourself why the Roman Republic managed to conquer the known world but in the process destroyed itself.

SELECTION 1:

The Formation of the Republic

As the proclaimed restorer of the Roman Republic, Augustus patronized many important men of letters who praised Roman traditions and urged their compatriots to revive ancient virtue. Among them was the historian Livy (59 B.C.–A.D. 17), who wrote a massive history of Rome from its origins. Livy based his history on ancient Roman legends, interpreting them according to the attitudes of his own time. One of his many dramatic stories told of the overthrow of the monarchy that had originally ruled Rome and of the establishment of the Republic, an event traditionally dated to 509 B.C. The leader of the rebellion was Lucius Junius Brutus, who went on to become one of the first two consuls, the highest officials of the republican regime. Even through imperial times, two consuls were elected annually by the Senate for a one-year term. In the extract from his history that forms this selection, Livy explains the significance of Rome's transformation from a monarchy to an aristocratic republic.

My task from now on will be to trace the history in peace and of a free nation, governed by annually elected officers of state and subject not to the caprice of individual men, but to the overriding authority of law.

The hard-won liberty of Rome was rendered the more welcome, and the more fruitful, by the character of the last king, Tarquin the Proud. Earlier kings may all be considered, not unjustly, to have contributed to the city's growth, making room for an expanding population, for the increase of which they, too, were responsible. They were all, in their way, successive 'founders' of Rome. Moreover it cannot be doubted that Brutus, who made for himself so great a name by the expulsion of Tarquin, would have done his country the greatest disservice, had he yielded too soon to his passion for liberty and forced the abdication of any of the previous kings. One has but to think of what the populace was like in those early days—a rabble of vagrants, mostly runaways and refugees—and to ask what would have happened if they had suddenly found themselves protected from all authority by inviolable sanctuary, and enjoying complete freedom of action, if not full political rights.

In such circumstances, unrestrained by the power of the throne, they would, no doubt, have set sail on the stormy sea of democratic politics, swayed by the gusts of popular eloquence and quarreling for power with the governing class of a city which did not even belong to them, before any real sense of community had had time to grow. That sense—the only true patriotism—comes slowly and springs from the heart; it is founded upon respect for the family and love of the soil. Premature 'liberty' of this kind would have been a disaster: we should have been torn to pieces by petty squabbles before we had ever reached political maturity, which, as things were, was made possible by the long quiet years under monarchical government; for it was that government which, as it were, nursed our strength and enabled us ultimately to produce sound fruit from liberty, as only a politically adult nation can.

Moreover the first step towards political liber-

Livy, *The Early History of Rome*, Aubrey de Sélincourt ed. (Harmondsworth: Penguin Books, 1971), pp. 105–106.

ty in Rome consisted in the fact that the consuls were annually elected magistrates—in the limitation, that is, not of their powers but of their period of office. The earliest consuls exercised the full powers of the kings, and carried all their insignia, with one exception—the most impressive of all—namely the 'rods.' These were allowed to only one consul of the two, to avoid the duplication of this dreadful symbol of the power of life and death. Brutus by his colleague's consent was the first to have the rods, and he proved as zealous in guarding liberty as he had been in demanding it. His first act was to make the people, while the taste of liberty was still fresh upon their tongues, swear a solemn oath never to allow any man to be king in Rome, hoping by this means to forestall future attempts by persuasion or bribery to restore the monarchy.

He then turned his attention to strengthening the influence of the Senate, whose numbers had been reduced by the political murders of Tarquin; for this purpose he brought into it leading men of equestrian rank and made up its number to a total of three hundred. This, we are told, was the origin of the distinction between the 'Fathers' and the 'Conscripts': i.e. the original senators and those (the conscripts) who were later enrolled, or conscripted, as members of the senatorial body. The measure was wonderfully effective in promoting national unity and lessening friction between patricians [members of the leading families, who dominated the early Republic] and populace.

After reading this selection, consider these questions:

1. Why does Livy associate the rule of law with the formation of the Republic?
2. Why does the author believe that liberty needs time to mature?
3. How did the symbol of the rods affect republican Rome?

SELECTION 2:

Cicero Describes Pompey's Triumph

Few Romans of the first century B.C. knew more about the Republic's intricate politics, or wrote so well about it, than Marcus Tullius Cicero (106–43 B.C.). Not a member of the old Roman elite, Cicero was a clever lawyer and a marvelously persuasive orator whose letters, speeches, and essays would define Latin style for more than a millennium and a half in Europe. (Students in advanced Latin courses still wrestle with his elegant syntax.) But while he was polishing his prose, he was also ceaselessly intriguing for money and high political office. In a letter to a friend in 55 B.C., Cicero describes the return to Rome of the conquering general Pompey, who had won a series of victories in the eastern Mediterranean and was now bidding for supreme power in the Republic. Pompey was given a "triumph," the kind of pompous military parade with which Rome traditionally honored a general who had won a great battle. In turn, Pompey entertained the Roman populace with "games" that included gladiators

fighting to the death against each other and exotic wild animals. Histori-
ans believe that Cicero himself would have liked to stage a triumph, so
perhaps a bit of envy lurks between his lines. In any case, his letter paints
a vivid picture of public life in the late Roman Republic.
In the end, both Pompey and Cicero would die violent deaths amid the
Republic's final convulsions.

If it was ill health that kept you from the games, I congratulate you on your good fortune; but if it was your dislike for such diversions that detained you I rejoice doubly: that you are well and that you are sane enough in mind to scorn the silly admirations of the people. I say this, however, on the supposition that during the days of the games you were putting in your time profitably. You would withdraw, no doubt, to that den of yours, which looks out over the Bay of Naples, and in the seclusion of your charming retreat you would spend the morning hours in cursory reading; whereas we, who left you for the show, were going to sleep over the performance; the rest of the day you were passing according to your fancy; whereas we had to put up with what could pass the Board of Censors.

In fact, the offerings were most elaborate but, to judge your taste by mine, not at all to your liking; for first, to do honor to the occasion those actors returned to the stage from which they had retired to do honor to themselves. Why, the voice of your particular favorite, Aesop, failed him in an especially impressive passage.

Why should I say more? Being familiar with such programs, you know what events came next. These did not have the charm even of ordinary shows, for the elaborateness of the spectacle took away all delight. I am sure you missed the display with perfect equanimity. How could one be pleased with six hundred mules in the *Clytemnestra,* or three thousand punch bowls in the *Trojan Horse,* or varied paraphernalia of cavalry and infantry in some battle scene! These spectacles won popular approval, but they would have pleased you not at all. If during the days of the games you had heard your slave Protogenes read anything whatsoever except my orations, you would have had more delight than any one of us.

As to the Greek and the Oscan shows, I am sure you did not miss them; for you can see the Oscans show off any day in your town council, and as for Greeks, you take to them so little that you will not take the Greek highway to your villa. Why should I suppose that you missed the athletic games when I know that you scorn gladiators? In these performances even Pompey acknowledges that he wasted his money and his pains. The final event consisted of hunting shows, two of them, continuing through five days, magnificent, to be sure; but what pleasure can a gentleman take in seeing a puny man torn to pieces by a monstrous beast or a beautiful animal pierced by a spear? The last was the day of the elephant-baiting, which brought the crowd much wonder, but little pleasure. Nay rather the beasts aroused some sense of pity as if there were some community of feeling between them and man (so that the crowd rose up and cursed Pompey).

I have written you a longer letter than usual out of an abundance, not of leisure, but of affection, because in a certain letter, if you but remember, you gave me a half-way invitation to write you something that would console you for having missed the games. If I have attained my object, I rejoice; if not, I comfort myself with the reflection that hereafter you will come to the show and visit me and not stake your hope of enjoyment on a letter from me.

After reading this selection, consider these questions:

1. Why did Cicero find Pompey's games so distasteful?
2. What does this letter tell you about public culture in Rome?
3. In what way do you suspect Cicero's complaints are a bit artificial?

Letters of a Roman Gentleman Selected from the Writings of Cicero, Arthur Patch McKinlay, trans. (Boston: Houghton Mifflin, 1926), pp. 85–87.

SELECTION 3:

A Roman Bath

Among the pleasures of life in Italian cities were the baths, which afforded citizens, most of whom had no running water in their homes, time to relax and socialize. From three of four o'clock in the afternoon until dinnertime, every Roman man headed for the baths. Women were supposed to go in the mornings, but the more daring joined their male companions, if there were no separate facilities for women. The baths were both public and private, with only a very small charge that went to the attendants. They were extremely egalitarian, with rich and poor alike enjoying the waters and the games available to the bathers. In this selection a modern French scholar describes an excavated bath at Pompeii.

Next to the buildings used for shows, the most characteristic structures of Roman cities were undoubtedly the *thermae* or public baths. Here again, we are discussing an Italian architectural invention, which is derived from the Hellenic gymnasium. Like the Roman theaters and amphitheaters, they first appeared in southern Italy: the oldest known example is that of the Stabian Baths at Pompeii. In their earliest form, they antedate the Roman conquest (about 89 B.C.), but modified several times, they kept being modernized and enlarged until the end of the city (A.D. 79). One may clearly see there the development of comfort and luxury, a typical evolution of baths under the Empire. To the earliest period belong several narrow dark cabins used for private baths. In addition, the large courtyard surrounded by columns and used for exercises form part of an old, Greek-style, *palaestra*.

Originally, the water was drawn from a neighboring well. But this rudimentary equipment was gradually improved. Pipes brought in water from aqueducts, and large halls were built, each of which was used for the various *steps* of the complicated process which a bath then was. By 89 B.C., the Stabian Baths had already been provid-

ed with the essential parts. But it is particularly in the Forum Baths, built around 80 B.C., and remarkably preserved, that we can clearly see the interior plan for buildings of this type.

The Forum Baths, like the Stabian Baths, are divided into two parts: the larger one was for men and the smaller for women. There is still a *palaestra*: it fills up the rear section of the men's baths, but its dimensions are relatively modest: a square of about twenty meters on each side. It was not used for old-fashioned exercises, but rather for strolling, for playing ball and, especially, the constantly repeated pleasure of conversation. The women's baths had only an uncovered area, perhaps arranged as a garden.

The men's bath is more complete. It has the four parts necessary for any Roman bath-building: an *apodyterium*, a large cloakroom where the bathers took off and left their clothes, then a cold room, the *frigidarium*, then a warm room, the *tepidarium*, and finally a steam room, the *caldarium*. Everyone went from one to the other according to the customary ritual. The plan of the Pompeian baths shows that the *apodyterium* opened into both the *frigidarium* and the *tepidarium*: thus it was possible for one to go directly into the cold room for the first ablution, accomplished by plunging into a pool which took up almost the whole room, or else one could first enter the warm

Pierre Grimal, *Roman Cities*, G. Michael Woloch, trans. (Madison: University of Wisconsin Press, 1983), pp.l 68, 70–72.

room, where the body gradually became used to a high temperature. After a few moments, the bather went into the *caldarium*, where the heat caused abundant sweating. A basin was placed there, holding lukewarm water and a tub into which one could plunge. It was then possible, by following the route in the opposite direction, to return to the *frigidarium* for a last cold bath.

In the more complicated and sumptuous baths built during the imperial era, other rooms were used for massages, for applying oil, and the rooms for conversation and strolling were multiplied. This is quite apparent, for example, in one of the largest baths of Timgad (called the Large North Baths or the Northern Baths), whose arrangements and symmetry obviously relate to the most magnificent bath-buildings in Rome, those of Caracalla or those of Diocletian. There one finds, next to the *caldarium*, where basins kept the hot room humid, rooms for dry heat, called *laconica* or Spartan baths, where the temperatures could climb even higher.

The need to locate in the baths sources of heat, powerful yet still capable of maintaining varied temperatures in the different kinds of rooms, led the architects to invent ingenious methods, of which the most common was the use of pavement supported on pillars of brick, which were called *suspensurae*. Thus, the hot air from the furnace circulated freely and warmed the floor, then it escaped through a large number of vertical pipes built into the walls, while the dust and smoke were carried along. In order to control the temperature of a room, it was sufficient to vary its location along the path of hot air, and the rooms closest to the furnace were obviously the hottest.

After reading this selection, consider these questions:
1. Why were baths so popular with the Romans?
2. What institutions in the modern world are similar to the Roman baths?
3. How were Roman baths heated?

SELECTION 4:

The Last Day of Julius Caesar

In the latter part of the first century B.C. institutions of the Republic withered and the generals and their armies began to struggle to take over the city and the lands that now were under Roman control. At times they might join forces in a triumvirate (a three-man coalition), but they were extremely fragile and no one was surprised when they fell apart. Julius Caesar (ca. 100–44 B.C.) was a powerful general who rose to prominence because of his successful wars in Gaul. Once back in Rome, the number and strength of his loyal troops convinced the politicians of Rome that cooperation with him was prudent. Caesar disposed of his enemies and soon governed as if he were Rome's only ruler, a king in all but name.

An opposition group formed among leading politicians who had been denied Caesar's favor. Cicero, although not an active member of the opposition, sympathized with it (a stand that would later cost him his life). Some of Caesar's friends also took the opposing side because they feared that he had become a threat to Rome's traditional liberties. One of these friends was Marcus Junius Brutus, a descendant of the patrician leader who in 509 B.C. had killed Rome's last king and proclaimed the Republic (selection 1). A conspiracy formed to kill Caesar on the date known, Roman-style, as the Ides of March (March 15), 44 B.C. What happened next is dramatically narrated by the ancient biographer Plutarch (A.D. 46–120). In reading this account, remember that Plutarch was writing more than a century after the events that he described.

When Caesar entered, the Senators stood up to show their respect to him, and of Brutus's confederates, some came about his chair and stood behind it. Others met him, pretending to add their petitions to those of Tullius Cimber, in behalf of his brother, who was in exile; and they followed him with their joint applications till he came to his seat. When he sat down, he refused to comply with their requests, and upon their urging him further began to reproach them severely for their importunities, when Tullius, laying hold of his robe with both his hands, pulled it down from his neck. This was the signal for the assault.

Casca gave him the first cut in the neck, which was not mortal nor dangerous, as coming from one who at the beginning of such a bold action was probably very much disturbed. Caesar immediately turned about, and laid his hand upon the dagger and kept hold of it. And both of them at the same time cried out, he that received the blow, in Latin, "Vile Casca, what does this mean?" and he that gave it, in Greek to his brother, "Brother, help!" Upon this first onset, those who were not privy to the design were astonished, and their horror and amazement at what they saw were so great that they neither fled nor assisted Caesar, nor so much as spoke a word. But those who came prepared for the business enclosed him on every side, with their naked daggers in their hands.

Whichever way he turned he met with blows, and saw their swords leveled at his face and eyes, and was encompassed like a wild beast in the toils on every side. For it had been agreed they should each make a thrust at him, and cover themselves with his blood. For this reason Brutus

also gave him one stab in the groin. Some say that he fought and resisted all the rest, shifting his body to avoid the blows, and calling out for help, but that when he saw Brutus's sword drawn, he covered his face with his robe and submitted, letting himself fall, whether were by chance or that he was pushed in that direction by his murderers, at the foot of the pedestal on which Pompey's statue stood, now wet with his blood. So that Pompey himself seemed to have presided, as it were, over the revenge done upon his adversary, who lay here at his feet, and breathed out his soul through his multitude of wounds, for they say he received three-and-twenty. And the conspirators themselves were many of them wounded by each other, while they all leveled their blows at the same person.

When Caesar was dispatched, Brutus stood forth to give a reason for what they had done, but the Senate would not hear him, but flew out of doors in all haste. They filled the people with so much alarm and distraction, that some shut up their houses, others left their counters and shops. All ran one way or the other, some to the place to see the sad spectacle, others back again after they had seen it. Antony and Lepidus, Caesar's most faithful friends, got off privately, and hid themselves in some friends' houses. Brutus and his followers, being yet hot from the deed, marched in a body from the senate-house to the capitol with their drawn swords, not like persons who thought of escaping, but with an air of confidence and assurance. As they went along, they called to the people to resume their liberty, and invited the company of any more distinguished people whom they met.

After reading this selection, consider these questions:

1. Why would the conspirators agree that each of them should strike Caesar?

"Caesar" in *Plutarch: The Lives of the Noble Grecians and Romans*, John Dryden, trans., rev. by Arthur Hugh Clough (New York: Modern Library, 1937), pp. 892–93.

2. Pompey was once Caesar's friend, then was defeated and died as his enemy. What does Plutarch find ironic about the scene of Caesar's assassination?

3. What role docs Brutus play in killing Caesar?

SELECTION 5:

Marc Antony's Funeral Oration

Although Caesar's assassins claimed that they had acted only to preserve Roman liberties, among the people of the city there were doubts. Much that Caesar had done benefited the populace. A calculating Marc Antony seized the opportunity at Caesar's funeral to remind the men and women of Rome all that they owed to Caesar. Better than any contemporary author, William Shakespeare captures the skill of Antony to rally public opinion against the conspirators. (It should be noted that Shakespeare took most of the material for his tragedy Julius Caesar from Plutarch).

Friends, Romans, countrymen, lend me your
  ears;
I come to bury Caesar, not to praise him.
The evil that men do lives after them,
The good is oft interred with their bones;
So let it be with Caesar. The noble Brutus
Hath told you Caesar was ambitious;
If it were so, it was a grievous fault,
And grievously hath Caesar answer'd it.
Here, under leave of Brutus and the rest,—
For Brutus is an honourable man;
So are they all, all honourable men,—
Come I to speak in Caesar's funeral.
He was my friend, faithful and just to me:
But Brutus says he was ambitious;
And Brutus is an honourable man.
He hath brought many captives home to Rome,
Whose ransoms did the general coffers fill:

Did this in Caesar seem ambitious?
When that the poor have cried, Caesar hath wept;
Ambition should be made of sterner stuff:
Yet Brutus says he was ambitious;
And Brutus is an honourable man.
You all did see that on the Lupercal*
I thrice presented him a kingly crown,
Which he did thrice refuse: was this ambition?
Yet Brutus says he was ambitious;
And, sure, he is an honourable man.
I speak not to disprove what Brutus spoke,
But here I am to speak what I do know.
You all did love him once, not without cause:
What cause withholds you then to mourn for
  him?
O judgment, thou art fled to brutish beasts,
And men have lost their reason. Bear with me;
My heart is in the coffin there with Caesar,
And I must pause till it come back to me. . . .

If you have tears, prepare to shed them now.

Julius Caesar, act 3, scene 2, in The Yale Shakespeare, Wilbur L. Cross and Tucker Brooke, eds. (New York: Barnes and Noble, 1993), pp. 959–60.

---

*a traditional Roman festival

You all do know this mantle: I remember
The first time ever Caesar put it on;
'Twas on a summer's evening, in his tent,
That day he overcame the Nervii.
Look, in this place ran Cassius' dagger through:
See what a rent the envious Casca made:
Through this the well-beloved Brutus stabb'd;
And, as he pluck'd his cursed steel away,
Mark how the blood of Caesar follow'd it,
As rushing out of doors, to be resolv'd
If Brutus so unkindly knock'd or no;
For Brutus, as you know, was Caesar's angel:
Judge, O you gods, how dearly Caesar lov'd him.
This was the most unkindest cut of all;
For when the noble Caesar saw him stab,
Ingratitude, more strong than traitors' arms,
Quite vanquish'd him: then burst his mighty heart;
And, in his mantle muffling up his face,
Even at the base of Pompey's statue,
Which all the while ran blood, great Caesar fell.

O, what a fall was there, my countrymen!
Then I, and you, and all of us fell down,
Whilst bloody treason flourish'd over us.
O now you weep, and I perceive you feel
The dint of pity; these are gracious drops.
Kind souls, what, weep you when you but behold
Our Caesar's vesture wounded? Look you here,
Here is himself, marr'd, as you see, with traitors.

After reading this selection, consider these questions:

1. How does Shakespeare's Marc Antony turn public opinion against the assassins?
2. Marc Antony refers to the time he offered Caesar a crown. Why do you suppose Caesar refused it?
3. Does Marc Antony show in his eulogy that he has the right to be Caesar's successor rather than Brutus?

SELECTION 6:

A Woman's Protest

This selection describes an event during the Roman civil wars. Roman society was torn apart by irreconcilable political partisanship within the city. Reflecting this condition, the Republic's government, headed by the Senate and the consuls, could not control its generals. Marius, Cinna, and Sulla, all of whom are mentioned in the selection, were earlier generals who seized power during the course of these civil wars.

In 43 B.C., Hortensia, daughter of a former consul (and thus a member of one of Rome's leading families), took the lead in protesting the action of the alliance formed against Julius Caesar's assassins. This alliance, called the Triumvirate ("the three-man group"), brought together Octavian, Marc Antony, and Lepidus. Their announced goal was to avenge Julius Caesar, but in fact they aimed to divide the Roman world among themselves.

Hortensia's protest is an eloquent testimony to the role that women played in Roman society. The voices of some women from the most important families could not be ignored; ordinary women, of course, had no such role.

The triumvirs addressed the people on this subject [paying off their debts] and published an edict requiring 1400 of the richest women to make a valuation of their property, and to furnish for the service of the war such portion as the triumvirs should require from each. It was provided further that if any should conceal their property or make a false valuation they should be fined, and that rewards should be given to informers, whether free persons or slaves. The women resolved to beseech the women-folk of the triumvirs. With the sister of Octavian and the mother of Antony they did not fail, but they were repulsed from the doors of Fulvia, the wife of Antony, whose rudeness they could scarce endure. They then forced their way to the tribunal of the triumvirs in the forum, the people and the guards dividing to let them pass. There, through the mouth of Hortensia, whom they had selected to speak, they spoke as follows: "As befitted women of our rank addressing a petition to you, we had recourse to the ladies of your households; but having been treated as did not befit us, at the hands of Fulvia, we have been driven by her to the forum. You have already deprived us of our fathers, our sons, our husbands, and our brothers, whom you accused of having wronged you if you take away our property also, you reduce us to a condition unbecoming our birth, our manners, our sex. If we have done you wrong, as you say our husbands have, proscribe us as you do them. But if we women have not voted any of you public enemies, have not torn down your houses, destroyed your army, or led another one against you; if we have not hindered you in obtaining offices and honours,—why do we share the penalty when we did not share the guilt?

"Why should we pay taxes when we have no part in the honours, the commands, the statecraft, for which you contend against each other with such harmful results? 'Because this is a time of war,' do you say? When have there not been wars, and when have taxes ever been imposed on women, who are exempted by their sex among all

mankind? Our mothers did once rise superior to their sex and made contributions when you were in danger of losing the whole empire and the city itself through the conflict with the Carthaginians. But then they contributed voluntarily, not from their landed property, their fields, their dowries, or their houses, without which life is not possible to free women, but only from their own jewellery, and even these not according to fixed valuation, not under fear of informers or accusers, not by force and violence, but what they themselves were willing to give. What alarm is there now for the empire or the country? Let war with the Gauls or the Parthians come, and we shall not be inferior to our mothers in zeal for the common safety; but for civil wars may we never contribute, nor ever assist you against each other! We did not contribute to Caesar or to Pompey.1 Neither Marius nor Cinna imposed taxes upon us. Nor did Sulla, who held despotic power in the state, do so, whereas you say that you are re-establishing the commonwealth."

While Hortensia thus spoke the triumvirs were angry that women should dare to hold a public meeting when the men were silent; that they should demand from magistrates the reasons for their acts, and themselves not so much as furnish money while the men were serving in the army. They ordered the lictors [Roman police] to drive them away from the tribunal, which they proceeded to do until cries were raised by the multitude outside, when the lictors desisted and the triumvirs said they would postpone till the next day the consideration of the matter.

After reading this selection, consider these questions:
1. What does this passage reveal about the role certain women could play in Roman politics?
2. Was it only because they risked losing some of their wealth that Hortensia and her supporters were angered?
3. What caused the triumvir to postpone immediate action against Hortensia and her followers?

Appian, *Roman History*, Horace White, trans., Loeb Classical Library (Cambridge, MA: Harvard University Press, 1961), pp. 195–99.

CHAPTER 10

Imperial Rome and Early Christianity: How Can the Achievements of Augustus and Jesus Be Compared?

The dying Roman Republic had created an empire, but with Julius Caesar's death it was an empire without an emperor. Rebellion, war, and corruption among leading public officials flourished unchecked. The last decades of the Republic suggested—and the failure of Caesar's assassins to reestablish the old political order proved—that Rome could be governed only by a strong ruler. The city of Rome and its traditional institutions simply could not govern the entire Mediterranean world.

The struggle for power in Rome entered its final phase. Caesar's grandnephew and adopted son, Octavian, who was still a youth at his studies at the time of Caesar's death, hurried back to Rome only to learn that Marc Antony had given away most of his inheritance. For a time Octavian, Antony, and Lepidus—the Triumvirate mentioned in chapter 9, selection 6—were allied against Caesar's assassins. But after Brutus and the other assassins had been defeated in war and either committed suicide or otherwise died, the victorious triumvirs' personal ambitions and jealousy drove them apart. By 27 B.C., after a new series of wars, Octavian was the sole ruler of the Roman Empire.

Octavian shrewdly called himself *princeps* ("first citizen") and claimed to be restoring the Republic. Actually he ran the government. The obedient Senate voted him the title of *Augustus* ("he who is revered"), and his name has gone down in history as Caesar Augustus, the first Roman emperor. He brought Rome peace and prosperity after decades of anarchy. The Empire over which he presided would endure for centuries, and some elements of the Roman system of government, notably its law codes, remain to this day fundamental to the political structures of most European states.

During Augustus's reign (for he would hold power until he died peacefully in A.D. 14), there was born in distant Roman-ruled Palestine a Jewish boy known as Yeshua (Jesus) of Nazareth. Augustus's name and lists of accomplishments were carved onto innumerable public monuments all over the Empire; his image appeared on all the Empire's coins. No documents mentioning Jesus survive from his lifetime, and he died an ignominious and painful death by crucifixion, the penalty for ordinary people whom the Romans considered rebels. Yet the religious movement that he set in motion, and which came to believe in him as God incarnate, was destined to transform not only the Roman world but all of Western civilization. Read the selections in this chapter with this question in mind: Whose was ultimately the greater historical accomplishment: Augustus's or Jesus'?

SELECTION 1:

Accomplishments of Caesar Augustus

The following selection is an extract from an account of Augustus's reign by the ancient Roman historian Suetonius (A.D. 75–150), who like Plutarch was writing several generations after the events he describes.

Augustus introduced many reforms into the Army, besides reviving certain obsolete practices, and exacted the strictest discipline. He grudged even his generals home-leave, and granted this only during the winter. When a Roman knight cut off the thumbs of his two young sons to incapacitate them for army service, Augustus had him and his property publicly auctioned; but, realizing that a group of tax-collectors were bidding for the man, knocked him down to an imperial freedman—with instructions that he should be sent away and allowed a free existence in some country place. He gave the entire Tenth Legion an ignominious discharge because of their insolent behavior, and when some other legions also demanded their discharge in a similarly riotous manner, he disbanded them, withholding the bounty which they would have earned had they continued loyal. If a company broke in battle, Augustus ordered the survivors to draw lots,

Gaius Suetonius Tranquillus, *The Twelve Caesars*, Robert Graves, trans. (Baltimore: Penguin Books, 1957), pp. 62, 66–67.

then executed every tenth man, and fed the remainder on barley bread instead of the customary wheat rations. . . .

Among his larger public works three must be singled out for mention: the Forum dominated by the Temple of Avenging Mars; the Palatine Temple of Apollo; and the Temple of Jupiter the Thunderer on the Capitoline Hill. He built his Forum because the two already in existence could not deal with the recent great increase in the number of law-suits caused by a corresponding increase in population; which was why he hurriedly opened it even before the Temple of Mars had been completed. Public prosecutions and the casting of lots for jury service took place only in this Forum.

Augustus had vowed to build the Temple of Mars during the [war] . . . against Julius Caesar's assassins. He therefore decreed that the Senate should meet here whenever declarations of war or claims for triumphs were considered; and that this should be both the starting point for military governors, when escorted to their provinces, and the repository of all triumphal tokens when they returned victorious. The Temple of Apollo was erected in the part of his palace to which, the soothsayers said, the god had drawn attention by having it struck with lightning. The colonnades running out from it housed Latin and Greek libraries; and in his declining years Augustus frequently held meetings of the Senate in the nave, or revised jury lists there. A lucky escape on a night march in Cantabira prompted him to build the Temple of Jupiter the Thunderer: a flash of lightning had scorched his litter and killed the slave who was going ahead with a torch. . . .

Augustus divided the City into districts and wards; placing the districts under the control of magistrates annually chosen by lot, and the wards under supervisors locally elected. He organized stations of night-watchmen to alarm the fire brigades; and, as a precaution against floods, cleared the Tiber channel which had been choked with an accumulation of rubbish and narrowed by projecting houses. Also, he improved the approaches to the city: repaving the Flaminian Way as far as Ariminium, at his own expense, and calling upon men who had won triumphs to spend their prize money on putting the other main roads into good condition.

Furthermore, he restored ruined or burned temples, beautifying these and others with the most lavish gifts: for instance, a single donation to Capitoline Jupiter of 16,000 lbs of gold, besides pearls and precious stones to the value of 500,000 gold pieces.

After reading this selection, consider these questions:

1. What do you think motivated Augustus in his dealings with the army?
2. Why would Augustus spend so much money on the construction of temples?
3. Would you expect public opinion of Augustus to be favorable or unfavorable?

SELECTION 2:

Augustus and the Roman Aristocracy

In this selection, a modern historian analyzes the relation between Augustus and the Senate and the aristocrats of Rome, many of whom had opposed Julius Caesar. Here were both opportunities and possible disasters.

Much has been written about the subservience of the Augustan Senate. Such views misconceive the nature of that august body. The Senate itself, even under the free Republic, had never been the independent originator of policy. That was decided in the private councils of a few leading men, chiefly the senior ex-consuls. The vast majority of senators were content to follow their lead, being known contemptuously as "foot-men."

There remained the Republican nobles. They were dangerous, and a century of sedition, revolution and civil war had given ample proof of their destructive proclivities. Moreover, they were the only class which had lost and lost heavily without compensation by the establishment of the Augustan Principate. And what they had lost

Donald Earl, *The Age of Augustus* (London, Elek Books, 1968), pp. 84–87.

was what they had most highly prized: independence of political action, freedom of competition for pre-eminent honor and glory, liberty to rule the Roman world according to their own desires and for their own profit. Some nobles had joined Augustus early, a few, perhaps, at the beginning; others, after varigated careers, had made convenient submission in due season, before or after Actium [the climactic battle in which Octavian's navy defeated Antony's]. But Augustus could never trust them, however apparently sincere their acceptance of the new order.

If he was ever tempted to, he had only to reflect how many of the Conspirators [against Caesar] had earlier received pardon and advancement from Caesar. Yet he could not ignore them. Despite their losses in civil war and proscription,* too many survived and the Roman people had always been susceptible to the glamour of a famous name. Augustus needed the nobles for advertisement and utility, now as during his rise to supreme power. They were, after all, the remnants of the ruling caste of the Republic, the heirs to its traditions and experience, the guarantee of the respectability of the new regime. To tame the nobles, to redirect their energies into channels conducive to the welfare of the state and his own survival, that was Augustus's problem.

From this point of view the encouragement of the new men, the organization of the Equestrian Order and of a civil service staffed largely by freedmen, the removal from the Senate's control of the most important armed provinces, these were largely negative measures; they reduced the scope and effectiveness of the nobles' capacity for mischief, but positively to bind them to himself Augustus adopted their own favorite political weapon, the marriage alliance. Beginning with his own marriage to Livia Drusilla, Augustus surrounded himself with an increasingly complex network of marriage alliances in which his female kinsfolk in particular were employed to assure the allegiance of important nobles and to satisfy his own dynastic ambitions.

But Augustus' attempt to tame the nobles failed. Conspiracy, death and disgrace reduced their numbers and frightened others from public life. At the same time the new governing and administrative class had consolidated and it consisted in part, at least, of men who had grown up wholly within the Augustan system. After A.D. 2 every man who reached the consulship at the minimum age of thirty-three had been born since the battle of Actium and had known nothing but the dispensation of Augustus.

To make revolution permanent, to promote to the Senate and the ruling class the new men from the length and breadth of Italy, was one of Augustus' leading objectives. His personal taste was to rule with a coalition of new men and nobles but in this he was frustrated, and by the accession of Tiberius the nobility was irreparably broken. The future lay with the new men. The transformation of the ruling class was not to be contained by geography. Under Caligula** two men from Narbonese Gaul reached the consulship, Valerius Asiaticus in A.D. 35, Domitius Afer in 39. Both were of native Gallic stock and Valerius achieved the ultimate distinction of a second consulate in A.D. 46 under Claudius. Caligula was interested in Gaul and the promotion of its inhabitants. So too was Claudius. Under Nero events were controlled and power exercised by Seneca from Corduba in Spain and Burrus from Gallic Vasio.

Vespasian, himself a new man from Italy, ruled with an oligarchy composed of municipal Italians and aristocrats from the provinces. Under him men like M. Ulpius Traianus from Spain and Cn. Iulius Agricola from Fréjus not merely reached the Senate but were numbered among the Patricians. The first stage of the process culminated in the elevation to the imperial power of Trajan, a Spaniard married to a woman from Nîmes in Gaul. But it did not stop there: Africa had already produced her first consul in A.D. 80 and ten years later the first consul from Asia is recorded. Between the accession of Hadrian and

*Proscription meant that a prominent person was condemned to death because of his political stand, and that anyone was legally free to kill him. It was a measure frequently carried out during the Roman civil wars.

**Caligula was a later Roman emperor. So were Nero, Vespasian, Trajan, Hadrian, and Commodus, all of whom are mentioned in the next paragraph.

the death of Commodus men from Africa and the East caught and perhaps overtook those from Italy and the West in numbers of senators if not in numbers of consuls. It was Augustus who had created the essential conditions and had taken the first steps which made this development possible. It was one of his greatest achievements for Rome and for the Western world.

After reading this selection, consider these questions:

1. Why were the nobles a problem for Augustus?
2. How did Augustus use marriage to win over some noble families?
3. How did new men come to power in the imperial structure? What is the importance of this process?

SELECTION 3:

Teaching of Jesus

Jesus of Nazareth was probably born before 4 B.C. (A computational error by the sixth-century Christian scholar who devised the B.C./A.D. dating system accounts for his birth "Before Christ.") Nazareth, his native town, was in Galilee, where the Romans had set up a puppet ruler, Herod Antipas.

Jesus wrote no books, and no accounts were written about him during his lifetime. Nevertheless, it seems reasonably certain that although humbly born, he was a learned man, regarded by the Jews of his time as a teacher, or rabbi. At about the age of thirty he underwent a religious experience and answered a call to preach and to heal the sick of Galilee who believed in him. Like every good Jew, he visited Jerusalem on holy days. He gathered a band of disciples who understood him to say that the kingdom of God was made present in him. Eventually, having angered both the Jewish religious authorities and their Roman political masters, he was arrested, tried, and executed by the procurator of Judea, Pontius Pilate, probably in A.D. 30.

On the Sunday following his crucifixion, certain of his friends and disciples claimed to have seen him risen from the dead. That was the first Easter and marks the beginning of the Christian belief in the resurrection of Jesus. The Gospel of Luke, a spiritual interpretation of his life and teachings that was written perhaps fifty years later, recalled these words of Jesus. Jesus frequently called himself the Son of Man, a title found in the Hebrew Bible in the Book of Daniel, one of the last books to be included in the canon.

"Therefore," he said to his disciples, "I bid you put away anxious thoughts about food to keep you alive and clothes to cover your body. Life is

The New English Bible with the Apocrypha (Oxford and Cambridge: University Presses, 1970), p. 91.

more than food, the body more than clothes. Think of the ravens: they neither sow nor reap; they have no storehouse or barn; yet God feeds them. You are worth far more than the birds! Is there a man among you who by anxious thought can add a foot to his height? If, then, you cannot do even a very little thing, why are you anxious about the rest?

"Think of the lilies: they neither spin nor weave; yet I tell you, even Solomon in all his splendor was not attired like one of these. But if that is how God clothes the grass, which is growing in the field today, and tomorrow is thrown on the stove, how much more will he clothe you! How little faith you have! And so you are not to set your mind on food and drink; you are not to worry. For all these are things for the heathen to run after; but you have a Father who knows that you need them. No, set your mind upon his kingdom, and all the rest will come to you as well.

"Have no fear, little flock; for your Father has chosen to give you the Kingdom. Sell your possessions and give in charity. Provide for yourselves purses that do not wear out, and never-failing treasure in heaven, where no thief can get near it, no moth destroy it. For where your treasure is, there will your heart be also.

"Be ready for action, with belts fastened and lamps alight. Be like men who wait for their master's return from a wedding party, ready to let him in the moment he arrives and knocks. Happy are those servants whom the master finds on the alert when he comes. I tell you this: he will fasten his belt, seat them at table, and come and wait on them. Even if it is the middle of the night or before dawn when he comes, happy they if he finds them alert. And remember, if the householder had known what time the burglar was coming he would not have let his house be broken into. Hold yourselves ready, then, because the Son of Man will come at the time you least expect him."

After reading this selection, consider these questions:

1. How does Jesus promote a set of values different from those held by people in the modern world?
2. Is there any comparison between Jesus' teaching and Daoism?
3. Why would Jesus urge his followers to prepare for his return?

SELECTION 4:

Giving the Church a Structure

A select group of Jesus' disciples came to be known as the Twelve. Only four of the Twelve receive much attention in the New Testament, the Christian Scriptures; the others are little more than names. Besides the Twelve, a convert to Christianity from Judaism, Paul of Tarsus, also figured in the early Christian community, for Paul became the great Apostle to the Gentiles (non-Jews).

After Paul's death about A.D. 67, his name became attached to some letters written by an unknown author. Seven of the Epistles traditionally ascribed to Paul were actually written by him. But three (those addressed to his well-known companions Titus and Timothy) were written by someone else. All of them reflect a period when the Christian Church was taking on a structure, breaking away from Judaism, and setting up its own hierarchy. Its leaders would be known as presbyters, meaning elders, or bishops, the Greek word for supervisors. The pastorals were written in the last thirty years of the first century in an effort to keep Paul's infant Christian com-

munities alive and stable. In the following selection, a modern biblical scholar examines how the early Christian churches were organized.

The qualities demanded of the presbyter-bishop are institutional virtues such as would be appreciated in a tight organization with a familial tone. He must be blameless, upright, and holy; he must be self-controlled and not arrogant or quick-tempered. He must be able to manage his own home well and control his children. It is implied that he must be able to manage the budget of his own home; in particular, he must not be a lover of money—character requirements all the more important if, as may well be suspected from Dead Sea Scroll parallels, the presbyter-bishop had to administer the common money of the Christian community. A blotch like drunkenness cannot be tolerated on his moral record. Indeed, at times the requirements border on matters of religious respectability: he cannot have been married more than once; he cannot be a recent convert; his children must be Christian.

These latter requirements reflect the emergence of the church as a society with set standards that it is imposing on its public figures. Jesus during his ministry called prominent followers from various walks of life without any consideration how society might look on fishermen, tax collectors, and a zealot.* But Jesus was not structuring a society; he did not live in an organized church; the Twelve were selected not as administrators but as eschatological judges of the renewed Israel. Once the movement associated with Christ became organized enough to be a society called "church," however, it began to decide that certain standards of religious respectability were very important for the common good.

Individuals, however talented, who did not meet those standards would have to be sacrificed. The presbyter, after all, had to serve as a model fa-

ther of a family. A man converted after his children had grown might be a natural leader; but if he did not meet the qualification of having believing children, he was not to be appointed presbyter-bishop. Sometimes recent converts are insecure or not mature in their Christian judgment; other times they are filled with an extraordinary zeal that might galvanize a community. The Pastoral Epistles would allow no recent convert, talented or not, to function in the presbyteral office—almost an ironic requirement, granted the history of the man who is supposed to be writing the letters.

Indeed, Paul might not have been able to meet several requirements the Pastorals would impose on the presbyter-bishops. "Not quick-tempered" would scarcely describe the Paul who called the Galatians "fools." "Dignified" would not fit the Paul who wished that his circumcising adversaries would slip with the knife and castrate themselves* and who could utter such vituperation as "Their God is their belly." Rough vitality and a willingness to fight bare-knuckled for the Gospel were part of what made Paul a great missionary, but such characteristics might have made him a poor residential community supervisor. The Pastorals are listing qualities necessary for someone who would have to get along with a community for a long time; fortunately for all, perhaps, Paul's missionary genius kept him on the move.

After reading this selection, consider these questions:

1. What was the function of a presbyter-bishop in the early Christian Church?
2. How does the author contrast the recruitment of Jesus' followers from those sought by the author(s) of the Pastorals?
3. What made Paul such an important personality in the early Christian Church?

---

*Zealots in Jesus' time were Jewish rebels, eager to struggle against Roman rule. Some advocated terrorism, and most looked toward an armed insurrection. At least one of the apostles, Simon, was a zealot.

*Paul disputed other early Christian leaders over whether male Gentile converts to Christianity should be required to submit to the Jewish practice of circumcision. Paul's position was that they should not.

Raymond E. Brown, *The Churches the Apostles Left Behind* (New York: Paulist Press, 1984), pp. 34–35.

SELECTION 5:

Jesus, Women, and the Church

In recent years much scholarly attention has focused on the place of women in the early Christian Church. The active participation of women in any religious movement of the first century A.D. was unusual and suspect; men of the time normally thought that women should humbly do as they were told. The Gospels, however, make it clear that Jesus appealed strongly to the Jewish women who heard and saw him preach and heal, and that not all of them were respectable. In the early churches, too, women seem to have been quite prominent, even on occasion taking leadership roles. The socially conservative Paul apparently tried to reduce women's position in the Christian communities. In this selection, a modern American historian grapples with these issues.

Jesus' relations with women seem to have been remarkably free, given the reserve that Jewish custom in his day required. He is received by Martha and Mary, neither of whom is married, and demonstrates his friendship by resurrecting their brother Lazarus. When his disciples find him talking to a Samaritan at Jacob's well in Sichem, they "marvelled that he talked with the woman. Yet no man said, What seekest thou? or, Why talkest thou with her?" Barriers were broken down in the most surprising ways. Jesus preached to foreign women like the "schismatic" Samaritan* and healed even the daughter of a Canaanite. The traditional hierarchy was overturned in favor of the despised: "The publicans [Jewish tax collectors for Rome] and the harlots go into the kingdom of God before you," Jesus tells the high priests and elders of the Temple. In a well-known passage he forgives the many sins

*Samaria was a province to the north of Judaea where a distinctive variety of Judaism was practiced. "Orthodox" Jews (such as Jesus) and Samaritans normally despised each other. Thus Jesus' preaching to Samaritans and his parables describing them as good people were highly unsettling to the average Jew.

Pauline Schmitt Pantel, ed., *A History of Women in the West*, Arthur Goldhammer, trans. (Cambridge, MA: Harvard University Press, 1992), pp. 420–21, 423–24.

of a woman who "loved much" because she, to the horror of the Pharisees, is willing to anoint his feet with ointment. The pardon granted to the adulterous woman and the disarray of her male accusers can be seen in the same light. So can the message to the Samaritan woman who has been married five times and is now living as a concubine. Even female impurity is transcended: a bleeding woman touches the hem of Jesus' cloak and is cured. He also takes pity on the poorest of women, the widows protected by the Law: he resurrects the only son of the widow of Nain, as Elijah before him had resurrected the son of the widow of Sarepta. The poor widow who casts in "two mites" is praised more than the rich men making their gifts to the temple treasury.

The identity of the "saved" women who followed Jesus out of Galilee varies with the source. In Luke, after the passage about the anointment, we read: "And the twelve were with him. And certain women, which had been healed of evil spirits and infirmities, Mary called Magdalene, out of whom went seven devils, and Joanna the wife of Chuza, Herod's steward, and Susanna, and many others, which ministered unto him of their substance." It is a diverse group of women that sets out with Jesus on the road in defiance of custom. In all the lists Mary Magdalene comes first. Unlike the Twelve, these women have not received an explicit call, nor are they dispatched on clear missions. Yet in contrast to the abandonment of Jesus by the disciples, the presence of the women is emphasized—at a distance according to the Synoptics** but near the cross according to John. As was customary in Judaism, the women are present when Jesus is wrapped in his shroud, and it is they who prepare perfumes and fragrances for anointing the body. Matthew names Mary Magdalene and the other Mary; Mark, Mary Magdalene, Mary, mother of James, and Salome; Luke, Mary Magdalene, Joanna, and Mary, mother of James; and John, only Mary Magdalene.

All four versions break with Jewish custom by making women, and particularly Mary Magdalene, witnesses to the resurrection and responsible for informing the disciples. To be sure, masculine incredulity is apparent in Mark and Luke. But the special place of women, who are the first to see the resurrected Christ, is therefore all the more significant, especially in the celebrated *Noli me tangere* ["Touch me not"] scene in John. Memory of that special role would be preserved in prayer and imagery. . . .

As the Church moved toward greater institutionalization, however, women did not hold well-defined ministries. Certain distinct groups of women did form, however. One such was the *cherai*, or widows, who, according to biblical tradition, enjoyed the special protection of the Law and of God. From the widow of Sarepta to Judith and Anne the prophetess, an image took shape of the widow as a person closer than other people to God. Christian communities took it upon themselves to aid widows without other means of support. Although remarriage was tolerated, even encouraged for young widows, and although the children of widows were reminded to care for them, widows past the age of sixty who had demonstrated maternal and charitable qualities in

a single marriage were called upon to live lives of continence and prayer. In setting forth the duties of elders (*presbytai*), young people, and slaves, the Epistle to Titus [one of the pastoral letters attributed to Paul] stated that elder women (*presbytides*) should occupy themselves with instructing other women: "The aged women likewise, that they be in behavior as becometh holiness, not false accusers, not given to much wine, teachers of good things; that they may teach the young women to be sober, to love their husbands, to love their children; to be discreet, chaste, keepers at home, good, obedient to their own husbands, that the word of God be not blasphemed." Despite Paul's advocacy of virginity, there is no sign of any special group of virgins among unmarried women in these early Christian communities.

Apart form these informal roles for women, there was probably also "a category of female ministers without specific titles." In the First Epistle to Timothy, after the section on the *episcopoi*, in the middle of the section on the *diakonoi*, "those who serve," we read: "Even so must their wives be grave, not slanderers, sober, faithful in all things." Here "their wives" seems to suggest a category of women parallel to that of the male *diakonoi*, exhibiting similar traits and sharing similar duties.

After reading this selection, consider these questions:

1. What might have been the appeal of Jesus' message to the Jewish women of his time?
2. Why do you think that males of the first century might distrust female religiosity, and oppose allowing women a prominent role in a religious movement?
3. What role did women assume in first-century Christian communities?

**the Gospels of Mark, Matthew, and Luke

SELECTION 6:
The Married Life

There was a certain preoccupation with sexual behavior among early fol-lowers of Jesus. It is true that some Christians of the first centuries A.D. tended to consider sexuality—and anything else suggesting enjoyment of the material world—a barrier to an intense spiritual life. One of the great-est of the early Christian theologians, Augustine (354–430), who was born a pagan and whose mistress bore him a son, struggled against sexu-al desire for years before he finally accepted conversion—and celibacy. He left an intense account of his psychological and spiritual journey in his autobiographical Confessions. *But although Augustine preferred that Christians voluntarily renounce sexuality, he did not wholly condemn it. The following selection presents an extract from one essay among his enormous body of writings, "The Married Life." His views, here and on many other subjects, became fundamental to medieval Christianity.*

(1.1) Every human being is part of the human race, and human nature is a social reality and possesses a great and natural good, the power of friendship. For this reason God wished to create all human beings from one, so that they would be held together in human society, not only by the similarity of race, but also by the bond of blood relationship. Therefore, the first natural union of human society is the husband and wife. God did not create even these as separate individuals and join them together as if they were alien to each other, but he created the one from the other. The power of the union was also signified in the side from which she was taken and formed, for they are joined to each other's side, when they walk together and together look where they are walk-ing. The result is the bonding of society in chil-dren, who are the one honorable fruit, not of the union of male and female, but of sexual inter-course. For there could have been some kind of real and amiable union between the sexes even

without sexual intercourse, a union in which the one rules and the other obeys.

(II.2) There is no need at this time for us to ex-amine and set forth a definite opinion on the question of how the offspring of the first humans could have come into being, whom God had blessed, saying: *Increase and multiply, and fill the earth* [Gen. 1:28], if they had not sinned. For it was by their sin that their bodies deserved the condition of death, and there could be no inter-course except of mortal bodies. Many different views have been expressed on this subject, and if we were to examine which of them is most con-gruent with the truth of the divine Scriptures, there is matter for extended discussion. . . .

(3) This is what we now say: according to that state of birth and death, which we experience and in which we were created, the union of male and female is something good. The divine Scripture commends this alliance to such an extent that a woman who is divorced by her husband is not al-lowed to marry another, while her husband is still alive; and a man who is divorced by his wife may not take another, unless the wife who has left him has died. It is right, therefore, to inquire why the good of marriage is good, which even the Lord

Augustine of Hippo, "The Good of Marriage," in *Marriage in the Early Church*, David G. Hunter, ed. (Minneapolis: Fortress Press, 1992), pp. 102, 104–105.

confirmed in the gospel, not only because he prohibited divorce, except in cases of fornication [cf. Matt. 19:9], but also because when he was invited to the wedding, he attended [cf. John 2:1–11].

I do not believe that marriage is a good solely because of the procreation of children; there is also the natural association (*societas*) between the sexes. Otherwise, we would no longer speak of a marriage between elderly people, especially if they had lost or had never produced children. But now in a good marriage, even if it has lasted for many years and even if the youthful ardor between the male and female has faded, the order of charity between husband and wife still thrives. The earlier they begin to refrain from sexual intercourse, by mutual consent, the better they will be. This is not because they will eventually be unable to do what they wish, but because it is praiseworthy not to wish to do what they are able to do.

If, therefore, they keep faithful to the honor and the conjugal duties that each sex owes the other, even if both of their bodies grow weak and almost corpselike, yet the chastity of spirits joined in a proper marriage will endure; the more it is tested, the more genuine it will be; the more it is calmed, the more secure it will be. There is an additional good in marriage, namely the fact that carnal or youthful incontinence, even the most wicked, is directed toward the honorable task of procreating children. As a result conjugal intercourse makes something good out of the evil of lust (*libido*), since the concupiscence of the flesh, which parental affection moderates, is then suppressed and in a certain way burns more modestly. For a sort of dignity prevails over the fire of pleasure, when in the act of uniting as husband and wife the couple regard themselves as father and mother.

After reading this selection, consider these questions:

1. What is Augustine's attitude toward marriage?
2. On what grounds does Augustine justify sexuality as part of human life?
3. Why does Augustine recommend that married couples refrain from having sexual relations as frequently as possible? Support or oppose his argument.

CHAPTER 11
Byzantium: What Was the Basis of Its Civilization?

The period of Roman history that extends from the foundation of Constantinople in A.D. 330 until 1453 is known as the Byzantine era, a named derived from the fact that before the foundation of Constantinople, the Greek city of Byzantium occupied the site.

Byzantine civilization comprised three key ingredients, which you should keep in mind as you study this chapter. These three factors were Roman political structure, Greek culture, and the Christian religion. An all-powerful emperor ruled over the state, presumably holding his position because God had chosen him to occupy the throne. The Greek language and its educational goals determined Byzantium's cultural life, and religion played such a major role that every citizen was touched by it on a daily basis.

Modern historians acknowledge the emperor Justinian I (482–565) and the empress Theodora (500–547) as the outstanding rulers of early Byzantium. Justinian came to prominence because he was the nephew of Justin, a general who later was chosen emperor. His spouse Theodora's background is not so easy to assess. Some historians believe that the *Secret History*, composed by Procopius (499–565), a disgruntled aide, is near the truth in depicting her beginnings as a circus entertainer. Others argue that these accusations are part of a scurrilous campaign, based on innuendo, and have no basis in fact. Both sides agree that she made a powerful impact on the empire and strongly influenced its direction.

SELECTION 1:

The Church of the Holy Wisdom

Justinian is remembered for successfully regaining much of the Mediterranean lands lost to the Germans, for commissioning the codification of Roman law, and especially for the construction of the Church of the Holy Wisdom. This building, the largest in the world for five hundred years, still stands in modern Istanbul (as the Turks call Constantinople) and is now a museum. In this selection, Procopius describes it.

The Emperor, disregarding all questions of expense, eagerly pressed on to begin the work of construction, and began to gather all the artisans from the whole world. And Anthemius of Tralles, the most learned man in the skilled craft which is known as the art of building, not only of all his contemporaries, but also when compared with those who had lived long before him, ministered to the Emperor's enthusiasm, duly regulating the tasks of the various artisans, and preparing in advance designs of the future construction; and associated with him was another master-builder, Isidorus by name, a Milesian by birth, a man who was intelligent and worthy to assist the Emperor Justinian. Indeed this also was an indication of the honor in which God held the Emperor, that he had already provided the men who would be most serviceable to him in the tasks which were waiting to be carried out. And one might with good reason marvel at the discernment of the Emperor himself, in that out of the whole world he was able to select the men who were most suitable for the most important of his enterprises.

So the church has become a spectacle of marvelous beauty, overwhelming to those who see it, but to those who know it by hearsay altogether incredible. For it soars to a height to match the sky, and as if surging up from among the other buildings it stands on high and looks down upon the remainder of the city, adorning it, because it is a part of it, but glorying in its own beauty, because, though a part of the city and dominating it, it at the same time towers above it to such a height that the whole city is viewed from there as from a watch-tower.

Both its breadth and its length have been so carefully proportioned, that it may not improperly be said to be exceedingly long and at the same time unusually broad. And it exults in an indescribable beauty. For it proudly reveals its mass and the harmony of its proportions, having neither any excess nor deficiency, since it is both more pretentious than the buildings to which we are accustomed, and considerably more noble than those which are merely huge, and it abounds exceedingly in sunlight and in the reflection of the sun's rays from the marble. Indeed one might say that its interior is not illuminated from without by the sun, but that the radiance comes into being within it, such an abundance of light bathes this shrine.

After reading this selection, consider these questions:
1. Why would Justinian want to build the Church of the Holy Wisdom?
2. What impression did the church make upon visitors?
3. Who were the architects of the church?

Procopius of Caesarea, *Buildings*, 1, 1–23, vol. 85 of the Loeb Classical Library. H.B. Dewing, trans. (Cambridge: Harvard University Press, 1954), 3, 11–17.

SELECTION 2:

Introduction to the Digest

Justinian explains how the Digest, *that part of his legal work providing a commentary on the law, was put together. The imperial style was not distinguished by understatement. Roman laws were issued as* constitutiones.

Governing under the authority of God our empire which was delivered to us by the Heavenly Majesty, we both conduct wars successfully and render peace honorable, and we uphold the condition of the state. We so lift up our minds toward the help of the omnipotent God that we do not place our trust in weapons or our soldiers or our military leaders our own talents, but we rest all our hopes in the providence of the Supreme Trinity alone, from whence the elements of the whole world proceeded and their disposition throughout the universe was derived.

1. Whereas, then, nothing in any sphere is found so worthy of study as the authority of law, which sets in good order affairs both divine and human and casts out all injustice, yet we have found the whole extent of our laws which has come down from the foundation of the city of Rome and the days of Romulus to be so confused that it extends to an inordinate length and is beyond the comprehension of any human nature. It has been our primary endeavor to make a beginning with the most revered emperors of earlier times, to free their *constitutiones* (enactments) from faults and set them out in a clear fashion, so that they might be collected together in one *Codex,* and that they might afford to all mankind the ready protection of their own integrity, purged of all unnecessary repetition and most harmful disagreement.

2. This work has been accomplished and collected in a single volume under our own glorious name. In our haste to extricate ourselves from minor and more trivial affairs and attain to a completely full revision of the law, and to collect and amend the whole set of Roman ordinances and present the diverse books of so many authors in a single volume (a thing which no one has dared to expect or to desire), the task appeared to us most difficult, indeed impossible. Nevertheless, with our hands stretched up to heaven, and imploring eternal aid, we stored up this task too in our mind, relying upon God, who in the magnitude of his goodness is able to sanction and to consummate achievements that are utterly beyond hope.

After reading this selection, consider these questions:

1. Why did Justinian begin the codification of Roman law?
2. How did the emperor relate his task of codification to God?
3. Why do you think Justinian's Code has had such a lasting effect on the European legal structure?

The Digest of Justinian, Latin ed., Theodore Mommsen and Paul Krueger, English ed. and Alan Watson, trans., 4 vols. (Philadelphia: University of Pennsylvania Press, 1985), 1, 55, 56.

SELECTION 3:

Theodora

The career of Theodora—described here in an extract from the work of the modern historian Anthony Bridge—is not only fascinating in its own right but also reveals much about the refined court life of sixth-century Byzantium. This was one of the largest and richest cities in the world, importing luxuries from many distant lands and exporting far and wide the magnificent products of its government-regulated workshops. Moreover, an overwhelming display of imperial grandeur was essential to maintaining the Byzantine rulers' image of God's representative on earth. Theodora obviously enjoyed all this to the hilt.

It was a privileged life, and she loved every minute of it. When old Justin had died, she and Justinian moved from the Palace of Hormisdas into the Imperial Palace itself, where they were surrounded by every possible luxury and comfort. Theodora was just over thirty years old at the time of the Nika revolt, but she looked younger, and everyone agreed that she was still as ravishingly beautiful as ever. Since she was also intensely feminine, she had every intention of remaining both young and beautiful for as long as possible, and she took the greatest possible care of herself and her appearance. Before having breakfast in bed, she would rise and spend hours in her bath; and then she would sit for at least as long in front of her mirror making up her face and doing her hair with the help of two or three of her personal maids. She dressed superbly, and since Justinian loved to load her with jewelry, she seldom appeared unadorned by precious stones of one kind or another. In the celebrated portrait of her in the Church of San Vitale in Ravenna [Italy], where she is depicted as she must have looked as an older woman not long before she died, she is wearing a head-dress set with enormous pearls as well as some emeralds, sapphires, and stones which look like jasper; her ear-rings are two square emeralds

set in gold with a pearl and sapphire pendant to each of them; her necklace is also of emeralds set in gold, as is a large brooch on her bosom; and her small shoulders seem to be covered with a silken cape embroidered with pearls and a dozen huge diamonds. Her toilet completed, she would emerge from the *gynaeceum* [the women's section of the palace], cocooned by a silken bevy of attendants, looking as regal as any Roman Empress before her and twice as lovely as most.

Her day's work would then begin, and the morning would be entirely devoted to it; but though she enjoyed working, she always retired to bed again in the afternoon for a siesta, for she loved sleeping, and she was determined to preserve her youthful appearance by taking ample rest. In this respect, she differed from Justinian, who grudged every moment he spent in sleep, and who allowed himself only a few frugal hours in bed each night, rising long before dawn to devote himself to his various pursuits; his work with Tribonian on Roman law engrossed him, he was fascinated by theology, and he nearly always had schemes for new buildings somewhere in the Empire, which needed his attention and approval. They had different tastes in food and drink too. Luxury did not attract Justinian; he ate little and drank less, being perfectly happy with a slice of bread and a salad for his supper. Theodora thoroughly enjoyed her food. As a child in the Hippo-

Anthony Bridge, *Theodora: Portrait in a Byzantine Landscape* (Chicago: Academy Chicago Publishers, 1984), pp. 82–85.

drome she had probably had to be content with whatever her mother was able to afford to put before her three hungry daughters, and that had probably been insufficient to satisfy the healthy appetite of a growing child; perhaps it was against this background of remembered hunger and a barely adequate diet that Theodora became celebrated for the epicurean meals she provided for herself and her guests. Nothing pleased her more than to entertain her friends and to give them such exquisite food that they would never forget it, and her taste in wine soon became a by-word in Byzantine society. She was both a gourmet by inclination and a superb hostess by natural gift, and her position as Justinian's consort gave her every opportunity to indulge this side of her nature, although she never allowed anyone to forget for a moment that she was the Empress; her insistence upon the proper social observances and etiquette did not grow less as the years went by, and she never became easily approachable.

But Theodora did not spend all her time enjoying herself; she was extremely active in the government of the Empire. After the Nika revolt was over, Justinian never forgot that he owed his victory to Belisarius, Mundus, Narses, and above all to Theodora. At the height of the crisis she had proved to be more politically astute and more resolute than all his other advisers put together, and without her intervention he would almost certainly have lost his throne. It was only fair that, since he had retained it by following her advice, he should share it with her now that things had returned to normal.

The Empress as such had no constitutional right to a part in the Emperor's authority, for he alone was the absolute ruler of the Roman world; but simply because he was absolute and an autocrat in the fullest sense of that word, he could choose to share his power with whomsoever he wished, and no one could stop him. One Byzantine historian summed up the situation by saying that "in the time of Justinian, there was not a monarchy but a dual reign. His partner for life was not less, but perhaps even more powerful, than he was." There was no precedent for this complete sharing of authority, and yet no one could possibly mistake the fact that it was indeed shared; on taking office, bishops, magistrates, generals, governors of provinces, ministers of the crown, and other high officials had to swear "by Almighty God, by his only Son Jesus Christ, by the Holy Spirit, by the holy and glorious Mother of God, Mary-ever-Virgin, by the four Evangelists, by the holy archangels Michael and Gabriel to render loyal service to the most pious and holy sovereigns Justinian and Theodora, wife of his Imperial Majesty." In fact, as time went by, Theodora began to play a larger part in the affairs of everyday government than did Justinian, and she did so for very good reason. . . .

But she did not like Constantinople very much, and so she took every opportunity which presented itself to leave the city and to spend a few weeks or even months in the country. Justinian did not always accompany her, for custom dictated that the Emperor should reside most of the time in the Imperial Palace, but he went with her when he could. At Hieron, a small town on the Asiatic shore of the Bosphorus near the point where it joins the Black Sea, there was a palace which she loved, and so Justinian had it greatly enlarged and splendidly furnished for her. He transformed the town too, building a magnificent church there and dedicating it to the Mother of God, as well as building baths, market places, and elegantly colonnaded streets, where people could wander in the shade with their friends and enjoy the pleasures of city life away from the dust and the crowds of Constantinople. As the heat of summer approached Theodora would issue orders to her court to prepare to leave for Hieron, and on the appointed day she would sally forth from the Palace in great state, surrounded by as many as two or three thousand attendants of one kind or another—guards, eunuchs, ladies-in-waiting, court officials, and a host of servants—and would go with them in splendid procession to the Golden Horn, where she would embark upon the royal barge, and the others would go aboard a great flotilla of small craft to sail to Hieron; with pennants fluttering in the breeze against the blue Byzantine sky and bedecked with silks and brocades, awnings and cushions, this small armada would then sail northwards, while the gulls screamed overhead and parties of shearwaters flew up and down the Bosphorus low over the water beside the boats; they were believed to be the souls of the many sailors drowned there, and they put the members of Theodora's retinue in mind of their own mortality.

After reading this selection, consider these questions:

1. What was Theodora's role as empress, and how did she fulfill it?
2. Why do you suppose Justinian gave his wife so much authority?
3. What were the advantages of spending the summer in Hieron?

SELECTION 4:

Nicephorus at the Church of the Holy Wisdom

Lesser men governed the empire after Justinian. While Byzantine armies for a time held back Germanic kings' rule in North Africa, Italy, and parts of Spain, the rise of Islam tore away the rich provinces of Egypt and Syria. Moreover, after 800, when the pope crowned Charlemagne emperor of the Romans, a rival to Constantinople's claim to Christian sovereignty arose.

Not much affection was demonstrated between the Frankish emperors in the West and the Greek emperors in the East. Delegations sent back and forth often did more harm than good in establishing cordial relations. Liutprand of Cremona, representing the western emperor Otto I, arrived in Constantinople in the tenth century to meet with the Byzantine emperor Nicephorus to arrange a marriage between the royal houses. In this selection, the awestruck Liutprand describes his impression of an imperial procession in his report filed with Otto I. The Church of the Holy Wisdom (Sancta Sophia) to which he refers was still the largest church in all of Europe. Built by Justinian, it still stands, but has been turned into a museum.

May nothing keep me from describing this procession, and my masters from hearing about it! A numerous multitude of tradesmen and low-born persons, collected at this festival to receive and to do honour to Nicephorus, occupied both sides of the road from the palace to St. Sophia like walls, being disfigured by quite thin little shields and wretched spears. And it served to increase this disfigurement that the greater part of this same

crowd in the emperor's honour, had marched with bare feet. I believe that they thought in this way better to adorn that holy procession.

But also his nobles who passed with him through the plebeian and barefoot multitude were clad in tunics which were too large, and which were torn through too great age. It would have been much more suitable had they marched in their everyday clothes. There was no one whose grandfather had owned one of these garments when it was new. No one there was adorned with gold, no one with gems, save Nicephorus alone,

Liutprand of Cremona, *Mission to Constantinople*, A.D. 968 (Lawrence, KS: Dollarbooks, 1972), pp. 7–9.

whom the imperial adornments, bought and prepared for the persons of his ancestors, rendered still more disgusting. By your salvation, which is dearer to me than my own, one precious garment of your nobles is worth a hundred of these, and more too. I was led to this church procession and was placed on a raised place next to the singers.

And as, like a creeping monster, the emperor proceeded thither, the singers cried out in adulation: "Behold the morning star approaches; Eos rises; he reflects in his glances the rays of the sun—he the pale death of the Saracens, Nicephorus the ruler." And accordingly they sang: "Long life to the ruler Nicephorus! Adore him, you people, cherish him, bend the neck to him alone!" How much more truly might they have sung: "Come, you burnt-out coal, you fool; old woman in your walk, wood-devil in your look; you peasant, you frequenter of foul places, you goat-foot, you horn-head, you double-limbed one; bristly, unruly, countrified, barbarian, harsh, hairy, a rebel, a Cappadocian!"

And so, inflated by those lying fools, he enters St. Sophia, his masters the emperors following him from afar, and, with the kiss of peace, adoring him to the ground. His armour-bearer, with an arrow for a pen, places in the church the era which is in progress from the time when he began to reign, and thus those who did not then exist learn what the era is.

After reading this selection, consider these questions:

1. How does this selection show that life in Constantinople had changed since the time of Justinian?
2. What bias do you find in Liutprand's account?
3. What response do you suppose Otto gave to his envoy upon his return?

SELECTION 5:

A Byzantine Holy Woman

Intensely felt religious experience was central to the Byzantine way of life, even if not everyone devout. Stories abounded of dissolute sinners suddenly being struck with remorse and dramatically becoming saintly ascetics. Whether the details of such stories are true is perhaps less important than the fact that the stories were taken seriously and the values that they reveal. Here, a modern American historian analyzes one such story, from the sixth century, describing how a notable Byzantine saint, Mary of Egypt, was transformed from a prostitute to a hermit who lived her last forty-seven years alone in the desert. As the author points out, there are interesting twists to the story, for Mary managed to achieve sainthood without the help of male priests. Ascetic Christian life in this period had a place for solitary figures in direct communion with Christ and the Blessed Virgin, as well as for people under closer church discipline.

Before living for over forty years as an ascetic in the Jordan Valley, Mary experienced a life that was wholly contrary to the conventional tales of the childhood days of female saints. She abandoned her parents at the age of twelve—when many holy women vow marriage to Christ—and journeyed to Alexandria. There she earned a living by begging and by spinning flax, and offered her body for pleasure, not payment. By classical standards, Mary was the worst kind of harlot because she engaged in intercourse not from financial need but to satisfy lust. She always carried a spindle, as if to mock the distaffs of the chaste, charitable women of sacred and classical discourse. The ex-prostitute informs the undefiled priest [Zosimas, who has come upon her in the desert] that all unnatural acts were welcome to her.

Eventually Mary met a group of sailors at Alexandria's harbor who were headed for the Holy Land to attend the festivities of the Exaltation of the Holy Cross. The harlot pushed her way through the crowd of pilgrims and, in an inversion of pious preaching, enticed the Egyptian and Libyan seafarers with lewd language. Mary claimed that at the time her strong desire to go with them was motivated not by religious ceremony but by the beautiful bodies of the seamen to whom she offered her own as payment for the voyage. She, like Jezebel, led men to sin, for once she arrived in Jerusalem, she seduced male pilgrims at the religious festivals. Mary's journey to Jerusalem is a perverted pilgrimage, and her activities in the city invert the Christian apostolic mission; as she tells Zosimas, "I was hunting for the souls of young men." During the festival of the Exaltation of the Holy Cross, Mary attempted to enter a church, but her polluted body was miraculously suspended outside the sacred space, held fast by the discriminating power of a relic of the true cross. Resting in the basilica's forecourt, she saw an icon of the *Theotokos* which impelled her to confess her sins to the Virgin, weep, and beat her breast. She called upon the Mother of

God as the mediator of salvation, imploring the Virgin to grant her access to the *sanctus sanctorum*.

Finally, the miraculous power of Christ's Mother guided Mary's sinful body over the threshold of the church, where the harlot "threw [herself] on the floor and kissed the sacred dust." She then returned to the icon and vowed to remake her body into a vessel of repentance. The Virgin's celestial voice instructed her to go out into the wilderness and cross over the Jordan River. Mary left the forecourt of the church and walked through the streets of Jerusalem. Her supernatural experience had so transformed her physical appearance that, as she wandered the city, a Christian gave her three coins and called her amma. The transfigured woman used the coins to buy three loaves of bread and then ran out the city gate.

When Mary reached the Jordan River, she washed her hands and face in its salvific waters, an action designed to evoke symbolic baptism and spiritual rebirth. The amma received communion at the church of Saint John the Baptist and then, under the Virgin's direction, she crossed the Jordan. She had been living in the desert for forty-seven years when Zosimas found her walking along the river banks. She tells the virginal monk that during those five decades in the wilderness she had been tempted by memories of her former life of sin, but that a miraculous light surrounded her and provided her with spiritual peace: "This light saved me from the lusts of mind." But unlike Antony's "saving light" which rescued the great hermit from vicious, demonic attacks, Mary's saving light delivered her from her inherent depravity. During her generation of desert life, Mary received neither instruction nor communion from a priest until she encountered Zosimas. Zosimas, on hearing this "life-giving narrative," pleads with the holy woman to tell him more. . . .

At the end of the narrative, the hagiographer provides a second significant gender reversal. Zosimas journeys again to the desert to administer communion to Mary, only to find her dead. Zosimas responds to this discovery by expressing for Mary the same piety Mary Magdalene demon-

---

Lynda L. Coon, *Sacred Fictions: Holy Women and Hagiography in Late Antiquity* (Philadelphia: University of Pennsylvania Press, 1997), pp. 86–88.

strates for Christ (Matthew 26.6–13; Mark 14.3–9; Luke 7.36–50; John 12.1–8): "He saw the holy one lying dead, her hands folded and her face turned to the East."

After reading this selection, consider these questions:

1. Why do you think Byzantine Christians would admire Mary?
2. Do you find Mary's story credible?
3. What does Mary's story suggest to you about the position of women in Byzantine society?

SELECTION 6:

East and West

*A*lrefor *in the fourth century differences between the Latin-speaking part of the church and the Greeks emerged. As long as the Byzantine Empire lasted tension between the West and East was always present despite efforts at several councils in 1274 and 1438–39 to reconcile the divergent points of view. In the following selection, British historian Joan Hussey discusses the challenge presented to the Byzantine church from the western European, or Latin, Christian church.*

This challenge largely turned on the interpretation of Trinitarian and Christological doctrine. In the case of the West it also concerned ecclesiastical authority because the eastern conception of the equality of all bishops and a collegial authority clashed with the Latin development of a single supreme bishop of Rome. The gap between Greek and Latin was there long before the aggravation of 1204. Primarily rooted in theological differences this gap was further widened by cultural, political, and linguistic problems, due in part—as far as Latins and Greeks were concerned—to the differing fortunes of the eastern and western halves of the Roman Empire. . . .

Factual evidence reveals the increasing extent to which the differences between Greek and Latin contributed to a rift which became the concern of all circles in Byzantium, making increasing demands upon diplomats as well as church-

men. For in the later middle ages the restoration of union between the Greek and Latin Churches was closely linked to the pressing need for a united Christian front in the face of a rapidly advancing Islam. Neither Lyons II (1274) nor Ferrara-Florence (1438–39) could provide an acceptable solution. But failure does not mean that these abortive negotiations can for that reason be omitted or watered down. They were significant for various reasons. They underlined the tenacity with which the Orthodox Church maintained its doctrinal and ecclesiological traditions. . . .

East–West ecclesiastical relations also reveal how little the Greeks knew of Latin theology (using "theologia" in the western doctrinal sense, for to the Greeks it meant the spiritual contemplation of God). The Church, despite differences between its members, was regarded as being one, but it early ceased to draw on its common heritage, at least as far as the Greeks were concerned. The major Greek fathers [Christian theologians] of the fourth and fifth centuries were rapidly translated into Latin, as was the seventh-

J.M. Hussey, *The Orthodox Church in the Byzantine Empire* (Oxford: Clarendon Press, 1986), pp. 2–5.

century Maximus the Confessor. But the Latin father [St.] Augustine . . . was not known in Greek until the late middle ages and then only in part, for instance the translation of the *De trinitate* [*on the Trinity*] by the fourteenth-century Manuel Calecas who also translated other later Latin works, as Boethius and Anselm of Canterbury, while his contemporaries the Cydones brothers made [St. Thomas] Aquinas available.

Thus for most of the middle ages the Greeks knew little of the western tradition. It was partly that they had long tended to regard the Latins as "barbarians" using a language which was in the Greek view ill-suited to express doctrinal truths. It was also partly due to a certain antagonistic undercurrent of political rivalry and hostility, for instance in the earlier period in Italy and the Balkans and then later on over the crusades. Further, the Greeks on the whole did not gravitate much to the West, though there were frequent contacts in Italy. But it was otherwise with the westerners who came East for various reasons. There was always the incentive of a pilgrimage to Jerusalem or the journey on crusade which could mean traveling through Byzantine lands, and finally there was the opportunity of actually settling in the conquered Aegean lands.

It was only in the late middle ages that the Greeks were brought up against some of the more acceptable aspects of Latin culture (together it must be said with much which they disliked). It was then that the Latin theological works, such as Augustine or Aquinas, began to be translated, though not on a large scale. Much remained unknown and might indeed have been found to be out of line with Greek doctrinal teaching. The Greeks were also in disagreement with the western use of the scholastic method, as they showed when debates took place, particularly in the fourteenth-century disputes. They regarded logic as a useful, indeed an essential, tool, but considered that dialectic could not be applied to the mysteries of faith. Much as some Greeks in the later period might admire individual Latins whom they got to know, with few exceptions (as for instance Demetrius Cydones) they probably felt that their own rich patristic heritage provided for their doctrinal and spiritual needs and for the most part they had no desire to explore western thought.

Thus during the 800 years and more from Heraclius to the end of the Empire the Orthodox Church went its own way. Closely integrated with the daily life of the East Romans, it was able to perfect and adapt its central administration, to organize its provinces and dioceses to meet changing needs, and to introduce its religion and way of life to its Slav neighbors. Above all it deepened its spiritual life which was centered in a developing liturgical round, particularly in the Eucharist. This service kept its original character and purpose, but during the course of the middle ages it was gradually enriched by additional actions, responses, hymns, and ceremonies. The Byzantines had a strong feeling for dignified ceremony and symbolism and this left its mark in ecclesiastical as well as imperial developments, bringing out and enhancing the meaning of the liturgy and indeed of the Christian faith. But it did not obscure the purpose of the sacramental life as is evidenced by the writings of the more spiritually minded members of the Church, often monks, but by no means always so. . . . What mattered was the liturgical life and faithful adherence to the traditions of the Church.

After reading this selection, consider these questions:
1. Why were there differences in the eastern and western expressions of the Christian faith?
2. How did language contribute to the growing differences between East and West?
3. Why was worship and tradition so important to eastern Christians?

CHAPTER 12
Western Europe in the Early Middle Ages: What Did Charlemagne Accomplish?

The Byzantine Empire resembled China in its ability to fend off barbarian attackers. Not so the western part of the Roman Empire, which in the early fifth century A.D. was overwhelmed by German invaders from beyond the Rhine River and the Alpine passes. Britain, Gaul, Spain, and North Africa, as well as Italy itself, were occupied by the Germanic Angles, Saxons, Franks, Vandals, and Goths. In these former Roman provinces they set up loosely organized kingdoms whose boundaries constantly shifted. For the most part the Latin-speaking upper classes of these areas adapted to their new German rulers, in some cases intermarrying with them. Cultural standards deteriorated markedly.

This was a time of almost constant warfare, for the Germanic peoples glorified the warrior and martial virtues (like the Aryans who had conquered India two thousand years before, as we saw in chapter 4). Germanic kings and chieftains seldom ceased raiding each other's lands or seeking to expand their area of control. During the turbulent fifth through eighth centuries the Christian Church was the only institution strong enough to survive and to begin the slow process of educating and taming the invaders. The process of restoring knowledge of the vanished Greco-Roman classical past culminated in the ninth century. Then, around A.D. 800, the Frankish ruler Charles the Great (known in French as Charlemagne) effectively unified much of western Europe. But Charlemagne's revived Roman Empire was swept away by new barbarian onslaughts during the century after his death in 814. Only in the late twentieth century has Europe begun moving again toward what may be long-lasting and voluntary unity.

As you read chapter 12, consider how fragile were the foundations on which civilization rested after the collapse of the western Roman Empire—and how desolate western Europe would have seemed to a contemporary visitor from such relatively civilized lands as China, India, Southwest Asia, or Byzantium.

SELECTION 1:

Clovis and His Chieftains

The first Christian king of Germanic Gaul was Clovis (465–511). This Frankish warrior was converted to Christianity at the beginning of the sixth century, in part through the efforts of his wife and in part because he needed educated Christian clergy to help him rule his lands. It was also important for him that the emperor in faraway Constantinople give him the ancient Roman title of consul, bolstering his claims to legitimacy. Distance made this a theoretical alliance, not a real political dependency.

For all his Christian and Roman trappings, Clovis remained essentially a barbarian whom his followers had acknowledged as their war chief by the traditional custom of raising him on their shields. The history of Gaul written after Clovis's death by Bishop Gregory of Tours (538–ca. 594) testifies to the important role that the church played in the early Frankish kingdom, and to the survival of remnants of ancient Roman culture. But it also reveals a violent society permeated by the supernatural. This selection, which is taken from Gregory's history, suggests how Clovis and his chiefs behaved. As the story opens, Clovis's pagan father Childeric has just died, and Clovis confronts rival Germanic kings such as Alaric in present-day southern France.

After these events Childeric died and Clovis his son reigned in his stead. In the fifth year of his reign Siagrius, king of the Romans, son of Egidius, had his seat in the city of Soissons which Egidius, who has been mentioned before, once held. And Clovis came against him with Ragnachar, his kinsman, because he used to possess the kingdom, and demanded that they make ready a battle-field. And Siagrius did not delay nor was he afraid to resist. And so they fought against each other and Siagrius, seeing his army crushed, turned his back and fled swiftly to king Alaric at Toulouse. And Clovis sent to Alaric to send him back, otherwise he was to know that Clovis would make war on him for his refusal. And Alaric was afraid that he would incur the anger of the Franks on account of Siagrius, seeing it is the fashion of the Goths to be terrified,

and he surrendered him in chains to Clovis' envoys. And Clovis took him and gave orders to put him under guard, and when he had got his kingdom he directed that he be executed secretly. At that time many churches were despoiled by Clovis' army, since he was as yet involved in heathen error. Now the army had taken from a certain church a vase of wonderful size and beauty, along with the remainder of the utensils for the service of the church. And the bishop of the church sent messengers to the king asking that the vase at least be returned, if he could not get back any more of the sacred dishes. On hearing this the king said to the messenger: "Follow us as far as Soissons, because all that has been taken is to be divided there and when the lot assigns me that dish I will do what the father [the bishop] asks." Then when he came to Soissons and all the booty was set in their midst, the king said: "I ask of you, brave warriors, not to refuse to grant me in addition to my share, yonder dish," that is, he was

Gregory of Tours, *History of the Franks*, Ernest Brehaut, trans. (New York: Octagon Books, 1965), pp. 36–38.

speaking of the vase just mentioned. In answer to the speech of the king those of more sense replied: "Glorious king, all that we see is yours, and we ourselves are subject to your rule. Now do what seems well-pleasing to you; for no one is able to resist your power." When they said this a foolish, envious and excitable fellow lifted his battle-ax and struck the vase, and cried in a loud voice: "You shall get nothing here except what the lot fairly bestows on you." At this all were stupefied, but the king endured the insult with the gentleness of patience, and taking the vase he handed it over to the messenger of the church, nursing the wound deep in his heart. And at the end of the year he ordered the whole army to come with their equipment of armor, to show the brightness of their arms on the field of March. And when he was reviewing them all carefully, he came to the man who struck the vase, and said to him: "No one has brought armor so carelessly kept as you; for neither your spear nor sword nor ax is in serviceable condition." And seizing his ax

he cast it to the earth, and when the other had bent over somewhat to pick it up, the king raised his hands and drove his own ax into the man's head. "This," said he, "is what you did at Soissons to the vase." Upon the death of this man, he ordered the rest to depart, raising great dread of himself by this action. He made many wars and gained many victories. In the tenth year of his reign he made war on the Thuringi and brought them under his dominion.

After reading this selection, consider these questions:

1. From this reading, what do you suppose Clovis's relationship with the Christian Church was before he accepted Christianity?
2. What evidence does this account suggest for the survival of ancient Roman culture in Frankish Gaul?
3. How would you evaluate the way Clovis inspired loyalty to his rule?

SELECTION 2:

Frankish Legislation on Crime

The Franks slowly changed after Clovis's time, eventually becoming predominantly a farming people. From their code of laws, which the Christian clergy who served the Frankish kings recorded in Latin as the Pactus Legis Salicae *(The Ordinance of Salic Law), the importance of farming is apparent. In the following selection, a modern British historian explains the meaning of this law code.*

The primacy of agriculture in the life of the Franks is usefully displayed by the *Pactus Legis Salicae*. It shows us a wholly rural world. The law code begins with livestock: 20 clauses about pigs (crimes ranging from striking a sow so that

it no longer gives milk through to the theft of 50 pigs) 14 clauses on the theft of cattle (including the very stiff fine of 90 solidi for stealing the king's bull); 14 clauses on the theft or mutilation of different types and ages of horses; five on the theft of sheep; two on goats; four on dogs (hunting dogs, greyhounds, sheep dogs); 10 on birds (thefts of falcons, poultry, domesticated cranes, swans, ducks and geese); four on the theft of

Edward James, *The Franks* (Oxford: Basil Blackwell, 1988), pp. 209–11.

swarms of bees; nine on damage to crops or enclosures by someone else's livestock. There are 28 clauses relating to miscellaneous offenses such as stealing a cow-bell; breaking off a graft from an apple- or pear-tree; breaking into a locked or unlocked workshop; and stealing items such as flax, grapes, firewood, eel nets, stake-nets or trawls.

Other clauses relate to the burning of outhouses, granaries and pig-sties; the theft of boats and sailing vessels; stealing grain or an iron tool from someone's mill, and breaking the sluice in someone's water-mill; and the taking of stags or boars that another's dogs have already exhausted. The phraseology and scale of values in the first clause of title 10 is also revealing: "If anyone steals another's male or female slave, horse or draught-horse, let him be liable for 35 solidi, in addition to its value and a fine for the loss of use."

Lex Ribvaria describes a similar society, though one that appears somewhat more complex and more Romanized (as befits a code which, conventionally at least, is dated to the 620s rather than to the early sixth century). The clause on the purchase of farms or vineyards or other properties, for instance, mentions the possibility of a written property deed or charter, although the ceremony it decrees in the absence of a charter is as concrete and colorful as anything in the Salic law:

> Let him go with witnesses to the place that was sold. . . . Let him pay the price in the presence of these and let him acquire the property. And let him give a box on the ear of each one of the little ones, and let him twist their ears in order that they can give testimony.

Memory, even in a largely oral society, sometimes needed to be reinforced. . . .

Laws, particularly laws so apparently haphazardly collected and written down as those in the Frankish law-codes, can never give any precise guide as to how society operated, but they do perhaps provide an indication of those things which a particular society thought important and worth protecting. The enumeration above gives a fairly clear if generalized idea of the nature of the Frankish rural economy. *Lex Ribvaria* even gives a scale of monetary values, which is unique for the Merovingian period,* as a guide to those who wish to pay fines in kind for the wergild (the amount a murderer has to pay to the victim's family, an amount dependent on the victim's social status) rather than in the enumerated *solidi*:

> If anyone begins to pay a wergild, let him give a horned ox, able to see and healthy, for two solidi. Let him give a horned cow, able to see and healthy, for one solidus. Let him give a stallion, able to see and healthy, for seven solidi. Let him give a mare, able to see and healthy, for three solidi. Let him give a sword with a scabbard for seven solidi. Let him give a sword without a scabbard for three solidi. Let him give a metal tunic in good condition for twelve solidi. Let him give a helmet in good condition for six solidi. Let him give a shield with a lance for two solidi. Let him give leggings in good condition for six solidi. Let him give an untrained hawk for three solidi. Let him give a crane-seizing hawk for six solidi. Let him give a trained hawk for twelve solidi. If he pays with silver, let a solidus be equal to twelve denarii, just as was decided long ago.

After reading this selection, consider these questions:

1. How does law reflect society's values?
2. What is the value of a witness when signing a contract?
3. What did Frankish society think about equal protection under the law?

---

*Merovingian refers to the Frankish kings and their kingdom after Clovis.

SELECTION 3:
The Death of Rusticula

In the centuries after the Roman Empire effectively disappeared from western Europe, Christianity was spread in the lands north of the Alps by men and women missionaries, usually monks and nuns. Women who were abbesses and led communities of nuns were greatly revered.

One such abbess was Rusticula of Arles (ca. 556–632). A woman from a Roman family in what was now territory ruled by the Frankish kings, she grew up amid the turbulence of those violent centuries. Convents and monasteries offered relatively secure refuge from the seemingly perpetual struggles of kings and other warlords. Like Rusticula, many of those who became monks and nuns came from the old Roman upper class.

This selection is an extract from a life of Rusticula written by her admirers after her death. Stories of the last moments of holy men and women were highly valued in those times because, after death, these saints were expected to perform miracles on behalf of those who venerated them. Saints' relics—bits of their bones or clothes that they had worn—were thought to ensure protection to those who came in contact with them, and oaths were sworn on the relics in the expectation that the saint would punish anyone who dared to break them. People were sure that to be buried close to the tomb of such a saint would ensure his or her protection in the afterlife. Just as a powerful warlord was supposed to offer military protection to those who submitted to his authority, so the saints were expected to be spiritual guardians to all who humbly sought their protection.

Thus on the dawning of that Saturday, she [Rusticula] began to feel moderate chills and all her limbs weakened. Lying in bed she was then overcome with raging fever but not so much that her mouth ever ceased praising God. With eyes intent on Heaven, she never relaxed her unconquered spirit from prayer. She commended her daughters whom she was leaving orphaned to the Lord and her strong spirit consoled those who wept. For then she was worthy to say with the Apostle: "I have fought the good fight, I have finished the course, I have kept the faith: henceforth there is laid up for me a crown of righteousness." It was

time for her to be called to rest, and to become one of the company of God's elect. By the next day, Sunday, she was yet more gravely ill. Though it was her custom that her bed was made only with the turning of the year, yet they asked the servant of God whether she would indulge herself a little with some softer straw to support her heavily fatigued body. But she could not bring herself to agree. Then on Monday the feast of the birth of Saint Laurence Martyr, the strength of her body was yet further dispersed and phlegm sounded more strongly in her chest. Seeing this, all the virgins of Christ were sorrowful. They wept and groaned and, when the third hour of the day was come, because of their excessive sorrow, the flock repeated their psalms in silence. Compassionately, the holy mother asked

Jo Ann McNamara, John E. Halborg, and E. Gordon Whaley, eds., *Sainted Women of the Dark Ages* (Durham, NC: Duke University Press, 1992), pp. 134–35.

why she could hardly hear their chanting voices. They answered that the grief of their mourning disabled them. "Sing more clearly," she said, "that I may receive comfort, for truly the psalms are sweet enough to me." Yet another day her body remained with barely any vital motion, though her eyes kept their usual vigor, shining like stars. Looking here and there, lacking power to speak, she motioned silently with her hand to comfort the weeping. And, when one of the sisters touched her feet in order to see whether they were hot or cold, she said: "This is not the hour." But a little later, at the sixth hour of the day, her face lit up, her eyes shone as though smiling and her gloriously happy soul was borne aloft to heaven to join the countless choirs of saints. . . .

So the holy body was laid out according to the custom of mourners and the diligent orphans multiplied their services with a great display of faith. And the next day the bishop of the city, Theodosius the Pontiff, together with all his clergy, came and took possession of the holy body laid out on gold and precious stones among crosses and tall burning candles of wax. And not only the faithful but even Jews joined the throngs of people assembled to venerate her at these services and they all strove to outdo one another with their tears. Then, just outside the monastery, as her corpse was being borne before the weeping multitude of her virgins, honored by the psalm-singing chorus, one of the monastery's elderly servants loudly bewailed the loss of his eyesight. Asking to be set before the bier, he begged with the greatest display of faith that the Lord of all would restore his sight. And immediately the lost light and the power of sight were restored. Meanwhile, the venerable corpse was borne with due honors to the basilica of saint Mary and the mysteries of the holy altar were celebrated. The holy, radiant, shining corpse was laid in her tomb at the right side of the altar.

After reading this selection, consider these questions:

1. The modern emphasis is more often on a person's life than on the moment of his or her death. What would prompt an early medieval Christian author to focus so vividly on the death of Rusticula?
2. What evidence in the account of her death suggests that the people of Arles considered Rusticula a saint?
3. How do you explain people's desire for miracles in the Early Middle Ages?

SELECTION 4:

St. Columban and His Women Followers

Separated from the continent of Europe by stormy seas, Ireland escaped the Germanic conquest suffered by the rest of formerly Roman-ruled western Europe. Instead, the clans and chieftains who ruled ancient Ireland were converted to Christianity by missionaries like the almost legendary St. Patrick (ca. 385–ca. 461). Once the Irish accepted Christianity, they became missionaries to other parts of Europe that had been overrun by Germanic conquerors.

One of the Irish monks and nuns who helped Christianize the West was

St. Columban (ca. 543–ca. 615). With twelve companions he settled at Luxeuil in northern France, where he established a monastery with a distinctive rule (disciplinary system) that he himself had devised. He died in northern Italy. The women who were his partners in spreading Christianity are the subject of this selection, taken from a study of women in Frankish society by a modern American historian.

In keeping with the spirit of Irish Christianity, dominated both morally and administratively by monasticism rather than by clericalism, Saint Columban did not harbor prejudices against women. Instead of shunning their company, he sought their friendship. Instead of emphasizing their impurity, he recognized their spiritual equality. He accepted the hospitality of Theudemada, a lady of great wealth who led a religious life. Acting as the spiritual adviser to married women, he baptized and blessed their children. The women thus honored proved to be enthusiastic supporters of monasticism, encouraging the religious vocation of their children and embracing the ascetic life themselves. A case in point is Flavia, whose husband, Waldelen, was duke of Upper Burgundy. Approached by the young couple to pray for them so that their marriage might be blessed by children, Columban made them promise that they would offer their firstborn to God's service. Her wished granted, Flavia not only sent her oldest son, Donatus, to Columban's foundation at Luxeuil, but when widowed she built Jussanum at Besançon. "Surrounding the convent with fortifications, she established many nuns there," wrote Ionas, Saint Columban's biographer.

Saint Columban's example inspired a new attitude toward women among his Frankish collaborators and disciples, many of whom were trained at Luxeuil, the center of the Irish movement. Influential because of high birth and their positions as abbots and bishops, these men cultivated spiritual friendships with women and sought feminine cooperation in building a network of monasteries throughout the kingdom. As a result of their efforts, men and women began to work together in partnership, promoting the contemplative life and discovering a practical solution to the problem of instituting female communities outside the cities. To protect nuns, help them run their vast establishments, and provide sacerdotal services, these enterprising men and women attached a contingent of monks to some of the newly founded communities. They created thus a new institution, the double monastery, which had some precedents in the East and in Ireland. They also set up separate, affiliated communities for men and women in close proximity to each other.

In the new monasteries women were not overshadowed by higher ranking men. Rather, they collaborated with men and acted as spiritual leaders. The double monasteries, as Mary Bateson has aptly expressed it, provided the female element of the ruling class with something to rule. Usually double monasteries were governed by an abbess, and the affiliated institutions by an abbot and an abbess. In keeping with the penitential practices the Irish introduced to continental monasteries abbesses heard confession three times a day and gave absolution and benediction to members of their community. They performed, therefore, quasi-sacerdotal functions in addition to the normal administrative, disciplinary, and spiritual duties of their office. Under female leadership, some of the double houses became famous centers of learning and devotion; they attracted members from as far as England and served as models for the double monasteries of the island. Neither total segregation of the sexes nor strict cloistering was practiced in these communities. Nuns and monks occupied separate living quarters, but in the scriptoria and the schools, and during the divine service, the two sexes shared common functions.

The rule compiled for nuns, probably by Waldabert of Luxeuil (629–670), indicates that women did not live as parasites on men in the double

Suzanne Fonay Wemple, *Women in Frankish Society* (Philadelphia: University of Pennsylvania Press, 1981), pp. 159–60.

monasteries. Nuns were required to perform manual labor. In addition to cooking, cleaning, serving, spinning, and sewing, activities traditionally associated with women, fishing, brewing, and building the fire were among the daily assignments of nuns. Work outside the monastery was always undertaken by teams of three or four, and special liturgical rites were prescribed for those going off to work in the morning and coming home in the evening.

Faremoutiers-en-Brie (Evoracium) was probably the first double monastery. It was established around 617 by Burgundofara under guidance of Eustachius, abbot of Luxeuil. At an impressionable age, when she was not more than ten, Burgundofara had met Saint Columban and received his blessing. This experience left such a deep mark on her that she resisted her parents' attempts to force her to marry a few years later. Probably through her brother Chagnoald, a monk at Luxeuil, she appealed to Eustachius. Coming in person to her rescue, Eustachius took her to Meaux, where she was veiled and consecrated. The abbot then assigned two of his monks, Chagnoald and Waldabert, to help her build a nunnery and to instruct the new community in the principles of religious life. Eventually a second house was added for the monks, and Burgundofara presided over both.

After reading this selection, consider these questions:

1. In what ways does the author of this selection consider Columban's attitude toward women exceptional in his time?
2. Why do you think that it was important for Columban and other Christian missionaries to cultivate good relationships with the women they encountered?
3. What does reading this selection tell you about the society of seventh-century western Europe?

SELECTION 5:

A Capitulary of Charlemagne

Under the Frankish king Charlemagne (771–814), western Europe was unified to a greater extent than it would be until our own day. What we now call France was the heart of his empire, and Charlemagne also dominated the Low Countries, western Germany, Switzerland, most of Italy, and northern Spain. Outside his grasp lay Britain and Ireland, Muslim Spain, the still-barbaric lands of Scandinavia and eastern Europe, and Byzantine-controlled southern Italy and the Balkans.

The Carolingian* Europe was, of course, a place unrecognizable by modern expectations. Vast forests covered most of the land, with only small clearings on which small, isolated communities of peasants eked out a living. Towns that the Romans had founded had been reduced almost to ruins. Only a few well-guarded merchant caravans ventured through the region, trading mostly in salt, furs and animal hides, and slaves. Widely scattered monasteries were the most substantial structures on the Conti-

*The adjective Carolingian refers to Charlemagne's empire and his times.

nent, and the monks who lived in them were almost the only people in western Europe who could read and write. The mighty men of the land barricaded themselves in wooden and earthwork forts, venturing forth either to make war or to collect tribute from their subjects. The bishops and abbots who led the church were kinsmen of the leading warriors, whose way of life (including perpetual fighting) they often shared.

By ceaseless war against external and internal foes, Charlemagne hammered this wilderness into a unified kingdom. In 800 Pope Leo III— western Christendom's spiritual leader, whom Charlemagne protected from other Germanic peoples in Italy—crowned him Roman Emperor. Byzantium, which also claimed imperial authority over Europe, was not happy to learn of this. To maintain order in his empire, Charlemagne issued edicts, or capitularies, and sent out delegates known as missi *("those sent") to see whether they were being obeyed. Usually the* missi *included both a layman and a cleric. Their reports on what the counts and dukes who administered Charlemagne's empire were doing would enable the emperor to take action if necessary—that is, to swoop down with his troops. The following selection, a typical Carolingian capitulary, gives some idea of the kind of society over which Charlemagne ruled.*

Concerning the commission dispatched by our lord the emperor. Our most serene and most Christian lord and emperor, Charles, has selected the most prudent and wise from among his leading men, archbishops and bishops, together with venerable abbots and devout laymen, and has sent them out into all his kingdom, and bestowed through them on all his subjects the right to live in accordance with a right rule of law.

Wherever there is any provision in the law that is other than right or just he has ordered them to inquire most diligently into it and bring it to his notice, it being his desire, with God's help, to rectify it. And let no one dare or be allowed to use his wit and cunning, as many do, to subvert the law as it is laid down or the emperor's justice, whether it concerns God's churches, or poor people and widows and orphans, or any Christian person. Rather should all men live a good and just life in accordance with God's commands, and should with one mind remain and abide each in his appointed place or profession: the clergy should live a life in full accord with the canons

[church laws] without concern for base gain, the monastic orders should keep their life under diligent control, the laity and secular people should make proper use of their laws, refraining from ill-will and deceit, and all should live together in perfect love and peace.

And the *missi* themselves, as they wish to have the favor of Almighty God and to preserve it through the loyalty they have promised, are to make diligent inquiry wherever a man claims that someone has done him an injustice; so everywhere, and amongst all men, in God's holy churches, among poor people, orphans and widows, and throughout the whole people they may administer law and justice in full accordance with the will and the fear of God. And if there be anything which they themselves, together with the counts of the provinces, cannot correct or bring to a just settlement, they should refer it without any hesitation to the emperor's judgment along with their reports. And in no way, whether by some man's flattery or bribery, or by the excuse of blood relationship with someone, or through fear of someone more powerful, should anyone hinder the right and proper course of justice.

Concerning the promise of fealty [obedience] to our lord the emperor. He has given instructions that in all his kingdom all men, both clergy and

H.R. Loyn and John Percival, *The Reign of Charlemagne*, (New York: St. Martin's Press, 1975), pp. 74–75.

laity, and each according to his vows and way of life, who before have promised fealty to him as king, should now make the same promise to him as Caesar [that is, as emperor]; and those who until now have not made the promise are all to do so for from 12 years old and upwards. And that all should be publicly informed, so that each man may understand how many important matters are contained in that oath—not only, as many have thought until now, the profession of loyalty to our lord the emperor throughout his life, and the undertaking not to bring any enemy into his kingdom for hostile reasons, nor to consent to or be silent about anyone's infidelity towards him, but also that all men may know that the oath has in addition the following meaning within it.

First, that everyone on his own behalf should strive to maintain himself in God's holy service, in accordance with God's command and his own pledge to the best of his ability and intelligence, since our lord the emperor himself is unable to provide the necessary care and discipline to all men individually.

Second, that no man, through perjury or any other craft or deceit, or through anyone's flattery or bribery, should in any way withhold or take away or conceal our lord the emperor's serf, or his landmark, or his land, or anything that is his by right of possession; and that no one should conceal the men of his fisc [servants attached to the imperial treasury] who run away and unlawfully and deceitfully claim to be free men, nor take them away by perjury or any other craft.

That no one should presume to commit fraud or theft or any other criminal act against God's holy churches or against widows or orphans or pilgrims; for the lord emperor himself, after God and his saints, has been appointed their protector and defender.

That no one should dare neglect a benefice [a grant of land] held of our lord the emperor, and build up his own property from it.

That no one should presume to ignore a summons to the host [the army] from our lord the emperor, and that no count should be so presumptuous as to dare to excuse any of those who ought to go with the host, either on the pretext of kinship or through the enticement of any gift.

That no one should presume to subvert in any way any edict or any order of our lord the emperor, nor trifle with his affairs nor hinder nor weaken them, nor act in any other way contrary to his will and his instructions. And that no one should dare to be obstructive about any debt or payment that he owes.

After reading this selection, consider these questions:

1. Why did Charlemagne appoint the *missi,* and what were they to look for?
2. From the tone of this capitulary, how effective do you think this method of governing Europe was?
3. What is the common thread in the laws enumerated in this document?

SELECTION 6:

The Forest

*I*n the following selection, a modern French historian reminds us what it was like to live in Carolingian Europe.

Let us then plunge into that immense domain of the ancient Hyrcanian forest, stretching from the Rhineland crags to Bohemia. The disciples of Saint Boniface, seeking a suitable site for their monastery, moved painfully through a beech forest at the borders of Hesse and Thuringia. For days on end, Sturm and his two companions forged ahead, sleeping in huts of branches behind thorny hedges which protected them from the wild beasts. They met no one but a few Slavs bathing naked near Fulda, who chased them away. The monks took no hurt beyond a bad odor. Finally, at the foot of the Rauschenberg, they found a favorable site for their monastery.

How vividly this passage from the *Vita Sturmi* depicts the two faces of the Carolingian forest, its terror and its attraction!

Chief among the terrors of the forest were the savage animals who ruled there: stags and boars as well as bears, bison, buffalo (*bubalus*), aurochs (*urus*), and, above all, wolves. Texts are filled with references to the ravages of these beasts. In 846, a hungry wolf even got into a church in the Senonais during Sunday Mass. No means could be neglected to frustrate these audacious animals: dogs were trained, traps were baited. In the month of May, by order of Charlemagne, wolf cubs were to be tracked down and either destroyed with poisoned powders or lured into concealed pits. The pelts of the slaughtered beasts were to be presented to him. In 813, wolf hunters were dispatched into every part of the country. But in spite of all these measures, the wolf remained, until modern times, the scourge of the western countryside.

Princes and aristocrats hunted savage beasts both for sport and to provide themselves with meat and furs. Kings jealously guarded their own hunting grounds, the *brolium* or, from the seventh century on, *foresta*—from which our modern word stems. In 800, when Charlemagne granted

Pierre Riché, *Daily Life in the World of Charlemagne*, Jo Ann McNamara, trans. (Philadelphia: University of Pennsylvania Press, 1978), pp. 25–27.

hunting rights to the monks of Saint-Bertin, he excepted "the forests set aside for our own use." To secure these rights, the king charged his foresters with a survey of the reserves, particularly in the Vosges, the Ardennes, the forested Massif of the Oise and the Aisne. Hunters (*venatores*) were employed to maintain packs of hunting dogs, especially greyhounds (*veltres*), whose reputation reached even to Baghdad. Domain intendants were made responsible for fostering young dogs, while falconers (*falconarii*) furnished tame falcons. Hincmar mentioned the separate offices of hunters (*bersarii*), greyhound trainers (*veltrarii*), and beaver hunters (*beverarii*).

Both lay and ecclesiastical aristocrats shared a passion for the chase. As soon as he began to emerge from childhood, a young man was trained to mount his horse, handle bow and boarspear, run the dogs, and cast the falcons. Bishops, abbots, and even simple clerks maintained sizable packs, in defiance of conciliar condemnation. Jonas, bishop of Orleans, was scandalized by this "dementia" which caused men to leave Sunday Mass for the chase and "to find the hymns of angels less pleasing than the baying of dogs."

Nor did the forest interest only the great folk. The Carolingian peasant could not have survived without it, for there he found the wherewithal to nourish and warm himself.

The forest was not so unpopulated as one might have believed at first glance. It was the refuge of ascetic men and women who wished to flee the world. In the forest, they found the "desert" where they could pursue their vocations. In the middle of the eighth century, more than four hundred monastic establishments had been planted in the forest. This movement continued into the ninth century. In 817, the monastery of Benedict of Aniane was built "not far from Aix, where live the horned stags, buffalo, bears, and wild goats."

But in the end, the installation of monks signaled the beginning of forest clearing and the transformation of the countryside. Already their presence alone offered reassurance in a hostile world. There were no better weapons than their prayers against the maleficent forces of paganism—woodland sprites, trolls, and *Waldleuten* ["forest folk," who were not quite human], sacred groves, enchanted springs and all the "forest murmurs" which, throughout the Middle Ages, incessantly bewildered the straying traveler. And last but not least, the abbey or even the simple hermit's cell, promised safe harbor to all who went in fear of brigands, the cold, and the dark. There they could pass some hours of rest before taking the road again.

After reading this selection, consider these questions:

1. What was the environment of Carolingian Europe?
2. Why were people afraid of the forest?
3. What was the first sign of human habitation in forest regions?

UNIT 3

Asian Cultural
Supremacy and
European Recovery

CONTENTS

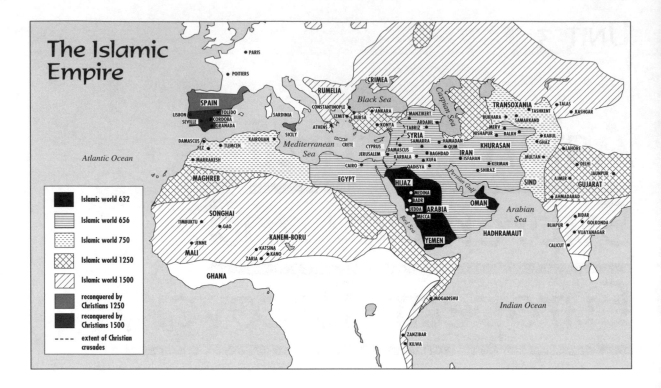

The Islamic Empire

Islamic world 632
Islamic world 656
Islamic world 750
Islamic world 1250
Islamic world 1500
reconquered by Christians 1250
reconquered by Christians 1500
extent of Christian crusades

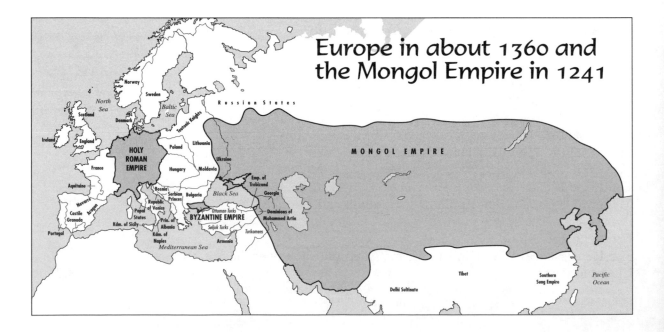

Europe in about 1360 and the Mongol Empire in 1241

Unit 3
Asian Cultural Supremacy and European Recovery

In units 1 and 2 we have seen how the two great empires at opposite ends of Eurasia, Rome, and Han China, went through profound crises in the third century A.D. For the Roman Empire, the result was division: The Byzantine state survived in the eastern Mediterranean, but western Europe sank into several centuries of profound cultural regression, from which the Carolingian world of the ninth century represented only a fragile, incomplete recovery.

By contrast, the centuries that followed Han China's crisis were for Asia an era of cultural flowering. Under the Tang and Song dynasties that succeeded the Han, China not only recovered its prosperity but strengthened the Confucian foundations that the Han had laid. Buddhism proved to be an enormously fruitful addition to the Chinese cultural synthesis. Off the eastern coast of Eurasia, Japan emerged as a major center of civilization—first in China's shadow, but eventually cultivating a unique way of life. Although India largely abandoned Buddhism, to which it had given birth in ancient times, it too not only prospered but also spread its Hindu cultural tradition to Southeast Asia.

Meanwhile, an immensely vital new religious and cultural tradition arose in Southwest Asia. Islam succeeded where Byzantine Christianity had largely failed—due to irreconcilable doctrinal conflicts—in making itself the heir to the region's ancient cultural traditions. Within a century of the Prophet Muhammad's announcement of what he believed to be God's final message to humanity, Islamic armies had conquered much of the Byzantine Empire, all of the Persian Empire, most of Spain, and Central Asia, and were preparing to assault Hindu India. Complementing this tide of conquest, Islamic culture achieved an impressive triumph in the region that once had been home to the world's oldest civilizations.

Europe eventually managed to construct its own civilization by fusing Greco-Roman traditions, Christianity, and the ethos of the Germanic invaders who had overrun the late Roman Empire in the West. Between the eleventh and thirteenth centuries, western Europe's achievement was quite impressive, though probably short of imperial China's relatively high standard of living.

153

Two dramatic shocks devastated most of Eurasia in the thirteenth and fourteenth centuries, shaking to their roots the civilized traditions that had by then become so imposing. One was the Mongol conquests, which destroyed Song China and the Abbasid caliphate in Southwest Asia—and probably would have overwhelmed Europe and Japan had the conquerors not been forced by internal developments to break off their assaults. The second disaster was the spread from China to Europe of microbes carrying the deadly bubonic and pneumonic plagues, which in the fourteenth century caused horrendous losses of life.

By the fifteenth century, however, Europe, spared invasion by outsiders, was able to surmount the worst consequences of the plague and begin a major cultural revival, the Renaissance. China eventually absorbed its Mongol conquerors and, when their vitality flagged, replaced them with the indigenous Ming dynasty. But Renaissance Europe began to look outward, while Ming China preferred to concentrate on an inward restoration of its civilization. The way was now prepared for Europe's bid for global power, which is a major theme of volume 2.

As you study unit 3, consider:

1. Why was Islam an almost instant success?
2. Is it fair to say that Tang and Song China constituted the most successful societies of their era?
3. How did the Mongols come so close to establishing an empire throughout Eurasia?
4. How did the civilization of medieval and Renaissance Europe compare with the Islamic, Chinese, and Japanese achievements of the era?

CHAPTER 13
Early Islam: How Did the Muslim Way of Life Emerge?

The Romans had never bothered to conquer the Arabian Peninsula because it was so far away and, to Mediterranean people, its climate and terrain were so uninviting. Living on the fringe of the Mediterranean, the native Arabs were only slightly touched by Greco-Roman civilization. Judaism, however, made some inroads in the towns, and by the seventh century A.D. so did Christianity, by then the religion of Rome. However, the Bedouin—the camel herders of the Arabian desert—continued to follow the religion of their ancestors, which consisted of worshiping natural forces.

About the year 570 (by the Christian calendar), a man named Muhammad was born in the Arabian city of Mecca. His city was a center of pilgrimage for believers in the native Arabian religion, as well as of long-range trade. After prospering as a merchant, Muhammad began to experience intense religious revelations, culminating in his announcement that he had been chosen as God's messenger, the last of the prophets. The religion that he proclaimed, Islam (which means "submission" to God's will), would during his lifetime unify Arabia in a common sense of community and destiny. Within a generation of the Prophet's death (A.D. 632),* Islamic conquerors would overrun the Persian and half of the Byzantine Empires. Today, Islam is the dominant religion of Southwest Asia, much of Africa, Albania in Europe, Central Asia, Pakistan, Bangladesh, Malaysia, and Indonesia. What explains its appeal and its strength? In this chapter we will begin to find out.

---

*The Islamic calendar reckons dates from the year of Muhammad's *Hijra*, or move from Mecca to the nearby city of Medina, where in A.D. 622 he organized the first enduring Muslim community. By this calendar, Muhammad died in A.H. ("year of the *Hijra*") 10.

SELECTION 1:

The Call of the Prophet

In this selection, the Prophet's earliest biographer, Muhammad ibn Ishaq, who lived a century later, describes Muhammad's dramatic call. The Quraysh, were Muhammad's clan, and his safety depended on the strength of this kinship.

The apostle set forth to Hira; as was his wont, and his family with him. When it was the night on which God honored him with his mission and showed mercy on His servants thereby, Gabriel brought him the command of God. "He came to me," said the apostle of God, "while I was asleep, with a coverlet of brocade whereon was some writing, and said, 'Read!' I said, "What shall I read?" He pressed me with it so tightly that I thought it was death; then he let me go and said, 'Read!' I said, 'What shall I read?' He pressed me with it the third time so that I thought it was death and said 'Read!' I said, 'What then shall I read?'—and this I said only to deliver myself from him, lest he should do the same to me again. He said:

Read in the name of thy Lord who created,
Who created man of blood coagulated.
Read! Thy Lord is the most beneficent,
Who taught by the pen,
Taught that which they knew not unto men.

So I read it, and he departed from me. And I awoke from my sleep, and it was as though these words were written on my heart. Now none of God's creatures was more hateful to me than an ecstatic poet or a man possessed: I could not even look at them. I thought, Woe is me poet or possessed—Never shall Quraysh say this of me! I will go to the top of the mountain and throw myself down that I may kill myself and gain rest. So I went forth to do so and then when I was mid-

way on the mountain, I heard a voice from heaven saying, "O Muhammad! you are the apostle of God and I am Gabriel." I raised my head towards heaven to see who was speaking, and behold, Gabriel in the form of a man with feet astride the horizon, saying, "O Muhammad! you are the apostle of God and I am Gabriel." I stood gazing at him, and that turned me from my purpose, moving neither forward nor backward. Then I began to turn my face away from him, but towards whatever region of the sky I looked, I saw him as before.

And I continued standing there, neither advancing nor turning back, until Khadija [his wife] sent her messengers in search of me and they gained the high ground above Mecca and returned to her while I was standing in the same place. Then he parted from me and I from him, returning to my family. And I came to Khadija and sat by her thigh and drew close to her. She said, "O Abu'l-Qasim, where have you been? By God, I sent my messengers in search of you, and they reached the high ground above Mecca and returned to me." I said to her, "Woe is me, poet or possessed." She said, "I take refuge in God from that O Abu'l-Qasim [another way to identify Muhammad by using his father's name]. God would not treat you in this way since he knows your truthfulness, your great trustworthiness, your fine character, and your kindness. This cannot be, my dear. Perhaps you did see something." "Yes, I did," I said. Then I told her of what I had seen; and she said, "Rejoice, O son of my uncle, and be of good heart. Truly, by Him in whose hand is Khadija's soul, I have hope that you will

Muhammad ibn Ishaq, *The Life of Muhammad*, A. Guillaume, trans. (Karachi: Oxford University Press, 1955), pp. 106–107.

be the prophet of this people."

Then she rose and gathered her garments about her and set forth to her cousin Waraqa bin Naufal bin Asad bin Abdu'l-Uzza bin Qusayy, who had become a Christian and read the scriptures and learned from those that follow the Torah and the Gospel. And when she related to him what the apostle of God told her he had seen and heard, Waraqa cried, "Holy! Holy! Truly by Him in whose hand is Waraqa's soul, if you have spoken to me the truth, O Khadija, there has come to him the greatest Namus [angel] who came to Moses before, and behold, he is the prophet of this people. Bid him be of good heart."

So Khadija returned to the apostle of God and told him what Waraqa had said, and that calmed his fears somewhat.

After reading this selection, consider these questions:

1. From this passage what do you learn about the importance of the written word to Muslims?
2. How does Gabriel act in Muhammad's call?
3. Why do you suppose Muhammad was reluctant to accept the role of a prophet?

SELECTION 2:

The Succession Passes to Abu Bakr

Muhammad and his disciples went on to convert the tribes that lived in the Arabian Peninsula. Then in 632 Muhammad died, leaving his community without clear instructions for choosing a successor. The events following his death are recounted by the Arab historian Muhammad ibn Jabir al-Tabari (839–923). 'A'ishah was Muhammad's favorite wife, daughter of Abu Bakr. 'Umar was another of Muhammad's close relatives.

When the news [of the Prophet's death] reached Abu Bakr, he came and dismounted near the door of the mosque [where] 'Umar was speaking to the people. He paid no attention to anything and went [straight] to the Messenger of God in 'A'ishah's house where he was lying in a corner covered by a striped garment of the Yemeni fabric. Abu Bakr went close [to the Prophet], uncovered his face, kissed him, then said, "With my father may you be ransomed, and with my mother! Indeed, you have tasted the death which God had decreed for you. No [other] death will ever overtake you." Then he replaced the cloth on [the Prophet's] face and went out as 'Umar was speaking to the people. He said, "Gently, O 'Umar, [and] be silent!" 'Umar refused [to be silent] and kept on speaking. When Abu Bakr saw that he would not listen, he went forward to the people [speaking]. When they heard his words, they came to him and left 'Umar.

After praising God and extolling Him, he said, "O people, those who worshipped Muhammad,

Muhammad ibn Jabir al-Tabari, *The History of al-Tabari*, vol. 9, *The Last Years of the Prophet*, A.D. 630–632, A.H. 8–11, Fred M. Donner, trans. (Albany: State University of New York Press, 1990), pp. 184–85.

[must know that] Muhammad is dead; those who worshipped God [must know that] God is alive [and] immortal." He then recited the verse: "Muhammad is only a messenger; and many a messenger has gone before him. So if he dies or is killed, will you turn back on your heels? He who turns back on his heels will do no harm to God; and God will reward the grateful." By God, it was as if the people did not know that this verse was revealed to the Messenger of God until Abu Bakr recited it that day. The people took it from him, and it was [constantly] in their mouths. "'Umar said, "By God, as soon as I heard Abu Bakr recite it, my legs betrayed me so that I fell to the ground, and my legs would not bear me. I knew that the Messenger of God had indeed died."

After reading this selection, consider these questions:

1. Some Muslims must have believed Muhammad to be immortal. How does Abu Bakr bring them back to reality?
2. How do you interpret the reference to Muhammad as "only" a messenger of God?
3. What is the role of 'Umar in this passage?

SELECTION 3:

Creating the Islamic State

At the news of the Prophet's death many of the Bedouin, who had accepted Islam while Muhammad was alive, presumed that their bond with the Muslims was at an end. A series of battles then ensued to restore the Islamic faith throughout the Arabian Peninsula. Simultaneously, Abu Bakr was chosen to be caliph, the leader of the Muslim community, after Muhammad's death. A modern Western historian, W. Montgomery Watt, discusses these crucial events in this selection.

The Islamic state in 632 was a conglomeration of tribes in alliance with Muhammad on varying terms, having as its inner core the people of Medina and perhaps also of Mecca. After the Islamic state had become an empire, *every* Arab tribe naturally wanted to show that it had been in alliance with Muhammad himself in his lifetime, and produced the best story it could of how it had sent a deputation and become Muslim. Even if these stories are accepted as roughly genuine, there are difficulties; the deputation may have represented not the whole tribe but only themselves; and the terms of alliance may not have given Muhammad any say in the affairs of the tribe, and may not even have included profession of Islam.

An example of the weaker types of story produced is that of the deputation from Ghassan, the chief pro-Byzantine tribe on the Syrian marches. The deputation consisted of three unnamed members of the tribe, who went to Muhammad in December 631. They were convinced of the truth of his claims, but went home and did nothing about it. Only one lived to make a public profession of Islam, and that was in 635! If this is the best story Ghassan could produce, the conclusion is inevitable that no members of the tribe became

W. Montgomery Watt, *Muhammad: Prophet and Statesman* (London: Oxford University Press, 1961), pp. 222–25.

Muslims during Muhammad's lifetime.

When due allowance has been made for all these points, we get a picture of the situation roughly as follows. The tribes in a broad region round Mecca and Medina were all firmly united to Muhammad and had all professed Islam. In a similar position were those in the center of Arabia and along the road to Iraq, but those nearest Iraq had not become Muslims. In the Yemen and the rest of the south-west many groups had professed Islam, but they generally constituted only a section of each tribe, and in all were probably less than half the population; they were very dependent on support from Medina. The position in the south-east and along the Persian Gulf was similar, but the Muslims were probably much less than half the population. On the Syrian border beyond about the Gulf of Akaba there had been little success in detaching tribes from the Byzantine emperor.

If Muhammad, then, had not made himself ruler of all Arabia, yet he had to a great extent unified the Arabs. Through his Arabic Qur'an, and through the religious and political system he had created, he had developed the Arabs' hitherto only implicit awareness of themselves as an ethnological and cultural unit. It was to this unit that the "Arabic Qur'an" was addressed, and it marked them off from Abyssinians, Byzantines, Persians and Jews. The new religion was parallel to the religions of these peoples and could hold up its head in their company; and the political system associated with it avoided all dependence on foreigners or non-Arabs.

In view of these entanglements of religion with politics the reader may feel that the movement of the Arab tribes into the Islamic state was essentially political and not religious. This is not so, however. Since the exodus of the Israelites from Egypt religion and politics in the Middle East have always been closely linked with one another; and the fact that a movement had a prominent political aspect has never meant that it was not religious (as it often does in the modern West.)

Islam provided an economic, social and political system, the *Pax Islamica*. Of this system religion was an integral part, since it gave the ideas on which the whole was based. The peace and security under the system were "the security of God and of His messenger." This system attracted men of the nomadic tribes in various ways. It offered an adequate livelihood, mainly by booty. It did not involve subjection to a distant potentate; all Muslims were equal, and Muhammad treated his followers with the courtesy and respect shown by a nomadic chief to his fellow-tribesmen. When the Persian and Byzantine empires showed signs of disintegrating and men needed "something to hold onto," the Islamic community promised to have the requisite stability.

The Arabs of that day almost certainly thought of the system as a whole, and were incapable of distinguishing in thought its economic, political and religious aspects. The supreme question for them was whether to enter the system or to remain outside. They could not have the economic and political benefits of membership without the religious profession of belief in God and His messenger; and a profession of belief of this kind made no sense unless a man was a member of Muhammad's community, which was political as well as religious. There is thus nothing improbable in a mass movement into the Islamic community in 630 and 631 which was in some sense religious. In European analytical terms it may be primarily political (though this is perhaps only the expression of a European prejudice for the material), but in the integral reality of the events the religious and political factors were inseparable.

After reading this selection, consider these questions:
1. Why in later ages were all Arab tribes eager to claim that they had been early converts to Islam?
2. How did Islam affect Arab culture?
3. How do politics and religion interact in the years following the introduction of Islam into Southwest Asia?

SELECTION 4:

Prescriptions for the Meccan Pilgrims

The book that Muhammad left his followers is known as the Qur'an. For Muslims it is the exact word of God that was spoken through his prophet Muhammad. Within the Qur'an there are 114 suras, or chapters, each one complete in itself. From these chapters, Muslims learn how they must act in order to conform to God's will. An important requirement for a Muslim is the hajj, the pilgrimage to Mecca. If financially possible, once in a lifetime every man and woman should make the hajj. A visit to Mount Arafat is one part of the pilgrimage. In the Qur'an, God gives precise instructions how believers are to conduct themselves on the hajj.

For *Hajj*
Are the months well-known.
If any one undertakes
That duty therein,
Let there be no obscenity,
Nor wickedness,
Nor wrangling
In the *Hajj*
And whatever good
Ye do, (be sure)
Allah knoweth it.
And take a provision
(With you) for the journey,
But the best of provisions
Is right conduct.
So fear Me,
O ye that are wise.

It is no crime in you
If ye seek of the bounty
Of your Lord (during pilgrimage).
Then when ye pour down
From (Mount) 'Arafat,
Celebrate the praises of Allah

At the Sacred Monument,
And celebrate His praises
As He has directed you,
Even though, before this,
Ye went astray.

Then pass on
At a quick pace from the place
Whence it is usual
For the multitude
So to do, and ask
For Allah's forgiveness.
For Allah is Oft-Forgiving,
Most Merciful.

So when ye have
Accomplished your holy rites,
Celebrate the praises of Allah,
As ye used to celebrate
The praises of your fathers —
Yea, with far more
heart and soul.
There are men who say:
"Our Lord! Give us
(Thy bounties) in this world!"
But they will have
No portion in the Hereafter.

And there are men who say:

The Holy Qur'an, Abdullah Yusuf Ali, trans. (Brentwood, MD: Amana Corporation, 1989), pp. 80–82.

"Our Lord! Give us
Good in this world
And good in the Hereafter,
And defend us
From the torment
Of the Fire!"

To these will be allotted
What they have earned;
And Allah is quick in account.

Celebrate the praises of Allah
During the Appointed Days.
But if anyone hastens
To leave in two days,
There is no blame on him,

And if anyone stays on,
There is no blame on him,
If his aim is to do right.
Then fear Allah, and know
That ye will surely
Be gathered unto Him.

After reading this selection, consider these questions:

1. What does the Qur'an require of the pilgrim making the hajj?
2. What are God's (Allah's) qualities according to the Qur'an?
3. What is the goal of the pilgrimage?

SELECTION 5:

Al-Hajj

Muslims who have made the hajj describe it as an overwhelmingly intense experience, as believers from all over the world come together to celebrate God's majesty and mercy. In the following selection, a twentieth-century Muslim scholar describes the making of the hajj during the Abbasid caliphate, the period of Islam's greatest prosperity and power in the years A.D. 750–1243. By this time, the Arabs, Persians, and some Turks were now solidly in the Muslim camp, but the Bedouin often reverted to plundering pilgrims on the way to Mecca. Baghdad was then the Abbasid capital. A qadi is a judge of Islamic law.

In view of the hardship involved in making the pilgrimage to Mecca in the traditional style, the discomfort and strain of caravan travel through an inhospitable countryside in a difficult climate and, above all, the constant threat of Bedouin attacks (sometimes bought off by the government), Muslims from the eastern lands of the Abbasid empire would gather together at Baghdad. From the beginning of the month of Shawwal, two months before the actual time of the *hajj*, people from Iraq itself and from regions much more distant, such as Khurasan, would reach Baghdad. Such people, numbering several thousands, found shelter in tents pitched on the western side of Baghdad. Here the government supplied them with food and drinking water. The period from the first arrival of the pilgrims till their departure on the *hajj* was an exciting time for the inhabitants of Baghdad. Every day new groups of pilgrims would enter the city, and the inhabitants of Baghdad, dressed in their best attire, gave them a warm welcome.

Muhammad Manazir Ahsan, *Social Life Under the Abbasids* (London: Longman, 1979), pp. 279–82.

The departure of the caravan was marked by elaborate celebrations. A large procession, with high-ranking officials at the front and the populace behind, accompanied the caravan to the outskirts of Baghdad and bade them farewell. To protect the pilgrims from attack, a contingent of troops also accompanied them. The caravan then proceeded towards Mecca under the leadership of an *Amir al-Hajj,* a commander of the pilgrims, who was appointed by the government in a ceremonial gathering attended by the caliph, the chief qadi and his deputies, and also by other dignitaries. The *amir* not only directed the journey, but supervised the conduct of the pilgrims and led his own contingent of the *hajj* during the ceremonies.

Arriving at Mina the pilgrims sacrificed camels, sheep or other domestic animals, one goat or one sheep for one man or one household, but as many as seven men might be partners in one cow or one camel. The flesh of the animal sacrificed was either eaten, stored or distributed among the poor; the skins were given to charity. . . . The return of the pilgrims to Baghdad offered an occasion of festive celebration for the people in general. The caliph himself came out of the city to receive the pilgrims. In order to enter Baghdad the next day rested and refreshed for the festivity, the pilgrims sometimes passed the previous night in the suburb of Al-Yasiriyya. Relatives of the pilgrims offered their thanks to God for the safe return of the kinsmen, congratulated the pilgrims, and celebrated the occasion with great excitement.

The procession of the caliphal caravan for the *hajj* was marked both by expense and by display. The *hawdaj* (litter) was profusely decorated with multicolored silk and materials woven with gold. The caliph, escorted by his bodyguard, appeared before the caravan, wearing the *burda* (cloak) of the Prophet with the *qadib* (staff) and the *khatam* (signet-ring) in his hands. A drum was beaten to inform the caravan that the moment of departure had come. The caliph, surrounded by members of his family, important dignitaries and troops with black standards, would now set out towards Mecca. On his way to Mecca the caliph showed his benevolence by distributing money and food to the people. This benevolence increased when the caliph reached Mecca, where he would entertain the inhabitants with lavish expenditure of food, iced drinks and gifts. It is said that the Caliph Mahdi, in one of his famous *hajj* journeys, distributed 30,000,000 dirhams in cash amongst the people of Mecca and Medina. This sum was in addition to the various gifts and the ice that was brought especially from Mawsil.

The pilgrimage made by Jamila bint Nasir al-Dawla in the year 366 became proverbial in the history of the pilgrimage. She is said to have provided all the people present at the pilgrimage that year with *sawiq* [a sweet drink] mixed with snow. In addition to many other things, she brought with her, loaded on camels, fresh green vegetables contained in earthenware crocks. She commissioned 500 mounts for those pilgrims who were limbless; bestowed 10,000 dinars on the Ka'aba, freed 300 slaves and 200 slave girls, gave handsome subsidies to those who had come to reside in Mecca, and provided 50,000 fine robes for the common population. It is also said that she had with her 400 litters each lined with satin, so that it was never known in which one she herself was.

The social, cultural and economic effects of the pilgrimage in medieval Islam were of great importance. In fact the *hajj* provided different people with different opportunities. If a man were a merchant, he might utilize it as a business trip; if he were a scholar, he might impart or gather knowledge and ideas; if he were a traveler, he might gain knowledge of the people and the land. Pilgrimage was, therefore, one of the important factors making for cultural unity and social mobility in the Islamic world.

After reading this selection, consider these questions:
1. Why was there so much excitement over the hajj in Muslim lands?
2. What behavior was expected of people making the hajj?
3. How did the hajj serve as a bond for all Muslims?

SELECTION 6:

The Qur'an and the Islamic Community

Marshall G.S. Hodgson was an American historian noted for his insights into how Islam became a vital part of world history. In the following selection he notes the importance of the Qur'an for the Muslim community.

For the Qur'an continued, as in Mecca and Medina, to be a monumental challenge. In its form, it continued, even after the ending of active revelation with Muhammad's life, to be an event, an act, rather than merely a statement of facts or of norms. It was never designed to be read for information or even for inspiration, but to be recited as an act of commitment in worship; nor did it become a mere sacred source of authority as the founding of Islam receded into time. It continued its active role among all who accepted Islam and took it seriously. What one did with the Qur'an was not to peruse it but to worship by means of it; not to passively receive it but, in reciting it, to reaffirm it for oneself: the event of revelation was renewed every time one of the faithful, in the act of worship, relived the Qur'anic affirmations.

Accordingly, the worshipper reaffirmed for himself through the Qur'an, in whatever passage of the Qur'an he was uttering, its single massive challenge: the challenge best summed up in the word *tawhid*—the assertion of God's unity. He certified anew that the authority of the Creator-god and His demands on human consciences confront us without any lesser rival, any intermediate source of norms, any slighter duty; thus he undertook to live up to a standing claim which every individual faced anew in the Qur'an each time he renewed his recitation of it; a demand to

which he rededicated himself in every act of worship. Every verse of the Qur'an presented and illuminated in its own fashion this challenge, applied to numerous details of common life or envisaged through the lessons of nature and of history.

The unique potency of the Qur'an, calling for a person's undivided attention to its single and total challenge, brought a purely religious component to the growing movement of iconophobia in the Irano-Semitic traditions; a movement which typified their piety and how that piety was fulfilled in Islam. The use of images could be felt to be inappropriate to a prophetic religion of the moral God because of its association with the nature gods; but in the presence of the Qur'an they became directly distracting and divisive, quite apart from any such associations. For the Qur'an itself can serve as a sensible, almost tangible symbol of the One whose challenge it presents.

That challenge is single-mindedly a moral one. If, in the Qur'an, we are directed to the glories of nature, it is not that we may praise God's beauty or stand in awe of His wisdom, but that we may be warned of His power to enforce His ordinances. In the spiritually more sensitive individual, the exclusive focusing of his thoughts on the Qur'an could generate an overwhelming moral force that might mold his whole personality. Hence to juxtapose any other symbols in worship alongside the Qur'an, however honestly they might point to other aspects of divinity, must necessarily, in the nature of the power of symbols in human beings, share in, channel away, and final-

Marshall G.S. Hodgson, *The Venture of Islam*, vol. 1, *The Classical Age of Islam* (Chicago: University of Chicago Press, 1974), pp. 367–69.

ly dissipate the concentrated devotional energies. Such alternative releases of the emotions were not alternative means of coming before the One; rather, they divided and weakened the devotion to the One expressed in the Qur'an, and to its moral demands. It may be said that the doctrine of the unity of God, which has been so central to developed Islam, is largely the theological expression of the unity of the act of worship at its best, its undivided dedication to realizing the moral lordship of God over the worshipper.

Accordingly, the central presence of the Qur'an excluded such symbolic expression of more limited distinct aspects of the divine-human relation as in Christianity was given in the sacraments; and with the sacraments, it excluded the priest-craft which the sacraments presupposed. Necessarily it excluded those other symbolic expressions of spiritual awareness represented in the arts; much as later happened in a somewhat similar movement in Protestant Christianity. But the feeling of the pious went beyond the service of worship and the place where the worship was held. All life should be informed with the religious spirit; nowhere should be tolerated anything that could rival the Qur'an in evoking the deeper responses of the spirit. The whole imaginative life was suspect: science and fiction, music and painting. So far as any art that is true to itself is not, in fact, a mere pleasing of the senses but evokes the whole spirit, all art was potentially a rival to the Qur'an, a subtle form of idolatry. Nor is science merely an objective satisfaction of curiosity: it calls for its own morally single-minded devotion. The pious, therefore, could well fear all the arts and sciences wherever they appeared, and indeed all aspects of high culture that did not clearly subtend the moral purposes to which the Qur'an summoned.

Finally, the unity of the cult centered on the Qur'an issued in the exclusivity of the religious community itself: if within Islam no rival form of cult could be tolerated, however monotheistic, then still less could be admitted the legitimacy of any religious communities rival to the one which maintained the Qur'anic cult. The one God implied the one medium of worship and the one worshipping community.

After reading this selection, consider these questions:

1. Why does Hodgson see the Qur'an as a challenge?
2. Why does Islam reject images, and in fact looks upon them as a serious distraction?
3. What makes Islam an exclusive community among world religions?

CHAPTER 14
East Asia's Golden Age:
Models of Civilized Life?

While Europe was experiencing centuries of cultural regression after the fall of the western part of the Roman Empire, and as Islam, Byzantium, and Gupta India were passing through brilliant phases of their respective civilizations, East Asia can well be described as a model of civilized life. During the six hundred years that the Tang and Song dynasties ruled China, from the early seventh to the late thirteenth centuries A.D., the Chinese population increased steadily, for the country's success in expanding its agricultural production permitted it to support the largest number of people in the world at what was—for a premodern society—a remarkably high standard of living. During this period, Japan, which received strong cultural influence from China, also emerged as a prosperous and increasingly distinctive society. As you read this chapter, consider the ways in which both China and Japan deserve to be ranked as the most advanced societies of the time.

The Tang dynasty ruled China from A.D. 618 to 907. After several centuries of internal turmoil and of trouble with northern barbarians following the collapse of the Han (A.D. 220), the advent of the Tang meant the restoration of a great empire based on Confucian political principles—surely a major event in world history. On the whole, the Tang emperors (and China's first empress, Wu Zhao) ruled China justly by the light of Confucian values. After a short interruption, the Song, who reigned between 960 and 1279, continued the Tang tradition of Confucian rule over at least part of China.

During the Nara period (710–784), Japan absorbed an intense wave of Chinese influence, including Buddhism, and Japanese emperors emulated the style and Confucian ideology of their Chinese counterparts. The Heian period (794–1185) saw the Japanese gradually adapt Chinese models to their own traditions, and slowly imperial power waned while that of local feudal lords rose.

For both East Asian societies, these were centuries in which creative activity in literature and the arts exploded. Poetry flourished. Astronomy, engineering, mathematics, and what we would now call chemistry received close attention. During the Tang period China invented both printing and papermaking, greatly advancing the written word and producing more literate people than anywhere else in the world.

SELECTION 1:

Mathematics in China

In this selection, Colin A. Ronan summarizes the study of Tang- and Song-era Chinese mathematics that was carried out by one of the greatest of Western scholars of Chinese science, Joseph Needham.

When . . . we ask what mathematical ideas seem to have radiated from China southwards and westwards, we find a considerable list, which contains the following:

(a) the extraction of square and cube roots;

(b) expressing fractions in a vertical column;

(c) the use of negative numbers;

(d) an independent proof of Pythagoras' Theorem;

(e) geometrical questions like the areas of circles and some solid figures;

(f) the Rule of Three for determining proportions;

(g) the Rule of False Position for solving equations, and the solution of cubic and higher equations;

(h) indeterminate analysis;

(i) the Pascal triangle.

There are also the questions of the development of place-value notation and the written symbol for zero. As far as the first is concerned, this seems to have grown quite independently in China, deriving nothing from that form of it used by the Old Babylonian mathematicians except, just possibly, the bare idea. And although evidence is uncertain, it seems likely that India not only received place-value notation later, but obtained it from China

Colin A. Ronan, *The Shorter Science and Civilisation in China*, vol. 2 (Cambridge: Cambridge University Press, 1981), pp. 61–63.

rather than Mesopotamia. A written symbol for zero seems to have been the one mathematical invention we have mentioned that occurred outside China, although even in this case it was a development which took place at a mutual cultural area on the Chinese-Indian border.

It seems probable, then, that in spite of the "isolation" of China and various social factors which made transmission difficult, between 250 B.C. and A.D. 1250 a good deal more came out than went in. Only at about the latter date did some influence from the south and west begin to be noticeable, and even then little took root. There was a little trigonometry, some small change in writing numbers and in the way multiplication was displayed, but that is all. . . .

From the description given it is clear that Chinese mathematics was quite comparable with the pre-Renaissance achievements of the other medieval peoples in the Old World. Greek mathematics was on a higher level, if only on account of its more abstract and systematic character—as is shown in Euclid—although it was weak just where the mathematics of India and China were strong, namely, in algebra. But historians of science are beginning to question whether the predilection of Greek science and mathematics for the abstract, the deductive and the pure over the concrete, the empirical and the "applied" was wholly a gain. Certainly, in the flight from practice into the realms of the pure intellect, Chinese mathematics did not participate.

Chinese mathematics, for all its originality, displayed certain weaknesses. There was an absence of the idea of rigorous proof, possibly as a result of the mental outlook which avoided the development of formal logic in China and which allowed associative or organic thinking to dominate. The *Thien Yuan* notation had beautiful symmetry but extreme limitations; after an initial burst of advance Sung algebra experienced no rapid and extended growth.

Social factors were also involved, and it is striking that throughout Chinese history the main importance of mathematics was in relation to the calendar. For reasons connected with the ancient corpus of beliefs about the cosmos, the establishment of the calendar was the jealously guarded prerogative of the emperor, and its acceptance by tributary states signified loyalty to him. When rebellions or famines occurred, it was often concluded that something was wrong with the calendar, and mathematicians were asked to reconstruct it. Possibly this preoccupation fixed them irretrievably to concrete numbers, and prevented consideration of abstract ideas; in any case the practical genius of the Chinese tended in that direction. . . .

It will be recalled that there was no belief in the idea of a creator deity, and hence of a supreme law-giver; this, combined with the conviction that the whole universe was an organic, self-sufficient system, led to the concept of an all-embracing Order in which there was no room for Law, and hence few regularities to which it

would be profitable to apply theoretical mathematics in the mundane sphere.

Mathematics in China was therefore utilitarian, its social origins bound up with the bureaucratic government system, and devoted to the problems the ruling officials had to solve. Of mathematics for the sake of mathematics there was very little. This does not mean that Chinese calculators were not interested in truth, but it was not that abstract systematized academic truth which the Greeks sought. And during this time the masses remained illiterate, having no access to the manuscript books which the government commissioned, copied and distributed. Artisans, no matter how greatly gifted, flourished on the other side of an invisible wall which separated them from the scholars of literary training. When Daoists and Buddhists inspired the invention of printing, this without doubt fostered the second flowering of mathematics in the Sung, but the upsurge did not last. As soon as the Confucians swept back into power with the nationalist reaction of the Ming, mathematics was again confined to the back rooms of government offices and ministries.

After reading this selection, consider these questions:
1. What advances did the Chinese contribute to mathematics?
2. What was the relation in China between mathematics and the calendar?
3. What were the differences between Chinese and Greek mathematics?

SELECTION 2:

Poetry of China

It is difficult for foreign readers to grasp the full richness of Chinese poetry by reading it in translation. The nuances of the language are hard to convey in a foreign tongue, and the entire visual dimension of the poetry is lost if one cannot appreciate the beauty of Chinese calligraphy. (In China, producing a handwritten manuscript with deft brush strokes is an art in itself.) Nonetheless, something of the ideas, wit, and imagery of Chinese poetry can survive in English translation, as should be apparent in the two selections below. Li Bo and Du Fu were two of China's greatest poets; they lived in the eighth century, under the Tang, and knew each other. In the first verse, dating from 761, Du Fu speaks of his friendship.

Du Fu's Poem

I have not seen Li Bo for a long time—
What a pitiable man with his feigned madness!
All the world wants to kill him:
I alone dote on his genius,
Quick-witted, he has hit off a thousand poems;
A waif in the world, his only home is in a cup
 of wine,
O my friend! 'Tis time to return to Ku-ang Shan,
Where you used to read books with such gusto.

[Li Bo was often away from his home, and on one occasion he was captured by robbers, an incident he recalls in the poem. When he finally managed to return home, he rejoiced in his family's love, despite their poverty.]

Li Bo's Poem

After a whole year's journey, I arrived at my
 thatched hut,
And found my wife in rags and tatters.
Deeply touched, our loud cries were echoed by
 the sighing pines,
And our stifled sobs blended with the sad music
 of the flowing brook.
My little son whom I used to fondle so much
 looked paler than the snow.
Seeing his father, he turned away his face and
 wept silently.
Dirty and greasy, he wore no socks on his feet.
In front of the bed stood my two little girls, with
 their seamy dresses
barely covering their knees:
I saw the embroidered sea-waves were all bro-
 ken and disconnected,
And the purple phoenixes and water-sprits dis-
 membered beyond recognition.
For several days, preyed upon by depression and
 illness,
I had lain in bed, vomiting and purging.

With no money in my purse,
How can I save my family from being frozen?
But my wife has taken out some old silk quilts,
And opened the cosmetics she had laid away
 during my absence.
I see beauty gradually returning to her emaciat-
 ed face;
And the girls, idiotic little things, are combing
 their own hair.
They ape their mother in every way:
In their morning coiffeur, they help themselves
 to the cosmetics:
They paint their faces haphazardly with vermil-
 lion and white powder,
And draw their eyebrows so broad that they
 look like comic masks
Coming back alive, and looking fondly at my
 kids,
I almost forget our dire penury.
And what naughty kids they are! They storm me
 with endless questions and even pull my
 beard!
But who can be angry with them just now?
When I remember how miserable I was in the
 hands of the brigands,
I find it very sweet indeed to be pestered by the
 noise and clamor of my little ones.
Newly reunited, it is for us to be nice to each
 other and make the best of life,
Before we think of the problem of livelihood.

After reading this selection, consider these questions:
1. What qualities made Du Fu a friend of Li Bo?
2. What does Li Bo find when he returns home? Does he show any guilt?
3. What does Li Bo's poem say about family values in China?

John C.H. Wu, *The Four Seasons of T'ang Poetry* (Rutland, VT: Charles E. Tuttle, 1972), pp. 58, 110–11.

SELECTION 3:

Footbinding and Widow Chastity

A less pleasant aspect of traditional Chinese life comes under consideration in the following selection, a modern author's survey of foot binding and the prohibition of remarriage for widows. The influence of Confucianism was so strong that it is not surprising that women (toward whom Confucius held very condescending views) occupied an inferior position in the Chinese family. However, binding women's feet, which ensured that they would walk with a mincing gait that men apparently found sexually appealing, and prohibiting widows from remarrying cannot be traced back to the Sage. These practices were products of the late Tang and early Song periods, and they grew out of historical circumstances and popular opinions about what constituted feminine beauty and fidelity to tradition.

Textbook surveys of Chinese history often note a decline in the status of women that is usually dated to the T'ang-Sung transition or to the Sung period. The two signs of this decline most frequently mentioned are the pressure on widows not to remarry and the practice of binding young girls' feet to prevent them from growing more than a few inches long.

In looking for explanations of the spread of these practices, so misogynist to modern Western eyes, should we be looking to the T'ang, the Sung, the Yuan, the Ming, or the Ch'ing periods? The key question is not when such practices first appeared, as any number of ideas can appear without becoming historically important, but when they became firmly established.

Footbinding began its spread in the Sung, first among dancers and courtesans. Nevertheless, in the large body of Sung poems and songs scholars have found only a few lines that refer to bound feet. The poet Hsü Chi (1028–1103) referred to a

woman as "knowing about arranging the four limbs [for burial], but not about binding her two feet." Su Shih (1036–1101) wrote a song that described in some detail the bound feet of a dancer; it reveals that he found tiny feet an object of wonder and wanted to hold them in his hand to get a better look. The first surviving inquiry into the origins of footbinding was written in the early twelfth century by a scholar who referred to bound feet as both small and "bowed" and associated with the lotus.

From the late twelfth century on, casual references to footbinding become gradually more common. The earliest protest against footbinding that I have found is by Ch'e Jo-shui from the late Sung: "I do not know when the practice of wives binding their feet began. Little children not yet four or five *sui*, who have done nothing wrong are nevertheless made to suffer unlimited pain to bind [their feet] small. I do not know what use this is." A thirteenth century tomb of the young wife of an imperial clansman contained several sets of shoes for bound feet, and the woman's feet were in fact bound with a strip of cloth.

Such is the evidence for assessing the spread of footbinding in Sung times. Through the

Patricia Ebrey, "Women, Marriage, and the Family in Chinese History," in *Heritage of China: Contemporary Perspectives on Chinese Civilization*, Paul S. Ropp, ed. (Berkeley and Los Angeles: University of California Press, 1990), pp. 216–18, 223.

eleventh century the evidence is extremely thin, and it is plausible that the practice was most common among dancers or courtesans. Literati were familiar with this world, and they recognized bound feet without necessarily having wives or mothers with bound feet. A late-fourteenth-century writer quoted a twelfth-century discussion of the relatively recent origins of footbinding and then quoted another source, otherwise unknown, that said a dancer in the palace of the ruler of the Later T'ang (923-935) bound her feet to make them small and curved like new moons. He concluded that people began to imitate her, and that although the practice was still rare through the eleventh century, it spread through imitation so that in his day people were ashamed not to practice it.

Can anything be inferred from these limited references concerning the reasons for the spread of footbinding? Howard Levy argues that erotic attraction was basic to the appeal of bound feet. In his discussion of the origins of footbinding, however, Levy connects it to intellectual currents in the Sung dynasty, especially the emphasis on womanly docility and chastity. He repeats a story that Chu Hsi, while prefect of Chang-chou in southern Fukein, encouraged footbinding as a way to promote chastity by making it more difficult for women to move about (because women with bound feet had to use canes to walk). This story is almost surely spurious as far as the reference to Chu Hsi goes. But does it contain a deeper truth? Did footbinding spread because of increased concern about controlling women and, in particular, limiting their mobility? Is there a socioeconomic explanation for the attraction of delicate women? Are there historical reasons why this attraction would have become more potent in Sung and Yuan times? Does it have anything to do with remarriage?

Discouraging young childless widows from remarrying and, especially, encouraging their suicides can be considered as misogynist as footbinding, but the history of its spread is different. The idea of widow chastity was not new in Sung times. The *Book of Rites* says, "Faithfulness is the basis of serving others and is the virtue of a wife. When her husband dies a woman does not remar-

ry; to the end of her life she does not change." The Han dynasty *Biographies of Great Women* contained several accounts of women whose primary accomplishment was their determined resistance to remarriage. These women generally cited maxims about wifely fidelity, such as "Even if there is a sagely mate, she does not go a second time," "The moral duty of a wife lies in not changing once she has gone [in marriage]," or "The moral duty of a wife lies in not having two husbands." Many of these women ended up sacrificing their lives rather than accepting disgrace. . . .

An intriguing historical contrast between China and the West is the relatively high level of standardization of family practices in China across regions, classes, and dialect groups. Throughout the country descent reckoning was patrilineal, offerings were made to recent ancestors, family property was divided among brothers, marriages among patrilineal kin were disapproved, essentially all women married, late marriages were rare, adoption was common, young married couples started their lives together in the home of senior relatives if feasible, and so on. In the West, by contrast, there was much greater variation in inheritance practices, naming practices, the proportion of people marrying, and the incidence of couples starting marriages in their own homes. Standardization in the West was generally limited to matters over which the church had asserted authority. The chief agent fostering standardization of family practices in China was not an organized church but the state. The integrating powers of the state are seen repeatedly through Chinese history but through different mechanisms in different periods. Ancestral rites were strongly rooted in the ancient cult of royal ancestors. Patrilineal surnames probably became universal because of the need of the imperial government to register the entire population. The patriarchal household was strengthened by the Ch'in and Han governments' desires to curb feudal forces and deal directly with family heads. Patriarchal principles were regularly reinforced by the law codes the government issued. Moreover, the bureaucratic technique of appointing natives of distant areas as magistrates tended to undermine distinct regional traditions of inheritance practices or other family legal matters. The state exerted tremendous influence on the education of the elite, especially from Sung times on, through the examination system. This education led the elites of the diverse regions to imitate common models of family behavior and to share an interest in reforming the family practices of commoners that the state deemed deviant. The state even played a major role in Ming and Ch'ing times in rewarding and celebrating the virtues of chaste widowhood.

After reading this selection, consider these questions:

1. Why does the author believe that foot binding will ensure the dependency of women?
2. How would the Chinese attachment to ancestors help explain the prohibition of women's remarriage?
3. What explains the common culture of China?

SELECTION 4:

Government and Taxes

O*f course, the government of Tang China intervened frequently in the lives of the people, especially to make sure that taxes were paid and that farmers showed up to perform free labor on government projects. A modern Western historian explains the Tang system of taxation in this selection.*

The Chinese system of population registration was a crucial administrative function in the operation of the government of traditional China. From the Qin and Han periods onward, successive governments maintained well-integrated systems of household registration and attempted to register the entire population that was under their control. In every prefecture and county of the empire multiple copies of household registers were drawn up; these were kept in the government offices and were used as basic data for administration—in particular, for financial administration. Chinese population statistics, enormous by comparison with the rest of the world and running into tens and hundreds of millions of persons, are known only because of the existence of this system of household registration.

Under the Northern Dynasties and the early Tang the implementation of the *zhun-tian* ("equal field") system of land allocation and the related *tsy-yong-diao* tax and labor service system made it imperative that the state should register every household and individual and oversee the allocation of every parcel of land. According to the formal provisions of this system, a rather substantial holding of land was given to every adult male in the country; they were in turn required to pay taxes in grain and cloth and to perform certain labor services. Whereas in later periods the government came to rely heavily on revenue from trade imposts and monopolies, they now depended almost exclusively on taxes in grain and cloth. It was therefore imperative that they keep an accurate account of every taxpaying family. . . .

Preliminary to the drawing up of the household registers, two detailed procedures were carried out, the personal inspection of the age and physical condition of individuals and the settlement of household categories. The personal inspection of

Arthur F. Wright and Denis Twitchett, eds., *Perspectives on the T'ang* (New Haven, CT: Yale University Press, 1973), pp. 121, 128–29.

individuals was the responsibility of the county magistrate and was carried out in groups. (The procedure was called t'uan-mao or mao-yüeh.) The laws concerning registration with regard to age were better developed under the Sui and Tang than they had been under the Southern Dynasties, and it is clear that the number of persons inscribed in the registers increased greatly.

Under the T'ang the personal inspection was carried out annually, although for a few years after 741 it was restricted to once in three years. The established convention regarding the ages which were to receive special attention in the inspection specified the "five nines" (i.e., for men, 19, 49, 59, 79, 89 and for women 79 and 89). But particularly careful attention was paid to young men of between fifteen and twenty. When a man became an adolescent at sixteen or an adult at twenty or twenty-one, this affected his liability for taxation, corvée service, military service, and the right to receive an allocation of land. Thus decision of these age categories was particularly important. When one reached the age of fifty

there were some cases in which one was released from military service and so on, while when one reached the age of sixty, as an old man he lost the greater part of the rights and obligations of an adult male. Eighty and ninety were ages at which one became entitled to a tax-exempt attendant adult and thus entailed the granting of tax exemption to another member of the household. That attention was concentrated upon young men in the fifteen-to-twenty age group is confirmed by the cases of revision of age that appear in the extant fragments of registers, seven out of eight of which are concerned with men aged from sixteen to twenty-one.

After reading this selection, consider these questions:
1. What was the purpose of population registration in China?
2. How did the Chinese government interfere in the life of the individual?
3. When could a Chinese person expect to retire and be cared for?

SELECTION 5:

Initiation of a Japanese Prince

The other major East Asian people to emerge in history were the Japanese. Although the islands off the mainland had been inhabited for thousands of years, not until contact was made with China did writing appear in Japan and historical records begin. For several centuries the Japanese lived in the shadow of China, but then they began their own development. Impressed by the Chinese capital at Qangan, the Japanese empress Gemmei put down a capital at Nara, in imitation of the great city of the Chinese emperors.

The Tale of Genji, the world's first novel, offers remarkable insight into the Japanese imperial court and its daily life. Genji was the golden boy of old Japan—handsome, clever, and accomplished in all he attempted. His interest in women was demonstrated frequently in this book of tales.

This selection tells us about court life as Genji passes from boyhood to adolescence. Note the importance of certain ceremonies and rituals in the course of court life. The Ministers of the Left and Right were two of the three important officials of the imperial Grand Council of State.

It seemed a pity that the boy must one day leave behind his boyish attire; but when he reached the age of twelve he went through his initiation ceremonies and received the cap of an adult. Determined that the ceremony should be in no way inferior to the crown prince's, which had been held some years earlier in the Grand Hall, the emperor himself bustled about adding new details to the established forms. As for the banquet after the ceremony, he did not wish the custodians of the storehouses and granaries to treat it as an ordinary public occasion.

The throne faced east on the east porch, and before it were Genji's seat and that of the minister who was to bestow the official cap. At the appointed hour in midafternoon Genji appeared. The freshness of his face and his boyish coiffure were again such as to make the emperor regret that the change must take place. The ritual cutting of the boy's hair was performed by the secretary of the treasury. As the beautiful locks fell the emperor was seized with a hopeless longing for his dead lady. Repeatedly he found himself struggling to keep his composure. The ceremony over, the boy withdrew to change to adult trousers and descended into the courtyard for ceremonial thanksgiving. There was not a person in the assembly who did not feel his eyes misting over. The emperor was stirred by the deepest of emotions. He had on brief occasions been able to forget the past, and now it all came back again. Vaguely apprehensive lest the initiation of so young a boy bring a sudden aging, he was astonished to see that his son delighted him even more.

The Minister of the Left, who bestowed the official cap, had only one daughter, his chief joy in life. Her mother, the minister's first wife, was a princess of the blood. The crown prince had sought the girl's hand, but the minister thought rather of giving her to Genji. He had heard that the emperor had similar thoughts. When the emperor suggested that the boy was without adequate sponsors for his initiation and that the support of relatives by marriage might be called for,

Murasaki Shikibu, *The Tale of Genji*, Edward G. Seidensticker, trans. (New York: Random House, Vintage Books, 1990) pp. 23–26.

the minister quite agreed.

The company withdrew to outer rooms and Genji took his place below the princes of the blood. The minister hinted at what was on his mind, but Genji, still very young, did not quite know what to say. There came a message through a chamberlain that the minister was expected in the royal chambers. A lady-in-waiting brought the customary gifts for his services, a woman's cloak, white and of grand proportions, and a set of robes as well. As he poured wine for his minister, the emperor recited a poem which was in fact a deeply felt admonition:

> The boyish locks are now bound up, a man's.
> And do we tie a lasting bond for his future?

This was the minister's reply:

> Fast the knot which the honest heart has tied.
> May lavender, the hue of the troth, be as fast.

The minister descended from a long garden bridge to give formal thanks. He received a horse from the imperial stables and a falcon from the secretariat. In the courtyard below the emperor, princes and high courtiers received gifts in keeping with their stations. The moderator, Genji's guardian, had upon royal command prepared the trays and baskets now set out in the royal presence. As for Chinese chests of food and gifts, they overflowed the premises, in even larger numbers than for the crown prince's initiation. It was the most splendid and dignified of ceremonies.

Genji went home that evening with the Minister of the Left. The nuptial observances were conducted with great solemnity. The groom seemed to the minister and his family quite charming in his boyishness. The bride was older, and somewhat ill at ease with such a young husband.

The minister had the emperor's complete confidence, and his wife, the girl's mother, was full sister to the emperor. Both parents were therefore of the highest standing. And now they had Genji for a son-in-law. The Minister of the Right, who as grandfather of the crown prince should have been without rivals, was somehow eclipsed. The Minister of the Left had numerous children by several ladies. One of the sons, a very handsome lad by his principal wife, was already a guards lieutenant. Relations between the two ministers were not good; but the Minister of the Right found it difficult to ignore such a talented youth, to whom he offered the hand of his fourth and favorite daughter. His esteem for his new son-in-law rivaled the other minister's esteem for Genji. To both houses the new arrangements seemed ideal.

After reading this selection, consider these questions:
1. Why do you suppose Genji's arrival at adolescence required a special ceremony?
2. What does this passage say about Japanese women? Are there contrasts with Chinese life, as revealed in selection 3?
3. Who was the likely audience for *The Tale of Genji*?

SELECTION 6:

Observations on Heian-Kyo

Japan's first capital was Nara, and it was here that Chinese and Buddhist influence on Japanese culture was strongest (hence the name of the Nara period). In 794 Emperor Kammu moved the capital from Nara to Heian-kyo, "the capital of peace and tranquillity." Later the city was renamed Kyoto, and it remained Japan's capital until Tokyo replaced it in 1867. Kammu apparently felt that there were too many Buddhist monks in Nara and feared undue influence, for the number of monasteries was limited in Heian-kyo. By 982, when the account excerpted in this selection was written by a Japanese visitor, the city was beginning to show some wear.

I have been observing the conditions of the eastern and western sections of the capital city for more than twenty years. The western section has lost most of its dwellings and is now reduced almost to rubble. People have left, but none enters the western section. Houses have crumbled into hovels but no new houses are built. Walking in this area, one finds that only those who do not mind being poor and destitute remain in the area. There are also some who prefer the life of the recluse, who under normal circumstances would have withdrawn into the mountains or returned to the fields, remaining in the western section. As to

those who wish to attain riches and work toward that end, they cannot wait a moment to leave the section.

In olden days, there was a great mansion owned by a nobleman, whose many chambers were adorned by vermilion doors and whose garden was full of bamboos, trees, springs and stones. It was a spectacular sight. However, its owner [Minamoto no Takaaki, the Minister of Left] was demoted in 967 to the position of Vice Governor of the Dazai area. Thereafter the mansion was burned down by a fire. Several tens of families used to have their mansions nearby, but they left the neighborhood one after another. Later the owner returned, but did not repair the mansion. He had many children and grandchildren, but none chose to remain in the area. The

David John Lu, *Sources of Japanese History*, vol. 1 (New York: McGraw-Hill, 1974), pp. 66–67.

gates were closed by thorns and bushes, and foxes and raccoon dogs were secure in their holes. Such devastation must be the manifestation of the will of Heaven to destroy the western section. It is certainly caused by the wrongdoings of the people.

In contrast, the eastern section from the Fourth Avenue northward, especially the northwestern and northeastern areas, is congested with people from all walks of life. The gates and buildings of great mansions follow one after another. Smaller buildings are erected so closely that their eaves touch one another. If the neighbor to the east suffers a fire, the western neighbor cannot escape a similar fate. If the neighbor to the south is invaded by armed bandits, the northern neighbor can expect to be affected similarly. . . . The rich are not necessarily endowed with virtue, while the poor still retain the sense of shame. Thus those poor people who live close to great families do not enjoy freedom of movement and behave continuously with trepidation. They do not dare replace their torn roofs or rebuild their broken fences. They are unable to laugh when happy or cry loudly when sorrowful. They are no different from sparrows who come near a flock of hawks. Instead of moving to another location to have a larger area to erect their dwellings, these insignificant people build their small dwellings close to each other, and contend for the small space. . . .

In extreme instances, families were annihilated because of lack of space. Some foolish people erect their dwellings by the River Kamo and when a flood comes they cast their fate along with fish and tortoises. Others choose to stay in the northern fields where in time of drought, there is not even a drop of drinking water. There is space in the two sections of the capital, yet how stubborn are the people to elect to remain only in a small portion of the capital.

By the River Kamo and on the northern fields, people not only build houses and dwellings but also cultivate fields and gardens. Old farmers toil on the land to create ridges between rice fields and dam up the river to irrigate their fields. But last year there was a flood and the river crested over the dike. The officials in charge of flood control used to boast of their accomplishment, but today they take no actions to rectify the situation. Must the people in the capital be consigned to a fate similar to that of fish?

When I study the regulations (*kyaku*), I discover that the western bank of the River Kamo can be cultivated by the Sujin-in only, and no exception is made. This prohibition is necessitated by the frequent flood damage. Furthermore, the banks of the River Kamo and the northern fields are two of the four major suburban areas which are utilized by the Emperor for the imperial outings. Even if people wish to cultivate these two areas, responsible officials must stop them. . . .

I cannot understand why people choose to stay in the congested eastern section which does not even belong to the capital proper while deserting the western section which is within the capital proper. The southern part of the western section is now given to waste where good grain can be produced. Why do people leave fertile soil to go to the infertile one? Is this due to the command of Heaven or due to the folly of the people?

After reading this selection, consider these questions:

1. Explain why some sections of cities decline while others prosper.
2. How does this description of Heian-kyo reflect the gap between rich and poor?
3. Why do people risk building their houses, then and now, in a floodplain?

CHAPTER 15
The Muslim World at Its Height: How Did Sufis, Jews, and Crusading Christians Interact?

As we have already seen (chapter 13), the period of the Abbasid caliphate, from A.D. 750 to approximately 1100, represented the height of Islamic civilization and prosperity. At the outset of the era, Muslims everywhere except Spain accepted the political supremacy of the caliphs ruling in Baghdad. Over time, however, other outlying parts of the Islamic world—Persia, Central Asia and northern India, Egypt, and North Africa—threw off the caliphate's authority, refused to pay tribute to Baghdad, and developed independent institutions.

This decentralizing trend paralleled an intensification of Muslim piety in most of the non-Arab lands conquered by Islamic armies in the seventh and eighth centuries. At least among Christians and Jews, conversions to Islam were at first infrequent. The Muslim authorities were satisfied and often preferred simply to tax their Christian and Jewish subjects and let them govern themselves. Educated members of these communities loyally served Muslim rulers without pressure to convert.

But in the Abbasid period this situation began to change. Just as in medieval Europe Christianity made a deep impression on townspeople and stimulated waves of intense piety, so in the Islamic world mass conversions of formerly Christian populations swelled the ranks of Muslim believers. Jews under Islamic rule seem to have been much more successful in maintaining the independent identity that Muslim rulers permitted them. Brotherhoods of Muslims, called Sufis, inspired many conversions from Christianity, especially in the eleventh and twelfth centuries, although Sufism also had a powerful impact on people whose forebears had been Muslim for generations. Like medieval Europe's Christian heretics, the Sufis had a tendency toward unorthodox religious ideas.

Until the late eleventh century, the Islamic world had often been on the offensive against Christendom, but now it faced a serious counterattack. The surging religious fervor of medieval Christians, an increasingly effective papacy, and the eagerness of Christian nobles to carve out new possessions for themselves in the wealthy East combined to produce a series of Crusades in which Christian warriors fought to regain Palestine from the Muslims. Although they seized Jerusalem in the process massacring as many Jews and Muslims as possible, the crusaders ultimately failed. In the process both sides learned more about each other—much of it distorted by mutual misunderstanding.

In reading this chapter, focus on developing an understanding of what it meant to be a Muslim or a Jew in the Abbasid period, and of how Muslims of that era regarded the Christians who threatened them.

SELECTION 1:

The Sufis

The following selection presents the evaluation of a modern American authority on Islamic history, John Esposito, of the impact of Sufism on medieval Islam.

The eleventh and twelfth centuries were a particularly turbulent time in Muslim history. The universal caliphate had disintegrated into a system of decentralized and competing states whose only unity was the symbolic, though powerless, Abbasid caliph in Baghdad. The Ismaili missionary propagandists were actively undermining the Sunni consensus. Muslim philosophers, deeply indebted to Hellenism and Neoplatonism,* were offering alternative, and sometimes competing, answers to philosophical and theological questions that often strained or tested the relationship between reason and faith. Sufism had become a mass movement with a strong emotional component and an eclectic propensity to accept superstitious practices. Much of what was taking place seemed out of the reach and control of the *ulama*

*Hellenism: ancient Greek cultural values; Neoplatonism: an ancient Greek philosophical school, loosely based on Plato's ideas, that insisted that true reality consisted of spiritual emanations from the world of transcendent ideas.

John L. Esposito, *Islam: The Straight Path*, 2nd ed. (New York: Oxford University Press, 1991), pp. 105–106, 110–12.

[The *ulama* were the Muslim theologians and jurists, always very conservative in their approach to Islam.], many of whom felt that these movements threatened their status and authority in the community. . . .

The focal point of a Sufi order was the domed tomb of its founder, who was venerated as a saint (*wali*, friend) of God. The tomb became a center for pilgrimage as visitors came to appeal to the saint for assistance. His spiritual power and intercession before God could be invoked for a safe pregnancy, success in exams, or a prosperous business, and offerings were made in thanksgiving for answered prayers. Once each year, a great celebration was held to commemorate the anniversary of his birth or death. Pilgrims would come from near and far for several days of rituals, songs or spiritual concerts, and celebration.

At the heart of Sufism is the belief that one's self must die, that is, one must undergo annihilation (*fana*) of the lower, ego-centered self in order to abide or rest (*baqa*) in God. Renunciation of that which is impermanent and transient, the phenomenal world, is a prerequisite to realization of the divine that indwells in all human beings. The goal of the Sufi was a direct knowledge or personal religious experience of God's presence. This mystical knowledge or understanding is reached by means of a series of stages and states. The shaykh [the spiritual guide of his Sufi disciples] leads the disciple through successive stages—renunciation, purification, and insight. Along the way, God rewards and encourages the disciple by granting certain religious experiences or psychological states.

In order to obtain their goal, the Sufis adapted many practices, some of which were foreign, in the eyes of the *ulama*, to early Islamic values. One of the fundamental tensions between the *ulama* and the Sufis was the extent to which the religious brotherhood offered an alternative sense of community, and the shaykh constituted a threat to the religious authority of the *ulama*. Among the more predominant Sufi practices employed to break attachment to the material world and rediscover or become aware of God's presence were: (1) Poverty, fasting, silence, celibacy, and other disciplines of mind and body whose object was the letting go of all attachment to and awareness of the self and the phenomenal world. Only then could the Sufi become aware of the divine, which was always present but ordinarily hidden from view by a preoccupation with the material world. While some orders practiced celibacy, many did not. The interpretation and practice of poverty varied as well. Each order and master had a distinctive approach. (2) Remembrance or recollection of God through a rhythmic, repetitive invocation of God's name(s), accompanied by breathing exercises, to focus consciousness on God and place the devotee in His presence. By themselves or sitting with their shaykh in community worship, Sufis repeated or recalled God's name hundreds and thousands of times for hours during the day or throughout the night. Another form of recollection is the recitation of a litany of God's names or attributes, often counted on a string of prayer beads, similar to a rosary. To become absorbed in recitation is to forget about worldly attachments and rest in God. (3) The use of music and song, spiritual concerts of devotional poems, as well as dance or bodily movements to induce or trigger ecstatic states in which the devotee could experience the presence of God or union with God. Though orthodoxy remained critical and Sufis like al-Ghazali warned of their dangers, music and dance proved especially popular among the people as a quick way to become intoxicated on God, to experience deep feelings of love for God and to feel His nearness. Groups of Sufis would gather to sing God's praises and loving hymns to Muhammad, or other great leaders like Ali, begging their intercession and assistance. The most famous example of the use of dance is that of the whirling dervishes, followers of the order founded by Jalal al-Din Rumi. Their whirling dance imitated the order of the universe. As dervishes spun in a circle around their shaykh, so did the planets revolve around the sun, the axis or center of the universe. (4) Veneration of Muhammad and Sufi saints as intermediaries between God and people. Muhammad had emphasized that he was only a human being and not a miracle worker. Despite this emphasis in official Islamic belief, the role of the Prophet as a model for Muslim life had early led to extravagant stories about Muhammad's life and extraordinary powers. This tendency became pronounced in Sufi piety. Muhammad was viewed as the link between God and man. The most extraordinary powers were attributed to him, given his closeness to God. These wonders were extended to Sufi saints, the friends or protégés of God. Miraculous powers (curing the sick, bilocation, reading minds, multiplication of food) and stories of saintly perfection abounded. Sufi theory organized the saints into a hierarchy, at the apex of which stood Muhammad, the pole of the universe, supervising the world. Shaykhs were venerated during their lifetime; they were honored, loved, and feared because of their miraculous powers. After their death, their burial sites or mausoleums became religious sanctuaries, objects of pilgrimage and of petitions for success in this life as well as the next, for worldly gains as well as eternal life.

After reading this selection, consider these questions:
1. Explain why the Sufi movement

expanded the Muslim world.

2. What practices did the Sufi brother-hoods require of their members?

3. Why was the *ulama* often at odds with the Sufis?

SELECTION 2:

Al-Ghazali's Conversion

The greatest of Muslim theologians of the late eleventh century was Abu Hamid al-Ghazali. Born in 1058 in Iran, he received a comprehensive education in law, philosophy, and theology, earning him an appointment to the most prestigious theological school in the Muslim world, the Nizamiyah of Baghdad. In 1095 al-Ghazali abandoned teaching due to an apparent crisis of faith and a feeling of futility. Eventually, his confidence returned after embracing the Sufi way of life. He then returned to the Nizamiyah, where he wrote an autobiographical work, The Deliverer from Wandering, *excerpted here. Through this classic, al-Ghazali wedded Sufism with Islamic orthodoxy.*

One day I would form the resolution to quit Baghdad . . . the next day I would abandon my resolution. I put one foot forward and drew the other back. If in the morning I had a genuine longing to seek eternal life, by the evening the attack of a whole host of desires had reduced it to impotence. Worldly desires were striving to keep me by their chains just where I was, while the voice of faith was calling: "To the road! to the road! What is left of life is but little and the journey before you is long. All that keeps you busy, both intellectually and practically, is but hypocrisy and delusion. . . ." On hearing that, the impulse would be stirred and the resolution made to take to flight.

Soon, however, Satan would return. "This is a passing mood," he would say. "Do not yield to it for it will quickly disappear: if you comply with it and leave this comfortable and influential position, these comfortable and dignified circumstances . . . then you will probably come to yourself again and you will not find it easy to return to all this."

For nearly six months . . . I was continuously tossed about between the attractions of worldly desires and the impulses towards eternal life. In the month of Rajab 486 AH the matter ceased to be one of choice and became one of compulsion. God caused my tongue to dry up so that I was prevented from lecturing. . . . This impediment in my speech produced grief in my heart, and at the same time my power to digest and assimilate food and drink was impaired: I could hardly swallow or digest a single mouthful of food. My powers became so weakened that doctors gave up all hope of successful treatment. "This trouble arises from the heart," they said, "and from there it has spread through the constitution. The only method of treatment is that the anxiety which has come over the heart should be allayed."

Thereupon, perceiving my impotence, and having altogether lost my power of choice, I sought refuge with God most High as one who is driven to Him because he is without further resources of his own. He answered me, for He "an-

W. Montgomery Watt, *Faith and Practice of al-Ghazali* (London: George Allen and Unwin, 1953), pp. 176–77.

swers him who is driven (to Him by affliction) when he calls Him". (Qur'an 27,63) He made it easy for my heart to turn away from position and wealth, from children and friends. I openly professed that I had resolved to set out for Mecca, while privately I made arrangements to travel to Syria. I took this precaution in case the Caliph and all my friends should oppose my resolve to make my residence in Syria. This stratagem for my departure from Baghdad I gracefully executed, and had it in my mind never to return there. There was much talk about me among all the religious leaders of Iraq, since none of them would allow that withdrawal from such a state of life as I was in could have a religious cause, for they looked upon that as the culmination of a religious career. That was the sum of their knowledge. . . .

I left Baghdad then. I distributed what wealth I had, retaining only as much as would suffice myself and provide sustenance for my children. . . . In due course I entered Damascus, and there I remained for nearly two years with no other occupation that the cultivation of retirement and solitude, together with religious and ascetic exercises, as I busied myself purifying my soul, improving my character and cleansing my heart for the constant recollection of God most high, as I had learned from my study of mysticism. I used to go into retreat for a period in the mosque of Damascus, going up the minaret of the mosque for the whole day and shutting myself in so as to be alone.

At length I made my way from Damascus to the Holy House (that is, Jerusalem). There I used to enter into the precinct of the Rock every day and shut myself in.

Next there arose in me a prompting to fulfill the duty of the Pilgrimage, gain the blessings of Mecca and Medina and perform the visitation of the Messenger of God most High. . . .

I continued at this stage for the space of ten years and during these periods of solitude there were revealed to me things innumerable and unfathomable. This much I shall say about that in order that others may be helped. I learnt with certainty that it is above all the mystics who walk on the road of God: their life is the best life, their method the soundest method, their character the purest character. Indeed, were the intellect of the intellectuals, the learning of the learned and the scholarship of the scholars, who are versed in the profundities of revealed truth, brought together in the attempt to improve the life and character of the mystics, they would find no way of doing so. For to the mystics all movement and all rest, whether external or internal, brings illumination from the light of the lamp of prophetic revelation, and behind the light of prophetic revelation there is no other light on the face of the earth from which illumination may be received.

After reading this selection, consider these questions:

1. How does al-Ghazali explain his indecision over giving up his position at the Nizamiyah?
2. What did al-Ghazali look for in his years of solitude?
3. Compare al-Ghazali's view of illumination with that of the Buddha (see chapter 5).

SELECTION 3:

Maimonides on Knowledge

Medieval Islamic authorities were generally tolerant of the Jewish communities over which they ruled. Jews and Christians were considered "people of the book" by Muslims, meaning that God had given them ear-

lier revelations, although because they had refused to accept Muhammad as the last and greatest of all the prophets they were now living in error. As Islamic piety deepened, however, Muslim impatience with Jewish dissent increased.

The most important medieval Jewish thinker, Moses Maimonides (in Hebrew, Moses ben Maimon), was born in Islamic Spain in 1159. Facing growing intolerance in Spain, he moved to Egypt and became the physician of Saladin, the Muslim commander who drove the Christian crusaders out of Jerusalem. Maimonides also served as leader of a Jewish community near Cairo. As a philosopher, his most important work was The Guide of the Perplexed, *from which this selection is taken. The book was closely studied by medieval Islamic, Jewish, and Christian thinkers alike.*

It is not an easy work to understand, for Maimonides was pursuing the difficult—some would say impossible—task of reconciling the ancient Greek philosopher Aristotle with rabbinical Judaism. Among other stumbling blocks around which all medieval philosophers and theologians had to maneuver, Aristotle insisted that the world had always existed and never been created, held that God was simply the impersonal "prime mover" to whom it was fruitless to pray, and denied that an afterlife awaited those who had died. Maimonides' solution—which he argues in this selection—was to claim that philosophers can by logical analysis understand matters that the untrained mind cannot hope to grasp. What do you think of his argument?

There are great differences in capacity between the individuals of the species. This also is manifest and very clear to the men of knowledge. It may thus happen that whereas one individual discovers a certain notion by himself through his speculation, another individual is not able ever to understand that notion. Even if it were explained to him for a very long time by means of every sort of expression and parable, his mind would not penetrate to it in any way, but would turn back without understanding it. This difference in capacity is likewise not infinite, for man's intellect indubitably has a limit at which it stops.

There are therefore things regarding which it has become clear to man that it is impossible to apprehend them. And he will not find that his soul longs for knowledge of them, inasmuch as he is aware of the impossibility of such knowledge and of there being no gate through which one might enter in order to attain it. Of this nature

is our ignorance of the number of the stars of heaven and whether that number is even or odd as well as our ignorance of the number of the species of living beings, minerals, plants, and other similar things.

On the other hand, there are things for the apprehension of which man will find that he has a great longing. The sway of the intellect endeavors to seek for, and to investigate, their true reality. . . . With regard to such there is a multiplicity of opinions, disagreement arises between the men engaged in speculation, and doubts crop up; all this because the intellect attached to an apprehension of these things, I mean to say because of longing for them; and also because everyone thinks that he has found a way by means of which he will know the true reality of the matter. Now it is not within the power of the human intellect to give a demonstration of these matters. For in all things whose true reality is known through demonstration there is no tug of war and no refusal to accept a thing proven—unless indeed such refusal comes from an ignoramus who offers resistance that is called resistance to demon-

Moses Maimonides, *The Guide of the Perplexed,* Shlomo Pines, trans. (Chicago: University of Chicago Press, 1963), pp. 65–67.

stration. Thus you can find groups of people who dispute the doctrine that the earth is spherical or that the sphere has a circular motion and with regard to other matters of this kind. These folk do not enter into our purpose. The things about which there is this perplexity are very numerous in divine matters, few in matters pertaining to natural science, and nonexistent in matters pertaining to mathematics. . . .

For man has in his nature a love of, and inclination for, that to which he is habituated. Thus you can see that people of the desert—notwithstanding the disorderliness of their life, the lack of pleasures, and the scarcity of food—dislike the towns, do not hanker after their pleasures, and prefer the bad circumstances to which they are accustomed to good ones to which they are not accustomed. Their souls accordingly would find no repose in living in palaces, in wearing silk clothes, and in the enjoyment of baths, ointments, and perfumes. In a similar way, man has love for, and the wish to defend, opinions to which he is habituated and in which he has been brought up and has a feeling of repulsion for opinions other than those.

After reading this selection, consider these questions:
1. What does Maimonides think of individual talent?
2. Why does Maimonides claim human knowledge is limited?
3. Maimonides maintains that people like what they are used to. Defend or dispute that claim.

Selection 4:

The Call to the Crusade

Into the Muslim world late in the eleventh century marched an army of western knights, crusaders, intent on seizing the city of Jerusalem and Christianity's most sacred shrine, the tomb in which Jesus had been buried after the Crucifixion. What set in motion these warriors had been a call for the Crusades made on November 27, 1095, by Pope Urban II at Clermont in France. There are several accounts of the pope's exhortation. This selection is a summary of the first part of his speech by Bishop Fulcher of Chartres, who was probably not at Clermont but received his information from several who were.

"Now that you, O sons of God, have consecrated yourselves to God to maintain peace among yourselves more vigorously and to uphold the laws of the Church faithfully, there is work to do, for you must turn the strength of your sincerity, now that you are aroused by divine correction, to another affair that concerns you and God. Hastening to the way, you must help your brothers living in the Orient, who need your aid for which they have already cried out many times.

"For, as most of you have been told, the Turks, a race of Persians, who have penetrated within the boundaries of Romania even to the Mediterranean to that point which they call the Arm of Saint George, in occupying more and more of the

Edward Peters, ed., *The First Crusade: The Chronicle of Fulcher of Chartres and Other Source Materials* (Philadelphia: University of Pennsylvania Press, 1971), pp. 30–31.

lands of the Christians, have overcome them, already victims of seven battles, and have killed and captured them, have overthrown churches, and have laid waste God's kingdom. If you permit this supinely for very long, God's faithful ones will be still further subjected.

"Concerning this affair, I, with suppliant prayer—not I, but the Lord—exhort you, heralds of Christ, to persuade all of whatever class, both knights and footmen, both rich and poor, in numerous edicts, to strive to help expel that wicked race from our Christian lands before it is too late.

"I speak to those present, I send word to those not here; moreover, Christ commands it. Remission of sins will be granted for those going thither, if they end a shackled life either on land or in crossing the sea, or in struggling against the heathen. I, being vested with that gift from God, grant this to those who go.

After reading this selection, consider these questions:
1. The pope in this passage emphasizes the need to help eastern Christians. Who are they and why do they need help?
2. Why does the pope mistakenly think the Turks are Persians?
3. How does a man profit from becoming a crusader?

SELECTION 5:

Muslims and Crusaders

The crusaders who arrived from Europe always formed a small minority among the Palestinians who had to deal with them. Since most crusaders were French, they imposed upon the Muslim population the feudal system that they had known at home. Sometimes friction between the two communities was common, but at other times good relations prevailed. Many Franks, the name that the Muslims called the crusaders, adapted very well to life in Southwest Asia.

In his autobiography, excerpted in the following selection, Usama ibn-Munqidh speaks of a close call he had with the crusaders in Palestine.

There are some Franks who have settled in our land and taken to living like Muslims. These are better than those who have just arrived from their homelands, but they are the exception, and cannot be taken as typical. I came across one of them once when I sent a friend on business to Antioch, which was governed by Todros ibn as-Safi, a friend of mine. One day he said to my friend: 'A Frankish friend has invited me to visit him; come with me so that you can see how they live.' 'I went with him,' said my friend, 'and we came to the house of one of the old knights who came with the first expedition. This man had retired from the army, and was living on the income of the property he owned in Antioch. He had a fine table brought out, spread with a splendid selection of appetizing food. He saw that I was not eating, and said: 'Don't worry, please; eat what you like, for I don't eat Frankish food. I have Egyptian cooks and eat only what they serve. No pig's flesh ever comes into my house!' So I ate, al-

Usama ibn-Munqidh, *Autobiography*, in *Arab Historians of the Crusades*, Francesco Gabrielli, comp., E.J. Costello, trans. (Berkeley and Los Angeles: University of California Press, 1984), pp. 78–79.

though cautiously, and then we left. Another day, as I was passing through the market, a Frankish woman advanced on me, addressing me in her barbaric language with words I found incomprehensible. A crowd of Franks gathered round us and I gave myself up for lost, when suddenly this knight appeared, saw me and came up. 'What do you want with this man?' 'This man,' she replied, 'killed my brother Urso.' This Urso was a knight from Apamea who was killed by a soldier from Hamāt. The old man scolded the woman. 'This man is a merchant, a city man, not a fighter, and he lives nowhere near where your brother was killed.' Then he turned on the crowd, which melt-

ed away, and shook hands with me. Thus the fact that I ate at his table saved my life.

After reading this selection, consider these questions:
1. How do you explain some crusaders' adoption of the Palestinian lifestyle?
2. Why do you suppose Usama was fearful of accepting Frankish hospitality?
3. Do you suppose friendship between crusaders and Muslims was common? Why or why not?

SELECTION 6:

A Muslim Appraises Europe

Very few Muslims in Southwest Asia ever visited France, which they considered an alien and hostile land. There were exceptions, but visitors such as Al Qazwini tended to confirm, not deny, prevailing prejudices. In the following selection, he describes France—or, as he called it, Frankland. Does it seem like a pleasant place to live?

Frank-land, a mighty land and a broad kingdom in the realms of the Christians. Its cold is very great, and its air is thick because of the extreme cold. It is full of good things and fruits and crops, rich in rivers, plentiful of produce, possessing tillage and cattle, trees and honey. There is a wide variety of game there and also silver mines. They forge very sharp swords there, and the swords of Frank-land are keener than the swords of India.

Its people are Christians, and they have a king possessing courage, great numbers, and power to rule. He has two or three cities on the shore of the sea on this side, in the midst of the lands of Islam, and he protects them from his side. Whenever the

Muslims send forces to them to capture them, he sends forces from his side to defend them. His soldiers are of mighty courage and in the hour of combat do not even think of flight, rather preferring death. But you shall see none more filthy than they. They are a people of perfidy and mean character. They do not cleanse or bathe themselves more than once or twice a year, and then in cold water, and they do not wash their garments from the time they put them on until they fall to pieces. They shave their beards, and after shaving they sprout only a revolting stubble. One of them was asked as to the shaving of the beard, and he said, "Hair is a superfluity. You remove it from your private parts, so why should we leave it on our faces?"

After reading this selection, consider these questions:

Al Qazwini, "Athar al-bilad," in *Islam from the Prophet Muhammad to the Capture of Constantinople*, vol. 2, Bernard Lewis, ed. and trans. (New York: Harper and Row, 1974), p. 133.

1. What positive views does Al Qazwini hold concerning the Franks?
2. What do his views reveal about how medieval Europeans and Muslims differed in their appreciation for cleanliness?
3. Why would a Muslim consider it important to wear a full beard, and be shocked at European men shaving their faces?

CHAPTER 16
The Mongols: How Did They Create an Empire?

Today Mongolia is a peaceful and thinly populated country wedged between Russian Siberia and China. But in the thirteenth and fourteenth centuries Mongols, also known as Tatars, riding tough little horses stormed out of their arid homeland and built the largest land empire in history. Their warfare combined surprise, ingenious logistics and long-distance communications, explosives for reducing fortifications, and utter ruthlessness. At their empire's height, the Mongol rulers, known as khans, were lords of China, Persia, Russia, and everything in between. Only fortunate accidents prevented the Mongols from invading, devastating, and probably subjugating Japan and western Europe.

The first great Mongol raid was led by Temüjin, one of the Mongol *begs,* or tribal chieftains. Temüjin took the title Genghis Khan, or "ruler of the world"—and he meant it. He and his sons came close to making the title a reality. When the thirteenth-century Venetian merchant Marco Polo traveled overland from the Mediterranean to the Mongol capital, near modern Beijing, he never crossed a single border.

A second great wave of Mongol conquest was led by Timur Lenk ("the lame," often called Tamerlane), a distant relative of Genghis Khan. Not much good can be said about him. Seldom in world history has a single man caused the death of so many people with cold, calculating means designed to crush all resistance, actual or potential. Using the most bloodthirsty tactics, between 1380 and his death in 1405 Timur made himself master of Central Asia, Persia, northern India, and most of Southwest Asia, and he came close to destroying the Ottoman Turks. Some of the lands that he conquered, including Iraq, never fully recovered.

Before concluding that the Mongols represented a purely destructive phase in world history, however, consider carefully the readings in this chapter.

SELECTION 1:

The Division of Labor Among the Mongols

The following selection is a description of the Mongols written by a medieval Englishman, William Rubruck. Traveling to the Mongol capital as an emissary of the pope, Rubruck wrote a perceptive report on the Mongol division of labor among men and women.

It is the duty of the women to drive the carts, get the dwelling on and off them, milk the cows, make butter and *gruit*, and to dress and sew skins, which they do with a thread made of tendons. They divide the tendons into fine shreds, and then twist them into one long thread. They also sew the boots, the socks, and the clothing. They never wash clothes, for they say that God would be angered thereat and that it would thunder if they hung them up to dry. They will even beat those they find washing them [and take their washing away from them]. Thunder they fear extraordinarily; and when it thunders they will turn out of their dwellings all strangers, wrap themselves in black felt, and thus hide themselves till it has passed away.

Furthermore they never wash their bowls, but when the meat is cooked they rinse out the dish in which they are about to put it with some of the boiling broth from the kettle, which they pour back into it. They also make the felt and cover the houses.

The men make bows and arrows, manufacture stirrups and bits, make saddles, do the carpentering on [the framework of] their dwellings and the carts; they take care of the horses, milk the mares, churn the *qumys* or mare's milk, make the skins in which it is put; they also look after the camels and load them. Both sexes look after the sheep and goats, sometimes the men, other times the women, milking them. They dress skins with a thick mixture of sour ewe's milk and salt. When they want to wash their hands or head, they fill their mouths with water, which they let trickle onto their hands, and in this way they also wet their hair and wash their heads.

After reading this selection, consider these questions:
1. What determined the roles of men and women in Mongol society?
2. Why do you think the Mongols were so afraid of lightening and thunder?
3. Why do you suppose washing was done as Rubruck describes?

William Woodville Rockhill, ed., *The Journey of William Rubruck*, quoted in Bertold Spuler, *History of the Mongols*, Helge and Stuart Drummond, trans. (Berkeley and Los Angeles: University of California Press, 1972), p. 96.

SELECTION 2:

The Mongol Armies

*O*ne of the persistent questions about the Mongol expeditions of the thirteenth century focuses on their military strategy and their recruitment of armies. The American historian Thomas T. Allsen offers his observation in the following selection.

By any standard of measurement, the series of military victories gained by the Mongols in such rapid succession during the thirteenth century was a most remarkable performance and, at first glance, not readily explainable. How did such a relatively small group of people bring so much territory under their control in so little time?

One possibility can be eliminated immediately: Mongol armies did not enjoy technological superiority over their enemies. Their weaponry did not differ appreciably from that of their sedentary adversaries, nor for that matter, from the basic pattern of armament that had prevailed in the Eurasian steppe since the first centuries of the Christian era. Rather, Mongol success was due to the fighting qualities of their soldiers and to the tactical, logistical, and organizational abilities of their leaders. But in addition to possessing a qualitative advantage over their opponents, they had a quantitative one as well. . . .

Where did the Mongols find the manpower to field such large armies? Certainly not from their own ranks, for their demographic base was quite limited. The answer, of course, is that the Mongols relied on subject peoples to meet their ever-growing manpower needs. The author of the *Tartar Relation*, writing in the latter half of the 1240s, was well aware of their reliance on this expedient. In tracing the rise of the Mongol Empire, he remarks that Genghis Khan "had the invariable habit of conscripting the soldiers of a

conquered army into his own, with the object of subduing other countries by virtue of his increased strength, as is clearly evident in his successors, who imitate his wicked cunning."

This procedure is not in itself unique, but the scale on which it was carried out by the Mongols was without precedent. It should be noted too, that although Mongol armies were international in character, the mercenary and slave soldiers so common in earlier empires were nowhere in evidence. The great size and ethnic diversity of Mongol field armies was achieved in the main by imposing something akin to a "national-service obligation" on all subject peoples immediately upon their incorporation into the empire. Initially the troops conscripted in this manner were almost entirely Mongol and Turkic nomads, the followers of rival tribal chieftains who had submitted to Genghis Khan out of political calculation or as the result of military defeat. The Mongol ruler's *levée en masse* of the "people who live in felt tents" established the pattern; thereafter, his successors applied this same technique to the sedentary regions of the empire, which contained vast reserves of manpower.

It is true that in Genghis Khan's day, surrendering Chinese armies, which had been fighting under the banner of the Qin dynasty, were incorporated into the imperial forces, but no systematic draft of the settled population took place until the middle years of Ögödei's reign [successor to Genghis Khan]. From that time on, however, sedentary auxiliaries were raised on a regular basis and assumed an important place in the Mongol military establishment. Besides supply-

Thomas T. Allsen, *Mongol Imperialism* (Berkeley and Los Angeles: University of California Press, 1987), pp. 189, 190–91.

ing additional manpower, which formed the empire's infantry arm, these auxiliaries also provided the Mongols with technical assistance in siege warfare.

As the Mongols pushed farther and farther into the sedentary regions of Eurasia, where they encountered walled cities and elaborate fortifications with increasing frequency, the need for such specialists grew, because the core of their army, the Mongol and Turkic nomads, had knowledge of neither the technology nor the tactics of siege warfare. Clearly the Mongols' success in mobilizing their sedentary subjects for military service is one of the major reasons why they were able to push forward the frontiers of the empire at such an astonishing pace.

After reading this selection, consider these questions:

1. How did Mongol armies recruit soldiers?
2. What do you suppose encouraged Mongol chieftains to ally with Genghis Khan?
3. What kind of warfare required specialists?

SELECTION 3:

New Year's Day with Kublai Khan

Kublai Khan was the grandson of Genghis Khan. He ruled China from Beijing and eventually acceded to the position of Great Khan, the chief of all the Mongol leaders. It was during his time that the Venetian Marco Polo (1254–1324) made his journey into China. Although some doubts have now been raised about the veracity of Polo's account (there are those who doubt that he made the trip), until proven otherwise we may assume that the Venetian traveler, if not an eyewitness, had access to information about the khan's activities.

In the following selection, one of Marco Polo's chapters details the New Year's celebration in Beijing. In Polo's account, he uses the term Tartars for the Mongols.

It is well ascertained that the Tartars date the commencement of their year from the month of February, and on that occasion it is customary for the Great Khan, as well as all who are subject to him, in their several countries, to clothe themselves in white garments, which, according to their ideas, are the emblem of good fortune. This is done in the hope that, during the whole course of the year nothing but what is fortunate may happen to them, and that they may enjoy pleasure and comfort.

Upon this day the inhabitants of all the provinces and kingdoms who hold lands or rights of jurisdiction under the Great Khan, send him valuable presents of gold, silver, and precious stones, together with many pieces of white cloth, which they add, with the intent that his Majesty

Manuel Komroff, ed., *Travels of Marco Polo, the Venetian* (New York: Horace Liveright, 1926), pp. 141–42.

may experience throughout the year uninterrupted enjoyment, and possess treasures adequate to all his expenses. With the same view the nobles, princes, and all ranks of the community, make reciprocal presents, at their respective houses, of white articles; embracing each other with demonstrations of joy and festivity, and saying, "May good fortune attend you through the coming year, and may everything you undertake succeed to your wish." On this occasion great numbers of beautiful white horses are presented to the Great Khan; or if not perfectly white, it is at least the prevailing color. In this country white horses are not uncommon.

It is moreover the custom in making presents to the Great Khan, for those who have it in their power to furnish nine times nine of the article of which the present consists. Thus, for instance, if a province sends a present of horses, there are nine times nine, or eighty-one head in the drove. And so also of gold, or of cloth, nine times nine pieces. His Majesty receives at this festival no fewer than a hundred thousand horses.

On this day it is that all his elephants, amounting to five thousand, are exhibited in procession, covered with housings of cloth, fancifully and richly worked with gold and silk, in figures of birds and beasts. Each of these supports upon its shoulders two coffers filled with vessels of plate and other apparatus for the use of the court. Then follows a train of camels, in like manner laden with various necessary articles of furniture. When the whole are properly arranged, they pass in review before his Majesty, and form a pleasing spectacle.

After reading this selection, consider these questions:
1. How did Kublai Khan's subjects demonstrate their loyalty?
2. Why would the khan appreciate a gift of horses?
3. Why would the New Year's celebration become an opportunity to display the khan's wealth?

SELECTION 4:

Life on the Steppe

Central Asia is a harsh land—arid, windy, and challenging to both humans and animals. In premodern times, people who lived in this vast region were either nomads or seminomads who had to follow the paths that offered pasture for their horses, camels, or sheep.

Despite their consequently low population density, the Mongol tribes were able, as we have seen, to build a mighty empire. A recent analysis of life on the steppe, excerpted in selection 4, comes from the world historian K.N. Chaudhuri.

For more than a thousand years, to the steppe people of inner Asia and the pastoralists of trans-

Oxiana, the rice and bread baskets of China and India held out an extravagant attraction which is difficult to comprehend and unravel. Neither the deserts, the fearsome Gobi, nor the Great Wall succeeded in containing the nomads beyond China's open frontiers in the north. India found

K.N. Chaudhuri, *Asia Before Europe: Economy and Civilisation of the Indian Ocean from the Rise of Islam to 1750* (Cambridge: Cambridge University Press, 1990), pp. 139–40.

only partial protection in the icy-heights of the Himalayas. The desert and the mountain without doubts symbolised in contemporaneous mind the spatial antithesis to sedentary life and even to civilisation itself. The Muslim urban sensibility of the fourteenth century would view the nomad and the desert through a very special reasoning. The Bedouin has no need to plan his vegetable garden, or take into account the direction from which the wind blows and construct water channels. In the desert the direction of the wind is not important, it comes from all sides. Only when people could not move as in a city that the wind turned bad. Towns built by Arabs with few exceptions quickly fall into ruin. The sites of al-Kufa and al-Basra in lower Iraq were chosen by the early Muslim conquerors with the sole thought of providing pastures for their camels and the proximity of the garrison-towns to the caravan routes. The 'Badawin' did not have to care about supplies of corn. Al-Muqaddasi had already expressed his own opinion of the neighbourhood of Kufa: 'the heat is very great, and the air foul and oppressive. There is a perfect pest of mosquitoes and life is a misery. Their food is fish, their drink is hot water, and their nights a torture.'

By this time advanced urban decay already marked many famous towns and cities of al-Iraq. The oasis agriculture of the central Euphrates-Tigris and the Diyala plains, the National Bank of Babylonia and the Islamic caliphate, were on their way back to the desert as the descendants of Chingiz Khan planned fresh onslaughts in Asia, this time in the direction of India. In 1321 Sultan Ghiyath al-Din Tughluq hurriedly built a great fortified town to the east of sprawling Delhi in case the Mongols once again broke through to the plains watered by the river Jamuna. A poor Turk by origin, the sultan had arrived in India as a groom in the service of a rich merchant and distinguished himself as a cavalry officer later. An inscription in the mosque at Multan described him as the victor of twenty-nine battles against the Tartar invaders. The terror and loathing aroused by the nomadic style of mobile warfare among the settled and regular imperial soldiers bred its own counter-terror. Mongol prisoners of war died terrible and cruel deaths at the hands of their captors. But even in captivity, as an Islamic portrait-painter saw with sensitive eyes, the valour of 'blood' remained defiant. The army of Hindustan did succeed in containing the Mongol invasions, until Amir Timur [Timurlane] and his steppe cavalry sacked Delhi in 1398, some would say with surprising ease. Soon the Tughluq urban-fortress was abandoned and lay in utter ruin, as the political gravitation of the empire moved away from Old Delhi. By night travellers encamped on the main caravan road to Agra had their rest disturbed by lions roaring under the massive ramparts, thirty feet thick. By day, the occasional shepherd led his flock through the deserted streets in search of grass, watched by eagles and vultures soaring high above the roofless halls, fallen masonry, and blind arches pointing to the sky like finger-less hands. In popular memory, the curse of the Sufi saint reverberated in disembodied anger. When nomads came to graze their animals over the land where royal palaces and cities had once stood, civilisation found the final plenitude of death. Political injustice, violence, and religious impiety still occupied extreme positions. There was no appeal against punishment and retribution from the victim and the transgressor alike.

After reading this selection, consider these questions:

1. What did the Mongols find attractive about India and China?
2. What explains the urban decay that afflicted so much of Central Asia and India?
3. Why was there fear and hostility between urban dwellers and steppe people, despite their economic dependence on each other?

SELECTION 5:

The Mongols in Russia

In 1237–40 a Mongol invasion under Batu Khan overwhelmed most medieval Russian lands, which had two important centers: Kiev in what is today Ukraine, and the area around Moscow and Novgorod in the north. The devastation wrought by the irresistible Mongols was immense, and Russian princes who escaped defeat in the initial onslaught tended quickly to submit to Mongol overlordship. What Russians still call "the Mongol yoke" profoundly affected the history of their country. A once flourishing medieval society was now impoverished, isolated from western Europe, and crushed by autocratic government—not only that of the Mongol overlords, but also of the native Russian princes who gathered the tribute due them. For example, the princes of Moscow, from whom descended the tsars of more recent centuries, were the chief collectors of money destined for the coffers of the Golden Horde, as the Mongol princes who ruled Russia under the sovereignty of the Great Khan were called.

One of the most notable Russian rulers of the thirteenth century was Alexander Nevskii (1236–1263), prince of Novgorod in northwestern Russia. Despite his collaboration with the Mongols, he became a saint of the Russian Orthodox Church and a Russian national hero because of his success in fighting off the Catholic Swedes and the Teutonic Knights, a crusading order of German monks who had established their headquarters in Prussia. American historian Charles Halperin analyzes Alexander Nevskii's policy toward the Mongols in the following selection.

Through indifference, rather than impotence, the Tartars allowed the Russian princes to keep their thrones, though each had to make a personal obeisance to the khan. Some, like grand prince Yaroslav and his son Alexander Nevskii, were required to visit the great khan at Karakorum [in Mongolia]. Though the Mongols were the ultimate arbitrators of succession in the Russian principalities, they strictly respected the dynastic legitimacy of the Riurikid clan* and in the thirteenth century even honored Russian collateral

*The extended family whose far-flung network of kinsmen supplied most of medieval Russia's princes.

Charles J. Halperin, *Russia and the Golden Horde* (Bloomington: Indiana University Press, 1985), pp. 48–50.

succession, from brother to brother (perhaps because it was a practice from the steppe). They let the Russian political infrastructure stand, in all its untidiness.

The grand prince of Vladimir, titular overlord of Vladimir-Suzdalian *Rus'* [northeastern Russia], continued his ambiguous dominance of other principalities in the northeast and his often nominal suzerainty in Novgorod. Changes in the south were more drastic; the devastation had left little worth ruling, and the throne of the grand prince of Kiev fell vacant. Some historians have credited the Mongols with uniting Russia, but the feuding between the principalities and city-states continued throughout the Mongol period. It was only after the demise of the Golden Horde that Muscovy, using some administrative methods learned from the Mongols, succeeded in unifying northeastern Russia.

Russia's acquiescence to Mongol hegemony ought not to be exaggerated. Until at least the middle of the fourteenth century, for a Russian prince to face the Mongols in open battle was suicide; yet in spite of this many princes and nobles in the northeast stood, fought, and died during the Mongol assault of 1237–1240. Under the circumstances, those princes who chose submission can hardly be castigated; timely propitiation usually helped to mitigate the Tartars' destructiveness. One attempt at concerted rebellion was a complete failure. Two southern princes who had originally fled when the Mongols appeared, Mikhail of Chernigov and Daniil of Galicia-Volhynia [in modern Ukraine], joined forces with Andrei Yaroslavovich of Vladimir-Suzdalia in an effort to liberate Russia. The coalition was unable even seriously to challenge the Mongol might, and each of its members paid for their audacity. Daniil had taken an oath of obedience to the pope in the expectation that Catholic crusaders would come to his rescue. Then, though his lands were the furthest removed from the Golden Horde, he personally submitted to the khan and waited for help which never came. Mikhail was summoned to the Horde and executed for rebellion. The Russian sources presented him as a religious martyr. Andrei Yaroslavovich took refuge abroad and was allowed to return only after submitting to his brother Alexander Nevskii, who was loyal to the Golden Horde.

Nevskii, rather than Russia, was the beneficiary of these machinations, and his collaboration with the Tartars has been an embarrassment to patriotic historiographers ever since. Still, his victories over both the Teutonic Knights and the Swedes prove his bravery and military skill, and he used his political capital with the Golden Horde to ameliorate the harshness of Mongol rule. Nevskii's willingness to cooperate with the Horde may well have saved Russia from more severe exactions. Nevskii died on the way home from pleading for leniency in response to the expulsion of the Muslim tax-farmers by cities in northeastern *Rus'* in 1262. Perhaps it was his mission which prevented the Tartars from sending an army to punish the uprising.

Nevskii seems to have been directly responsible for bringing the city-state or urban republic of Novgorod into the Mongol fold. Novgorod's stance toward the Golden Horde has been idealized and badly distorted, its reputation for staunch resistance resting on an uncritical interpretation of a single episode, the census under the aegis of Alexander Nevskii. It is true that the city was not sacked during the conquest, but many cities in northeastern Russia escaped this fate, and it cannot be taken as evidence of extraordinary heroics. Indeed, Novgorod's long-term relations with the Golden Horde, though in some ways unique, contain ample examples of the pragmatism and opportunism characteristic of the Russian response to the Golden Horde.

On the eve of the Mongol conquest, Novgorod had already perfected the strategy for maximizing its independence that it would use with modifications throughout the Mongol period: Novgorod was necessarily subservient to outside Russian princes, but by manipulating rivalries among the Riurikids, the city managed to maintain considerable autonomy. If a prince proved overweening, the Novgorodians offered the city to a more responsive one from a rival principality. In this way they resisted the encroaching power of the grand prince of Vladimir in the twelfth and early thirteenth centuries by inviting in princes from Smolensk or the Dnepr' valley.

After reading this selection, consider these questions:
1. Why would the Mongols allow Russian princes to retain their authority rather than rule the country directly?
2. Why was Russia difficult to unite?
3. What does the author think of Alexander Nevskii?

SELECTION 6:

The Embassy from Spain

The second of the great Mongol khans was Timur Lenk, or Tamerlane. In 1369 Timur's goal was to secure the boundaries of his khanate after he had taken the city of Samarkand from foreign invaders. Then he changed his course of action, beginning a period of twenty-four years of campaigns within the Muslim world. All over Southwest Asia Timur's armies brought catastrophe to the local populations. In 1383 at Sabzawar in Iran, he forced two thousand prisoners into a living mound and bricked them in. At Isfahan his troops massacred seventy thousand people, and even more fell in Delhi, the capital of India. In 1400 he ordered four thousand Christian soldiers of Sivas (in modern Turkey) buried alive.

Only one European embassy made its way to Timur's court at the beginning of the fifteenth century and left a record of the meeting. The delegation was led by a Spaniard, Ruy Gonzalez del Clavijo, on behalf of King Henry III of Castile.

Then coming to the presence beyond, we found Timur and he was seated under what might be called a portal, which same was before the entrance of a most beautiful palace that appeared in the background. He was sitting on the ground, but upon a raised dais before which there was a fountain that threw up a column of water into the air backwards, and in the basin of the fountain there were floating red apples. His Highness had taken his place on what appeared to be small mattresses stuffed thick and covered with embroidered silk cloth, and he was leaning on his elbow against some round cushions that were heaped up behind him. He was dressed in a cloak of plain silk without any embroidery, and he wore on his head a tall white hat on the crown of which was displayed a balas ruby, the same being further ornamented with pearls and precious stones.

As soon as we came in sight of his Highness we made him our reverence, bowing and putting the right knee to the ground and crossing our arms over the breast. Then we advanced a step and again bowed, and a third time we did the same, but this occasion kneeling on the ground and remaining in that posture. . . .

His Highness however commanded us to arise and stand close up to him that he might the better see us, for his sight was no longer good, indeed, he was so infirm and old that his eyelids were falling over his eyes and he could barely raise them to see. We remarked that his Highness never gave us his hand to kiss, for that is not their custom, no one with them should kiss the hand of any great lord which to do would here be deemed unseemly. Timur now inquired of us for the health of the King our Master saying: "How is it with my son your King? How goes it with him? Is his health good?" We suitably answered and then proceeded to set out the message of our embassy at length, his Highness listening carefully to all that we had to say. When we had finished Timur turned and proceeded to converse with certain of the great lords who were seated on the ground at his feet. . . .

Turning to them therefore Timur said: "See now these Ambassadors whom my son the King

E. Denison Ross and Eileen Power, eds. Ruy Gonzalez del Clavijo, *Embassy to Tamerlain, 1403–06*, Guy le Strange, trans. (New York: Harper, 1928), pp. 220–21.

of Spain has sent to me. He indeed is the greatest of all the kings of the Franks who reign in that farther quarter of the earth where his people are a great and famous nation. I will send back a message of good will to my son this King of Spain. Indeed it had been enough that he should have sent me his Ambassadors with a Letter merely and no offerings or gifts. It suffices me to know that he is well in health and state, and no gift from him do I ever require."

After reading this selection, consider these questions:

1. Why would a Spanish king send a delegation to Timur?
2. Describe the protocol for an audience with Timur.
3. What do you expect was achieved by such an embassy?

CHAPTER 17
Medieval Europe: What Explains Its Growth and Decline?

Charlemagne's Empire fragmented after his death because of internal warfare and inept rulers. Added to these domestic problems were assaults from Vikings, Hungarians, and Arabs. The Arabs, however, were eventually beaten back, and during the tenth and eleventh centuries the Vikings and Hungarians settled down to become Christian Europeans. Roughly around the year 1000, Europe experienced a remarkable surge of energy whose impetus lasted until the late thirteenth or early fourteenth century. The western tip of the vast Eurasian landmass became an important new center of civilization.

Scholars debate the reasons for Europe's medieval revival. The weather may have had something to do with it: By examining samples of glacial ice, we know that the climate grew milder during these centuries, which in turn spurred agricultural productivity. The invention and spread of more efficient plows and the clearing of forests for new settlement made it possible to sustain population growth. Towns, which had practically vanished with the fall of the Roman Empire, came back to life or were founded anew. Money and credit increasingly replaced barter. Wealth other than land ownership rewarded successful artisans and merchants, creating a new middle class of men and women often called the bourgeoisie, from the French, or, from German, burghers. With increasing frequency, peasants could use money to buy personal freedom from their lords, and so ceased to be serfs. The tensions and growing wealth of an urbanizing society helped intensify western Christianity and spurred the revival of the papacy, which claimed the right and duty to oversee the policies of Europe's kings.

Latin Christianity set the values for peoples' lives. One rather dubious expression of this religious fervor was the crusading movement, which we encountered in chapter 15. Another, more positive, channel for religious enthusiasm was the building of great monuments to Christian faith, the cathedrals, which are among the world's masterpieces of architecture and engineering (selection 1). A parallel achievement was the creation of great literature and of the first universities, from which our modern institutions of higher learning trace a direct descent (selections 2 and 3).

The foundations of Europe's new civilized way of life were, however, precarious. Peasants still lived at a thin margin of subsistence: Bad weather, crop failure, or wartime destruction could mean famine (selection 4). And when in the mid–fourteenth century Europe was struck by a devastating plague, which probably originated in China and spread rapidly across the Mongol-dominated lands, almost a third of the population may have died (selections 5 and 6). Western civilization did not perish, but it changed direction. As you read chapter 17, ask yourself what were the fundamental values of medieval European culture, and how these values affected ordinary Europeans' daily lives.

SELECTION 1:

Chartres Cathedral

The following selection is a modern art historian's account of the planning and building of one of the greatest of the medieval cathedrals, at the city of Chartres in northern France. Cathedrals such as this took centuries to complete. Their planners and most of their builders would never worship in them, and therefore they were truly undertakings of faith, devotion, and civic pride.

Many art historians believe that the relatively modest-sized Gothic cathedral at Chartres is the greatest of Europe's cathedrals. Struck by a devastating fire in September 1020, it was rebuilt by order of Bishop Fulbert. The word Gothic *refers to the distinctive architectural style, perfected in late eleventh- and twelfth-century Europe, that aimed to flood the cathedral's interior with the greatest possible amount of light. This was accomplished by raising walls as high as possible in thin stone piers, maximizing upper space for glass windows, and holding everything up with exterior supports, called flying buttresses.*

Fulbert's façade underwent transformation in the middle of the twelfth century. After a fire which broke out on September 5, 1134, it was decided to build on the northern side, and in front of the Romanesque* gate-tower, a great free-standing tower. A few years later, the decision was taken to add a symmetrical tower on the southern side.

The intention was to join these two towers by a great porch comprising, like the narthex at Vézelay, three sculpted doorways standing against the wall of the Romanesque nave.** But, towards the year 1150, the architect was seized by a new idea, deciding to place his doorways (already largely

Louis Grodecki, *Chartres* (New York: Harcourt, Brace & World, 1963), pp. 19, 22–23.

*Romanesque is the name of the earlier architectural style in medieval Europe. It featured massive walls and Roman-style rounded arches.

**Narthex: the vestibule leading into the cathedral; nave: the elongated central space of the cathedral.

prepared in the cathedral workshop) in line with the western fronts of the bell-towers. Behind the doorways he built a vaulted porch, surmounted by a gallery lit by three great stained-glass windows.

Certain admirable texts recounting the construction of this façade have come down to us. The enthusiasm of the faithful was almost incredible, even in the eyes of contemporary observers. In 1144, Robert de Torigny, Abbot of Mont St. Michel recounted how the faithful population of Chartres and its diocese harnessed themselves "to carts laden with stones and wood, corn and everything else contributing to the construction of the cathedral, the towers of which rose as if by magic. Enthusiasm spread throughout Normandy and France. On all sides could be seen men and women dragging heavy loads through mire and marsh. Everywhere penitances were performed and enemies forgiven."

Another text, dating from 1145—a letter from Haimon, Abbot of St. Pierre-sur-Dives, addressed to the monks of Tutbury in England—tells the story of self-inflicted corvées [labor services]: "Has anyone ever seen or heard of powerful lords and mighty princes . . . and even women of noble birth bowing their necks to the yoke and harnessing themselves to carts?" The citizens of Chartres set an example to all Normandy. Brotherhoods are created and the people set to work in silence, at night singing canticles and lit by the glow of candles; nothing can stem the tide of work, they are like the people of Israel crossing the Jordan. Healings and miracles abound, and at Ste. Marie-du-Port the sea retreats before them."

Haimon's letter may perhaps contain a certain amount of rhetorical exaggeration, but events of such an extraordinary character were naturally deemed miraculous—a testimony to the intervention of the Virgin of Chartres, the inspiration of this outburst of fervor, sweeping progressively through the whole of Normandy and France.

Almost the whole of this mid-twelfth century building has been preserved. The upper part of the older or north tower was rebuilt between 1506 and 1512 by Jean Texier, known as Jean de Beauce. This is now called the "clocher neuf," or "new tower." The south spire—the "clocher vieux" or "old tower"—still stands today as it was built between approximately 1140 and 1170. The central part of the façade was modified towards the beginning of the thirteenth century when the great west rose [window] was added. Thus, while the stones carted with such enthusiasm are still there, the proportions of the towers and the original formal balance of the work has been disrupted.

The south spire springs over 300 feet high, with no decoration other than scallops covering its flanks and the groins accenting the angles of the pyramid and emphasizing its heavenward flight. "For nearly 800 years," wrote [art historian] Emile Mâle, "it has braved storms and thunderbolts; its stones assembled with such precision that they seem to be endowed with the solidity of metal, assailed from without by mighty winds and swept from within by the hurricane of the bells. Seen from afar, this lofty signal not only awakened love of native land, but proclaimed the hope of the world to come."

After reading this selection, consider these questions:

1. Why did cathedral building start in the eleventh century?
2. What explains the enthusiasm of the men and women of Chartres for constructing a cathedral?
3. Why did many medieval people assume that miracles were routine occurrences?

SELECTION 2:

Dante's Inferno

Complementing the construction of the cathedrals was a large literary output on religious subjects. Poetry, which had been neglected since the time of the Roman poet Virgil, was again written by authors such as Geoffery Chaucer in England and Dante Alighieri in Italy.

In Dante's work, The Divine Comedy, *the author makes a journey through purgatory, hell, and heaven. In the section entitled "The Inferno," Dante visits the places where those who were damned are now punished for their sins. It is not just a place of fire and brimstone, but of cold and ice. Individuals here are reaping the results of having lived without the warmth of love and concern for other human beings. In this first section, or canto, the poet describes the beginning of his descent into hell. On his journey he has Virgil, the Roman poet, for his guide.*

In the middle of life's journey
I found myself in a thick woods
for I had lost myself on the straight way.
Ah, how hard it is to explain it
because this savage forest was both dense and
    overgrown.

When I recall it my fears still haunt me.
It was so bitter that it reminded me of death.
But there were also good things to discover,
and I shall also tell you of the other things I saw.

I cannot say just how I entered
since at that point I was nearly asleep
when I lost the right path.
But as I reached the bottom of a hill
where this valley ended
that had so filled my heart with terror
I looked up and saw its shoulders
already clothed with the rays of the planet
that leads one along every path.
For this reason my fear died down a bit
and the hard night that passed with such terror

stilled the lake of my heart.

And just as a person out of breath
once safe from the sea arrives on shore
turns back to view the dangerous water,
So my soul, formerly a fugitive,
turned back to look at the entrance
that does not let a person come out alive.

I decided to rest my tired body a bit.
And then continued the journey along the
    deserted slope
with a firm foot always the one below.

[In a later canto Dante describes the punishments inflicted on one group of condemned souls in hell.]

Now woeful cries reach my ears,
now distressed moans come into my hearing.
I have arrived at a place of muted light
where the sea crashes like a storm
when opposing winds clash over it.

The infernal wind, which never stops
drives on the spirits with its force.
Turning and pounding it gnashes at them.

Dante Alighieri, *La Divina Commedia*, (Milano: N. Bettoni, 1825), Canto. Translated by the editor.

When they approach the slope
there are shrieks, howls, and laments.
They curse the divine power.

I learned that those tormented so
were condemned for sins of the flesh.
They had abandoned reason for the sake of lust.

And as in the cold winter starlings' wings carry
   them along
in large and crowded waves
in the same way this horrid wind bears down on
   the guilty.
Now here, there, down, up, it carries them aloft.
No hope ever comforts them.
They may never rest, no chance for relief from
   even small pains.

And like cranes in flight call out their songs
making a long file in the air,
so did the spirits I saw come close
carried by that restless wind.
Then I asked him,
"Master, who are these people whom the dark
   wind torments?"

After reading this selection, consider these
questions:

1. Where would Dante get his inspiration for this section of *The Inferno*?
2. How did the poet feel as he entered
   on his journey into the underworld?
3. Why would the torments of hell be
   pictured in such graphic terms in
   medieval thought and art?

SELECTION 3:

The Universities

Town life and the growing power of the clergy and nobles who needed administrators created the environment that resulted in the formation of Europe's first universities. Here students and faculty, the masters, came together to explore the disciplines needed for success in the world of the Middle Ages. In this selection, a modern historian describes the workings of medieval universities.

As the medieval universities achieved a fuller and more highly defined structure, they customarily came to have four distinct subdivisions or "faculties": arts, law, medicine, and theology. The last three were considered higher or "superior" faculties for which, presumably, the arts course was preparatory. The masters, who were duly admitted members of each faculty, elected their own proctor or dean. Usually the four deans then selected a rector to represent the entire uni-

versity, but it did not always work out that way. At Paris, the rector was originally merely the head of the arts faculty, and it took some doing to gain recognition for him as head of the entire university. "It was not till after a long series of struggles," [an authority on the medieval universities] observes, "that the Rector fought his way to the headship of the university, and the fighting was very literal fighting; on several occasions it assumed the form of a physical encounter in church between the partisans of the Rector and those of the Dean of Theology."

As the scholars of the university faculties became more organized, they also became more ob-

Willis Rudy, *The Universities of Europe, 1100–1914* (London and Toronto: Fairleigh Dickinson University Press, 1984), pp. 29–30.

viously professional. One sign of this was the new economics of instruction. Previously, the masters had been somewhat haphazard in the fees that they charged for their services. Some, notably the monastic teachers of the early middle ages, had dispensed instruction *gratis*. But in the thirteenth century, the business of higher education became highly competitive and the supply of adequate church benefices or endowments was in increasingly short supply. As a result, the masters began to charge set fees for their instruction.

To have a voice in the affairs of a master's university or guild, one first had to be accepted as a member of the same; this meant, in essence, that one had been approved as a teaching professional. All medieval degrees were in their inception teaching degrees. Master, doctor, and professor "meant one and the same thing—teacher.". . . "Admission to the degree meant that you belonged to a guild of teachers, and began at once to teach the subjects you had just learned." Every faculty, by the way, had its own master's degree, but the masters in the higher, or professional, faculties such as law, medicine, and theology, came in time to be called *doctores* or *professores*.

Curriculum. The first formal stage of instruction in a medieval university was a general arts course leading to a ceremony (or debate) known as "determination," which was the equivalent of a bachelor's degree. After two more years of study under a master, the young man was eligible for recognition as a candidate for the master's degree or license itself. At this point the aspiring bachelor was formally invested as a "licentiate." There followed another period of study and lecturing, during which the candidate hoped by some master work or other achievement to demonstrate that he should be admitted into the master's guild. Once accepted, he was formally recognized as a fellow master at an imposing ceremony known as "inception."

After reading this selection, consider these questions:

1. How were medieval universities started?
2. Compare the faculties of the medieval and modern universities.
3. What do you like about the medieval university? What do you dislike?

SELECTION 4:

Peasant Women

At least 80 percent of medieval Europe's population were peasants. Their way of life made little allowance for personal comfort or security, although their monotonous diet, when crops did not fail, was basically healthy. Work was hard and constant for men and women alike. Here, the modern American historians Marty Newman Williams and Anne Echols offer a vivid sketch of medieval peasant life, reflecting the latest scholarship.

Of all classes, peasant women probably worked the hardest. A diligent wife and mother helped her family prosper, while a lazy woman could spell disaster. An industrious wife performed a variety of domestic tasks including: keeping house, cooking for her family, making cloth and clothes, and caring for her children. She also kept the hens and pigs, sheared sheep, milked cows and made

Marty Newman Williams and Anne Echols, *Between Pit and Pedestal: Women in the Middle Ages* (Princeton, NJ: Markus Wiener, 1994), pp. 28–31.

cheese, butter, and ale. The peasant wife carried her water from wells or streams, hoed and weeded her kitchen garden, gathered kindling, and tended the home fire. She even helped the men in the fields, doing everything from planting to harvesting. Not only did she grow her own herbs and vegetables, but when her husband was working on the lord's lands, she performed many of the same backbreaking tasks on the family's acreage.

In addition to their normal household chores, the most efficient housewives frequently supplemented their families' income. Some Italian peasant women sold their hair to rich town ladies. One rural woman, known as *Cavolaja* because she sold cabbages, even became quite wealthy and famous by marketing the vegetables she grew on her farm to the townspeople of late fourteenth-century Florence. In the English countryside, peasant women sometimes earned extra money by shearing sheep, thatching roofs, mixing mortar for new buildings, or whipping dogs out of churches—an "odd job" indeed. In mid-fifteenth-century Cambridge, Katherine Rolf frequently worked as a day laborer for a convent, earning around two *pennies* a day for weeding, thatching, making candles, threshing grain, and cleaning wool.

Village women who brewed ale or sold bread were especially common in England. In the village of Broughton, perhaps one out of every four women was occasionally listed as an alewife, although few had operations as large as that of Emma Roger. Her fines (or license fees) were three times higher than those paid by other village women from the years 1309 through 1340. Broughton had no taverns at this time, but in 1297 Joan Everard ran the village equivalent by selling her ale in a room she rented at John Crane's house.

The dwellings of these English peasant women ranged from the homes of the more affluent villeins and freemen to the mere hovels occupied by many *cottars* (usually the poorest because they held no land). In the past fifteen years, archaeological evidence has revealed that villagers—especially in early medieval centuries—moved more often than most historians had realized. Individuals, families, and sometimes whole villages moved from one locale to another searching for more food, better land, or safer conditions (free from wars or natural disasters). In addition, recent archaeological finds refute the belief that peasant homes were almost always constructed from local materials. The new evidence indicates that peasants often experimented with a variety of building materials—even with ones that had to be transported over great distances.

In both England and France, the typical peasant's house sheltered only one married couple and their children. It was most often a one-story structure of irregular dimensions that had corn cribs, mows for hay and straw, and cattle sheds at the back. A heavy door opened into the one large family room with its pressed earth floor. Walls were sooty because the smoke from the central fire had to escape by way of holes in the roof. Piglets, ducklings, and cats meandered about inside the house, while a hen might nest beside the fire. Even the larger animals were often kept inside during the winter, only slightly separated from the family's living space. Windows were extremely rare, and burning rushes soaked in resin usually provided the artificial light since candles were too expensive for daily use.

Most peasants slept in familial straw beds that were warm and fairly comfortable, but also provided ideal breeding conditions for vermin. The *board*, of the same design as that used in castles or town houses, consisted of a trestle table with benches or stools. Some peasant women had chests for valuables like clothing and cups, but only the most affluent owned any real chairs. The few kitchen utensils included kettles, pot hangers, shovels, and fleshhooks. During the winter, peasants made or restored cooking implements along with other household and farming tools.

The homes and furnishings of the peasantry did not change quickly, but there were some improvements in their living conditions by the late 1400s. Among these were houses built on raised platforms, stone floors, cobbled yards, and drainage ditches. Innovations in heating technology included hand and foot warmers, furnaces, and baths. The most prosperous fourteenth- and fifteenth-century Tuscan farmers and sharecroppers often lived in relatively large stone houses with tiled roofs, sleeping lofts, larders, and halls. Similar progress was evident in late fourteenth-century English and French dwellings, which began to include more rooms, and even fireplaces built into walls.

Rural peasants (and even the very poorest city residents) often had trouble finding enough food. Peasants who ate well in some years had to resort to soups made of dead leaves or acorns in other winters. Peasant women usually cooked for their own families. Prudent wives made the most of what was available by not wasting food and by learning how to keep it edible. In England and France, women stored fruit under straw and then preserved it in honey or cooked it in fruit juice. The mainstay of their diet was bread, which was usually made of coarse, dark flours such as rye, oats, barley, and even peas or acorns.

The major source of protein in much of France was cheese, though some peasants obtained a little meat from chickens, pigs, or sheep. Most families grew cabbages, leeks, onions, and turnips, and peasants also gleaned supplementary foods from nature's bounty, adding mushrooms, nuts, and snails to the menu. Italian peasants ate coarse bread, cheese, raw turnips, noodles or macaroni, and garlic. Tripe was a staple by the fourteenth century, as was a dish of pureed beans with bacon. The poorer classes in Germany consumed dark bread, oatmeal porridge or gruel, boiled peas, lentils, and occasionally pork, which they particularly savored as leftovers cooked with turnip greens or cabbage. During the fall, English peasants fattened their pigs on roots and acorns in the forest before killing the animals at the end of autumn. The pork was then cooked with the same things the pig itself normally ate—wild sage, garlic, and windfall apples. Peasant women smoked or salted any leftover meat to provide bacon for the winter. The villein's diet also included beans, leeks, curds, and oatmeal cakes or porridge. The nutritional content of peasants' diet improved over the centuries as more iron- and protein-rich foods were being grown.

Peasant attire, on the contrary, changed little, remaining largely utilitarian in style throughout the Middle Ages. The basic patterns were similar to the fashions of wealthier people, but peasant styles lacked the quality of materials and ornamentation that distinguished the clothes of the nobility. Male peasants wore loose tunics, shirts, britches, and hose, while their wives donned long, loose gowns with aprons and wimples. Shoes for both sexes were normally wooden clogs or simple leather slippers. Peasant women usually made their families' apparel from homespun wool that they colored with bright natural dyes. The poor had few accessories, although they frequently wore belts and girdles from which hung knives and other implements. In later years, many peasant women made their families' clothes more attractive by adding embroidery. Their patterns remained simple, but even the peasantry's clothing had become slightly more close-fitting and ornate by the end of the Middle Ages.

After reading this selection, consider these questions:

1. What economic role did women play in the medieval peasant household? Why was it a vital one?
2. What does this selection tell you about the place of money and of barter in the medieval economy?
3. What evidence suggests that medieval peasants typically lived in nuclear families (husband, wife, and children) rather than in extended households with grandparents, brothers, sisters, and other kin? What does this say about the kind of life that peasants led?

SELECTION 5:
The Plague Strikes Italy

About 1250 the growth of medieval Europe's population slowed and eventually it ceased. The climate turned colder and harsher; technological progress had ceased to keep up with demographic expansion, squeezing living standards; constant warfare and disease took their usual toll. Then, in 1346–48, the worst single disaster in European, and possibly in world, history struck, in the form of a devastating epidemic of bubonic plague. Approximately one-third of Europe's population died, and in many places (including Italy) the death rate was probably higher. Losses in China were comparable. This catastrophe was only the first of a series of plague outbreaks that would ravage Eurasia until the eighteenth century. Cities—crowded and dirty breeding places for plague-carrying rats— were hardest hit. In selection 5, the great Italian writer Giovanni Boccaccio uses a vivid narrative of the so-called Black Death as the prologue to his Decameron, *a collection of incongruously lighthearted tales that supposedly were swapped by upper-class citizens of Florence as they hid from the plague at a country retreat.*

It did not act as it had done in the East, where bleeding from the nose was a manifest sign of inevitable death, but it began in both men and women with certain swellings either in the groin or under the armpits, some of which grew to the size of a normal apple and others to the size of an egg (more or less), and the people called them *gavoccioli*. And from the two parts of the body already mentioned, within a brief space of time, the said deadly *gavoccioli* began to spread indiscriminately over every part of the body; and after this, the symptoms of the illness changed to black or livid spots appearing on the arms and thighs, and on every part of the body, some large ones and sometimes many little ones scattered all around. And just as the *gavoccioli* were originally, and still are, a very certain indication of impending death, in like manner these spots came to mean the same thing for whoever had them. Neither a doctor's advice nor the strength of medicine could do anything to cure this illness; on the contrary, either the nature of the illness was such that it afforded no cure, or else the doctors were so ignorant that they did not recognize its cause and, as a result, could not prescribe the proper remedy (in fact, the number of doctors, other than the well-trained, was increased by a large number of men and women who had never had any medical training); at any rate, few of the sick were ever cured, and almost all died after the third day of the appearance of the previously described symptoms (some sooner, others later), and most of them died without fever or any other side effects.

This pestilence was so powerful that it was communicated to the healthy by contact with the sick, the way a fire close to dry or oily things will set them aflame. And the evil of the plague went even further: not only did talking to or being around the sick bring infection and a common death, but also touching the clothes of the sick or anything touched or used by them seemed to communicate this very disease to the person involved.

Giovanni Boccaccio, *The Decameron*, Mark Musa and Peter E. Bondanella, trans. (New York: W.W. Norton, 1977), p. 4.

After reading this selection, consider these questions:

1. What about the plague frightened Boccaccio?

2. Why would amateur doctors appear on the scene?

3. How do you account for the different symptoms of the Black Death?

SELECTION 6:

The Black Death

*W*hat *Europeans called the Black Death engulfed the civilized world from China to the Atlantic. One of the great pioneers of world history, the American William H. McNeill, explains in the following selection how the epidemic spread and the devastation it caused.*

The disease broke out in 1346 among the armies of a Mongol prince who laid siege to the trading city of Caffa in the Crimea. This compelled his withdrawal, but not before the infection had entered Caffa itself, whence it spread by ship throughout the Mediterranean and ere long to northern and western Europe as well.

The initial shock, 1346–50, was severe. Die-offs varied widely. Some small communities experienced total extinction; others, e.g., Milan, seem to have escaped entirely. The lethal effect of the plague may have been enhanced by the fact that it was propagated not solely by flea bites, but also person to person, as a result of inhaling droplets carrying bacilli that had been put into circulation by coughing or sneezing on the part of an infected individual. . . .

Whether or not pneumonic plague affected Europeans in the fourteenth century, die-off remained very high. In recent times, mortality rates for sufferers from bubonic infection transmitted by flea bite has varied between 30 and 90 percent. Before antibiotics reduced the disease to triviality in 1943, it is sobering to realize that in spite of all that modern hospital care could ac-complish, the average mortality remained between 60 and 70 percent of those afflicted.

Despite such virulence, communications patterns of medieval Europe were not so closely knit that everyone was exposed, even though an errant ship and infected rat population could and did bring the plague to remote Greenland and similarly distant outliers of the European heartlands. Overall, the best estimate of plague-provoked mortality, 1346–50, in Europe as a whole is that about one-third of the total population died. This is based on a projection upon the whole Continent of probable mortality rates in the British Isles, where the industry of two generations of scholars has narrowed the range of uncertainty to a decrease in population during the plague's initial onset of something between 20 and 45 percent. Transferring British statistics to the Continent as a whole at best defines an approximate magnitude for guess-estimation. In northern Italy and French Mediterranean coastlands, population losses were probably higher; in Bohemia and Poland much less; and for Russia and the Balkans no estimates have even been attempted.

Whatever the reality may have been—and it clearly varied sharply from community to community and in ways no one could in the least comprehend—we can be sure that the shock to

William H. McNeill, *Plagues and Peoples* (Garden City, NY: Doubleday, 1976), pp. 166, 168–69.

accustomed ways and expectations was severe. Moreover, the plague did not disappear from Europe after its first massive attack. Instead, recurrent plagues followed at irregular intervals, and with varying patterns of incidence, sometimes rising to a new severity, and then again receding. Places that had escaped the first onset commonly experienced severe die-off in later epidemics. When the diseases returned to places where it had raged before, those who had recovered from a previous attack were, of course, immune, so that death tolls tended to concentrate among those born since the previous plague year.

In most parts of Europe, even the loss of as much as a quarter of the population did not, at first, make very lasting differences. Rather heavy population pressure on available resources before 1346 meant that eager candidates were at hand for most of the vacated places. Only positions requiring relatively high skills—farm managers or teachers of Latin, for instance—were likely to be in short supply. But the recurrences of plague in the 1360s and 1370s altered this situation. Manpower shortages came to be widely felt in agriculture and other humble occupations; the socioeconomic pyramid was altered, in different ways in different parts of Europe, and darker climates of opinion and feeling became as chronic and inescapable as the plague itself. Europe, in short, entered upon a new era of its history, embracing as much diversity as ever, since reactions and readjustments followed differing paths in different regions of the Continent, but everywhere nonetheless different from the patterns that had prevailed before 1346.

After reading this selection, consider these questions:
1. Why did plague outbreaks vary so much from one locality to another?
2. How was the plague spread?
3. How would the loss of so many people affect European society?

CHAPTER 18
The Renaissance: Why Did Europeans Attempt to Recover the West's Classical Past?

The French word *renaissance* means "rebirth." More than a hundred years ago, the word was coined by historians who wanted to explain why and how Europe recovered its vitality after the catastrophes of the mid–fourteenth century. Although the concept of a "Renaissance period" in Europe between the late fourteenth and early sixteenth centuries is a modern historians' interpretation (no one sounded a trumpet flourish and announced that the Renaissance had begun!), educated Europeans of the time were conscious of a growing movement to recover the values of Greek and Latin antiquity. "Recovery," "revival," "rebirth," "renovation," "restoration," and other "re-" words were on many contemporary lips.

The emphasis on "recovery" underscores one dimension of the Renaissance: its conservatism. Scholars, artists, and artisans thought of themselves as returning to the perfection of ancient cultural models, not as forging new paths. Imitation was the ideal; "innovation" was something you accused an opponent of doing. Imitation, however, could mean many things. In painting, nature should be "imitated" by using the tricks of perspective to achieve a sense of depth and roundness, and depictions of individuals were increasingly expected to reveal the subject's personality or the drama of a situation. The growing ranks of wealthy laypersons, especially in such Italian cities as Florence and Venice, thirsted for literary and philosophical works that they could understand in terms of human values; the dry logic of professional medieval philosophers left them cold. And what better models for accessible literature and philosophy were there than the elegantly phrased classics of Greece and Rome? These works, too, the creative spirits of the Renaissance imitated, responding to what wealthy bankers and merchants (who paid for it all) wanted. Talented painters, sculptors, architects, poets, and even historians arose who could satisfy the changing tastes of the day. They produced some of humanity's greatest accomplishments.

As you read the selections that make up chapter 18, ask yourself whether the culture of Renaissance Europe can properly be described as "progress." Remember that progress—the sense that things are getting better and that history is moving forward rather than turning in endless cycles, or perhaps degenerating from the standards of a "golden age" of the past—was not a concept in which educated people of the Renaissance era believed.

SELECTION 1:

Human Dignity

This selection is a characteristic piece of Renaissance thought from the late fifteenth century. Its author, a minor Italian prince named Giovanni Pico della Mirandola (1463–1494), was well educated in humanism, as well as in the methods of medieval professional philosophers. Humanism is a concept that is often misinterpreted. In medieval and Renaissance Europe, teachers of "the humanities"—that is, humanists—were those who specialized in Latin literature and grammar, rather than in the more technical subjects in the curriculum such as logic. (See chapter 17, selection 3.) With lay patrons increasingly interested in ideas drawn from ancient literature that they could understand, rather than in abstract philosophical debates that they could not follow, the formerly rather low prestige of teachers of the humanities rose.* Renaissance humanists did not teach anti-Christian paganism; most of them were intensely devout and rather pedantic. But they did insist that ancient literature and philosophy offered many lessons for Christians of their own time, complementing, but not replacing, Christian teachings.

Pico della Mirandola's Oration on the Dignity of Man *must be read with the differing aims of medieval and Renaissance thought in mind. He wrote his oration in 1487 as the opening speech in a grand debate to which he challenged the academic philosophers of his time. In this debate he proposed to argue that the human mind was capable of reconciling all the seemingly contradictory opinions that contemporary scholars were uncovering as they delved deeper into ancient learning—not only Latin, but also Greek and even ancient Hebrew and Babylonian thought. Not merely philosophy, but also magic and other arcane ancient lore, were part of Pico's mental universe. Unfortunately, the debate never took place. The pope forbade it, sensing that Pico was venturing too far into dangerous waters—and perhaps thinking that the young man (he was only twenty-four years old) did not know what he was talking about. Still, Pico had produced a classic statement of confidence in human abilities. Read his oration, and judge for yourself.*

*Remember that the humanities were basically the introductory courses in medieval universities, which did not lead to lucrative professions such as the law, medicine, or advanced theology.

At last I feel that I have come to understand why it is that man, the most fortunate of all living things, deserves universal admiration; of what his proper place is in the hierarchy of beings that makes him the envy not only of brutes, but as well of the astral beings and the very intelligences which inhabit the world's outer limits—a being beggaring belief and smiting the soul with awe.

And why should this not be so? Is it not precisely on this ground that man, with full justification is considered to be, as he is called, a great miracle? Hear then, O Fathers, just what the condition of man is; and grant me, in the name of your humanity, your gracious hearing, as I develop this theme.

God the Father, almighty architect, in accord with his mysterious wisdom had already created this sensible world, this cosmic habitation of divinity, this most revered temple; He had already dressed the supercelestial arena with intelligences, informed the celestial spheres with the life of immortal souls, and set the dung-heap of the inferior world into ferment, swarming with every form of animal life; but when all this was accomplished, the divine artificer still felt the lack of some creature capable of comprehending the meaning of so great an achievement—a creature which might be stirred with love at its beauty, and struck with awe at its grandeur. Thus, after the completion of all else—as both Moses and Timaeus [a figure in one of Plato's Dialogues] witness—finally, he conceived of man's creation.

However, in truth, there was left to him no archetype [model] according to which he might form this new being. His treasures, all but spent, contained nothing fit with which to endow a new son; nor among the seats of the universe was there left a place from which this new creature might comprehend the world. All space was already taken; all beings had been relegated to their proper high, middle, or low order. But the Father's power was such that it would not falter in this last creative urge; nor was it in the nature of the Supreme Wisdom to fail through lack of counsel in this matter; nor, finally, was it in the nature of his beneficent love to create a creature destined to praise the divine generosity in all other things, who lacked it in himself.

The Super Maker, at last, decreed that this creature to whom he could give nothing uniquely his own, should share in the heritage of all other creatures. Taking this creature of indeterminate image, man, he therefore set him in the center of the world and spoke to him thus:

"O Adam, We have given you neither visage nor endowment uniquely your own, so that whatever place, form, or gifts you may select after pondering the matter, you may have and keep through your own judgment and decision. All other creatures have their natures defined and limited by laws which We have established; you, by contrast, unimpeded by any such limits, may, by your own free choice, to whose custody We have assigned you, establish the features of your own nature. I have set you at the center of the world so that from that position you may search about you with the greater ease upon all that is in the world contained."

After reading this selection, consider these questions:

1. How does Pico della Mirandola's oration summarize the Renaissance view of humans?
2. Does his oration fit your view of humanity?
3. If Pico della Mirandola's oration is not correct, then how do you think it should be amended?

Arturo B. Fallacio and Herman Shapiro, trans., *Renaissance Philosophy*, vol. 1, *The Italian Philosophers* (New York: Modern Library, 1967), pp. 142–43.

SELECTION 2:

The Education of a Renaissance Prince

The demand for a classical education was evident in every court in fifteenth-century Italy. Diplomatic dispatches and official histories had to be written in elegant Latin, not in the crabbed and technical language of academic experts, providing attractive career opportunities for middle-class and aristocratic young men. Nobles and courtiers found it to their benefit to be able to correspond and converse with friends, rivals, and mistresses in good Italian larded with allusions to fashionable art and literature. In Mantua, a small principality in northern Italy, the marchioness Isabella d'Este was energetic in offering patronage to librarians, artists, and musicians. Especially concerned about the schooling of her son, Federico, she employed the tutor Francesco Vigilio to oversee his training. In this selection, Vigilio writes to Isabella about the young man's progress. Notice the importance of Livy and Cicero as models to be imitated (see chapter 9, selections 1 and 2). You may want to compare its contents with your own education.

During your Highness' absence, your son, my master Signor Federico, has not failed to attend my instructions twice a day. It is true that he cannot keep up his attention for more than an hour, or a little longer, but during this time he is really attentive and diligent. We have gone through the abridged history of Livy, and he has translated two books of Valerius with me at hand to help him when he seemed puzzled, and now he knows Roman history and the laws and constitution of the State so well that he can sometimes remind me of things that I have forgotten, and even find me the passage I require. I have taught him a work of Ovid, *In Ibim*, full of little-known stories and fables, and he seems particularly fond of history, which I think is especially useful for a prince. I have also read some beautiful elegies with him.

He does not find verses easy, although he knows how to scan them, but he construes orations very easily. Every day I dictate some epistles to him, which he writes correctly—unless he makes an accidental slip—and every day I expound an Epistle of Cicero to him, in order that he may acquire a good style. In the grammar examination he answered my questions more quickly and better than any of the other boys. I have made him run through Petrarch, as good practice in reading, and he himself has chosen to read some books of the *Orlandos*, on which he often spends as much as two hours at a time. This is our method of learning letters.

As for his conduct in other ways, I see nothing in him which does not lead me to hope for a glorious and honorable career, and although the natural ardor of youth inclines him to love, his conduct in this respect persuades me that he will avoid the license which is displeasing both to God and men. I earnestly entreat Your Excellency to condescend to help my labors with your exhortations.

Julia Cartwright, *Isabella de'Este, Marchioness of Mantua, 1474–1539*, 2nd ed. vol. 2 (New York: E.P. Dutton, 1923), p. 121–23.

Your devoted servant, Jo. Franc. Vigilius

After reading this selection, consider these questions:

1. How does Vigilio's teaching reflect the values of the Renaissance?
2. Compare his textbooks with those that you use.
3. What would be the positive and negative features of such an education?

SELECTION 3:

Life in a Renaissance City

Florence, beautifully situated in the hill country north of Rome, was the largest and richest city of fourteenth- and fifteenth-century Italy. Its wealth derived from its textile manufacture, which its merchants marketed throughout Europe, investing their profits in banking. On these solid economic foundations, the culture of the early Renaissance flourished.

Florentine politics, however, were exceedingly complex and tense. In the following selection, American historian Gene Brucker, a lifelong student of Florentine history, summarizes the function of institutions that originated in the Middle Ages in the era of the Renaissance.

Brucker uses some terms that must be understood. The Popolo *(people) meant the whole body of Florentine citizens, most of whom were not at all rich. The* Commune *was the city itself, to which every citizen was required to swear obedience. The* Signoria *was the the city's government, chosen by a complex system of lots that was subject to considerable manipulation by inner circles of important men. Guilds were associations of artisans or merchants that controlled various branches of the economy, which only men, and occasionally their widows, of proven skill and financial standing could join. The* Parte Guelfa *(Guelf Party) was a hereditary political association of loyal citizens dating from the city's medieval struggle for liberty against the German emperors; membership in it was essential for active citizenship in Florence.*

With these definitions in mind, consider the elaborate network of sworn associations, brotherhoods, and other arrangements for ensuring social and political reciprocity that dominated Florentine life in the Renaissance. If individuality and self-expression was the hallmark of the Renaissance man, what room for such qualities do you see in the story Brucker tells?

From the beginnings of their documented past, medieval Florentines (like other Italian city-dwellers) had displayed a strong and persistent impulse to band together into associations, and to invest those bodies with a corporate character. They drafted constitutions specifying the rights

Gene Brucker, *The Civic World of Renaissance Florence* (Princeton, NJ: Princeton University Press, 1977), pp. 14–15, 18–19.

and obligations of membership; they exacted oaths of fealty; they convened assemblies; they levied dues and services. These organizations gave their members a measure of security in a turbulent world where public authority was weak, and where survival depended upon cooperation and mutual assistance. In addition to providing support, both material and psychic, they performed an important social function by resolving conflicts and restraining violence among their members. As Florence grew in size, and her society and polity became more complex, new associations were formed in response to changing needs. A citizen of Dante's generation (*c.* 1300) would customarily belong to several of these societies: a guild, a confraternity, the Parte Guelfa, the commune.

The commune of the *trecento* [the 1300's; that is, the fourteenth century] was a composite of these collectivities, and the institutional embodiment of the corporate spirit. Its legislative councils, of the *Popolo* and the Commune, were the organs of political associations that had been formed in the past. Membership in the commune was restricted to citizens who were matriculated into one or more of the city's twenty-one guilds. Comprising the supreme executive, the Signoria, were eight priors chosen as representatives of the guild community, and the standard-bearer of justice. Among the groups which advised the Signoria on policy, and voted on legislation, were agents of corporations that had been integrated into the communal structure: the sixteen standard-bearers of the militia companies who represented the city's neighborhoods; the captains of the Parte Guelfa; the guild consuls. Every magistracy—from the Signoria to the officials charged with collecting gabelles [taxes on salt] at the city gates or those responsible for internal security—functioned collegially: debating issues, promulgating edicts, levying fines.

The corporate ethos was fundamentally egalitarian. Members of a guild, political society *(parte),* or militia company *(gonfalone)* were assumed to possess equal rights and privileges, and to bear equal obligations to the society and their fellows. "If any one of us is offended or outraged by any person," so read a clause in the charter of a fourteenth-century Guelf association, "each and every one is obligated to help, defend and avenge him with his life and property, and to respond to that quarrel as though it were his own person." By joining a corporation, the Florentine acquired "brothers" who, individually and collectively, could make claims upon him that he had sworn an oath to acknowledge. These obligations took no account of differences in wealth, social status, or personal qualities. "Members of late medieval confraternities and *corpora mystica*," [Canadian historian] Lionel Rothkrug has written, "were compelled by oath of entry to treat every other person in the community according to a whole set of reciprocal rights and duties without regard to personal choice." In theory if not always in practice, that principle applied to every corporate society in Florence, whether religious or secular.

This corporate spirit was revealed most graphically during the celebrations honoring Florence's patron, John the Baptist. Every year, on the day before the saint's feast (24 June), the guilds displayed the finest examples of their wares and skills: in cloth-making and leatherwork, in gold ornaments and woodcarving. Competing for the public's attention were members of religious confraternities, "who assemble [Gregorio Dati reported] at the place where their meetings are held, dressed as angels, and with musical instruments of every kind and marvelous singing. They stage the most beautiful representations of the saints, and of those relics in whose honor they perform." Later that day, representatives from each of the city's sixteen electoral districts (*gonfaloni*) brought candles to the Baptistery, as offerings to their patron saint. On the feast day itself, a more formal procession moved through the streets, headed by the captains of the Parte Guelfa, prominent citizens, Messer Rinaldo Gianfigliazzi and Messer Donato Acciaiuoli, carried the banners of the *popolo* and the Parte Guelfa around the square, followed by a large crowd shouting: "Long live the *popolo* and the Parte Guelfa!". . .

To perceive the family, the lineage, as a corporate unit in a social order formed by collectivities is to grasp an important truth about this urban community. Though the family had no charter or constitution, nor formal rules and regulations, it was—and remained—the most cohesive force in Florentine society through the Renaissance and beyond. Lineages were held together by *fidei commissum* [a pledge of fidelity]; by jointly owned property and businesses; by common political interests and objectives; above all, by identification with, and loyalty to, a family tradition. The bonds of kinship had changed significantly since the halcyon days of the *consorterie* [elite aristocrats] in the late twelfth and early thirteenth centuries. The infiltration of "new men" into the city, the rise of the *popolo,* the enactment of legislation concerning magnates, the demographic and economic crises of the mid-fourteenth century: these developments had combined to transform, and perhaps to weaken, kinship ties. Florentines in 1400 were rather more reluctant than formerly to participate in vendettas, less willing, perhaps, to risk money on behalf of relatives plagued by economic misfortune or threatened by neighbors or the commune. In 1373, Foligno de' Medici recalled with nostalgia a past time when his family was strong and unified, "and every man feared us." But some scholars have exaggerated the disintegration of the lineage in the fourteenth century, just as they have emphasized too strongly the debility of other corporate bodies. The trend is not a simple declension from strength to weakness, from cohesion to fragmentation, but a more complex pattern of flux and reflux, of breakdown and reconstitution.

After reading this selection, consider these questions:

1. Why did the Florentines join so many societies?
2. What means were used to bond members belonging to a society?
3. What was the relationship between guilds and the signoria?

SELECTION 4:

Shakespeare's Star-Crossed Renaissance Lovers

William Shakespeare's (1564–1616) poetic tragedy Romeo and Juliet, *which was written and first performed in London in the early 1590s, was based on a tale, supposedly true, from the Renaissance city of Verona in northern Italy. Shakespeare added a number of characters and situations that greatly enhanced the subtlety and dramatic impact of his play, but the heart of the tragedy came directly from the original source. Renaissance audiences would immediately understand that the play was about the ways in which feuds between wealthy, rival families could tear apart the kind of delicately balanced community that Gene Brucker has described in the previous selection.*

In Shakespeare's tragedy, the prince of Verona—who is supposed to uphold law and order—is at first insufficiently ruthless. He relies on mere promises that the feuding families will behave themselves, which of course they fail to do. And the young lovers suffer not only because they fail to understand how deadly is their elders' mutual hatred, but also because they let their passions outrun good sense. In an age in which marriages in every respectable family were arranged by one's grown-up kin, falling in love with the wrong person could be deadly. Read the following selection with this in mind.

Enter Prince Escalus with his Train.
PRINCE. Rebellious subjects, enemies to peace,
Profaners of this neighbor-stained steel—
Will they not hear? What ho! you men, you beasts,
That quench the fire of your pernicious rage
With purple fountains issuing from your veins—
On pain of torture, from those bloody hands
Throw your mistemper'd weapons to the ground
And hear the sentence of your moved Prince.
Three civil brawls, bred of an airy word,
By thee, old Capulet and Montague,
Have thrice disturb'd the quiet of our streets
And made Verona's ancient citizens
Cast by their grave beseeming ornaments
To wield old partisans, in hands as old,
Canker'd with peace, to part your canker'd hate.
If ever you disturb our streets again
Your lives shall pay the forfeit of the peace.
For this time all the rest depart away.
You Capulet, shall go along with me.
And Montague, come you this afternoon
To know our farther pleasure in this case
To old Freetown, our common judgment place.
Once more, on pain of death, all men depart. . . .

[*Enter Juliet at the window.*]
Romeo: It is my lady! O it is my love!
O that she knew she were!
She speaks yet she says nothing, what of that?
Her eye discourses, I will answer it.
I am too bold, 'tis not to me she speaks.
Two of the fairest stars in all the heaven,
Having some business, do entreat her eyes
To twinkle in their spheres till they return.
What if her eyes were there, they in her head?
The brightness of her cheek would shame those stars
As daylight doth a lamp; her eye in heaven

Would through the airy region stream so bright
That birds would sing and think it were not night.
See how she leans her cheek upon her hand!
O that I were a glove upon that hand
That I might touch that cheek.
   Juliet.   Ay me!
   Romeo.   She speaks.
O speak again, bright angel, for thou art
As glorious to this night, being o'er my head,
As is a winged messenger of Heaven
Unto the white-upturned wond'ring eyes
Of mortals that fall back to gaze on him
When he bestrides the lazy puffing clouds
And sails upon the bosom of the air.
   Juliet. O Romeo, Romeo, wherefore art thou Romeo?
Deny thy father and refuse thy name;
Or if thou wilt not, be but sworn my love
And I'll no longer be a Capulet.
   Romeo. Shall I hear more or shall I speak at this?
   Juliet. 'Tis but thy name that is my enemy,
Thou art thyself, though not a Montague.
What's Montague? it is nor hand nor foot
Nor arm nor face. O be some other name
Belonging to a man.
What's in a name? that which we call a rose
By any other word would smell as sweet.
So Romeo would, were he not Romeo call'd,
Retain that dear perfection which he owes
Without that title. Romeo, doff thy name,
And for thy name, which is no part of thee,
Take all myself.
   Romeo.   I take thee at thy word.
Call me but Love and I'll be new baptiz'd,
Henceforth I never will be Romeo.
   Juliet. What man art thou that thus bescreen'd in night
So stumblest on my counsel?
   Romeo.   By a name
I know not how to tell thee who I am.
My name, dear saint, is hateful to myself

William Shakespeare, *The Tragedy of Romeo and Juliet,* Richard Hosley, ed. (New Haven, CT: Yale University Press, 1954), pp. 6, 8–9.

Because it is an enemy to thee.
Had I it written, I would tear the word.

After reading this selection, consider these questions:
1. Based on the evidence of this selection, would you be inclined to sympathize with Prince Escalus?
2. What does Juliet mean when she asks, "O Romeo, Romeo, wherefore art thou Romeo?"
3. Is the romantic passion expressed in *Romeo and Juliet* out of fashion today? Justify your answer.

SELECTION 5:

The Scientific Genius of Leonardo da Vinci

The Renaissance virtually invented the concept of genius. The word itself is Latin, meaning the "inner spirit" that makes someone unique. With the greater consciousness about the value of creativity that Renaissance art and learning fostered, artists and thinkers ceased to be the rather anonymous craftspeople they were considered in medieval society. Their genius—their special dignity as creators of something profound or beautiful—defined their worth.

Leonardo da Vinci (1452–1519) was the archetypal Renaissance genius, both in the original sense that we have defined here and in the modern meaning of the word, that of a person of extraordinarily high intelligence. He was not a conventionally learned man: He had been trained as a painter, and he claimed to scorn humanists whose learning rested on having memorized mountains of books. As a painter, his ambition, which most critics would say he achieved with spectacular success, was to produce the most perfect imitations of nature, which meant portraits that not only rendered physical qualities as lifelike as possible but also revealed the subject's innermost personality. But Leonardo's fascination with nature also led him to study the natural world around him with the analytical eye of an artist and an engineer. His observations and speculations were recorded in his private notebooks. Often he went far beyond the conventional ideas of his time. A modern American historian of the Renaissance explains in this selection.

For remarkable universality of mind and perceptive insights into the structure and operation of nature, no other Renaissance figure surpassed the searching genius of Leonardo da Vinci. From earliest youth, Leonardo possessed an insatiable appetite for knowledge. In his lifelong quest for learning, he considered the great teacher to be na-

De Lamar Jensen, *Renaissance Europe* (Lexington: D.C. Heath, 1981), pp. 165–67.

ture itself, not books, traditions, or authorities. He was not only an acute observer of nature, perhaps the greatest of his age, he was also a discoverer of its characteristics and properties. . . .

Paramount in understanding Leonardo as a scientist is to remember that he was more interested in the nature of things—the operation of forces; the problems of weight, movement, and pressure; the theories of mechanics and dynamics—than he was in the successful operation of any particular machine. In the words of one modern writer, he was "a scientific explorer rather than a colonizer," a visionary more than a practitioner. Leonardo considered mathematics the basis of all science, and he was aware of mathematical proportions in nature, believing mathematical principles could be used to explain and measure all physical phenomena. "The economy of nature," he wrote, "is quantitative, or one may say, mathematical."

The range of Leonardo's interests is impressive. In his notebooks he recorded, sketched, and diagrammed his observations and experiments on hundreds of scientific topics. He contemplated the heavens and concluded that the universe was a celestial machine, governed by laws of mathematical precision. He declared also that the earth was similar to the sun in giving off rays of heat and light that could be observed if one were far enough away from the surface. From his observations of water, he drew many conclusions about the pressure of fluids and their movement through channels and orifices. Water power fascinated him and he devised numerous ways of harnessing it for useful mechanical purposes. He even suggested a wave theory of light based on its similarity to the movement of waves on water. Leonardo was also enchanted by air and by the challenge to conquer it. He recorded almost endless observations of birds in flight and of the functions of their various parts as they climbed, soared, and alighted. These analyses of the processes of flight in birds led him inevitably to suggestions for flying machines of various types, and the recommendation for a parachute made like a "tent roof of which the pores have all been filled." But Leonardo's enthusiasm for flight did not preclude his practicality, as the following note, accompanying one of his designs, reveals: "This machine should be tried over a lake, and you should carry a long wine skin as a girdle so that in case you fall you will not be drowned."

Exploring the high Alps in search of fossils and other geological artifacts, Leonardo concluded that the earth was much older than anyone had previously suspected, and that the presence of salt-water fossils suggested great physical upheavals and changes in the earth's surface since the first appearance of plant and animal life. While investigating the physical properties of matter and the nature of various forces, he gave meaningful thought to such factors as the tensile strength of different materials and to the effects of friction. Perhaps his most impressive experiments and observations, based on his personal dissection of some thirty cadavers during his lifetime, were in the fields of anatomy and physiology. He described the results in hundreds of unique drawings and sketches.

After reading this selection, consider these questions:

1. How do you explain genius?
2. How would Leonardo's concern for mathematics assist him as a painter?
3. Explain why you might think Pico della Mirandola's vision of the Renaissance man was fulfilled in Leonardo's life.

SELECTION 6:

Mona Lisa

Giorgio Vasari (1511–1574) today is little regarded for his painting, but his biographies of the leading artists of Renaissance Italy are a major historical legacy. His accounts of the lives of Michelangelo and Leonardo da Vinci, for example, helped create the image of the awesome genius for which these artists are still remembered. In the following selection he tells his reader how Leonardo painted that most famous of all Renaissance paintings, the Mona Lisa, which now hangs in the Louvre in Paris.

For Francesco del Giocondo, Leonardo undertook to paint the portrait of Mona Lisa, his wife, but, after loitering over it for four years, he finally left it unfinished. This work is now in the possession of King Francis of France, and is at Fontainebleau. Whoever shall desire to see how far art can imitate nature, may do so to perfection in his head, wherein every peculiarity that could be depicted by the utmost subtlety of the pencil has been faithfully reproduced. The eyes have the lustrous brightness and moisture which is seen in life, and around them are those pale, red, and slightly livid circles, also proper to nature, with the lashes, which can only be copied, as these are, with the greatest difficulty; the eyebrows also are represented with the closest exactitude, where fuller and where more thinly set, with the separate hairs delineated as they issue from the skin, every turn being followed, and all the pores exhibited in a manner that could not be more natural than it is: the nose, with its beautiful and delicately roseate nostrils, might be easily believed to be alive; the mouth, admirable in its outline, has the lips uniting the rose-tints of their colour with that of the face, in the utmost perfection, and the carnation of the cheek does not appear to be painted, but truly of flesh and blood: he who looks earnestly at the pit of the throat cannot but believe that he sees the beating of the pulses, and it may be truly said that this work is painted in a manner well calculated to make the boldest master tremble, and astonishes all who behold it, however well accustomed to the marvels of art. Mona Lisa was exceedingly beautiful, and while Leonardo was painting her portrait, he took the precaution of keeping some one constantly near her, to sing or play on instruments, or to jest and otherwise amuse her, to the end that she might continue cheerful, and so that her face might not exhibit the melancholy expression often imparted by painters to the likenesses they take. In this portrait of Leonardo's, on the contrary, there is so pleasing an expression, and a smile so sweet, that while looking at it one thinks it rather divine than human, and it has ever been esteemed a wonderful work, since life itself could exhibit no other appearance.

After reading this selection, consider these questions:
1. Does art always imitate nature?
2. Why would portrait painting be very popular with Renaissance artists?
3. Why would Mona Lisa need to be entertained while she sat for her portrait?

Giorgio Vasari, *Lives of . . . Painters, Sculptors, and Architects*, E.H. and E.W. Blashfield and A.A. Hopkins, eds, vol. 2 (New York: Charles Scribner's Sons, 1923), 164–65.

UNIT 4

African and American Centers of Early Civilization

CONTENTS

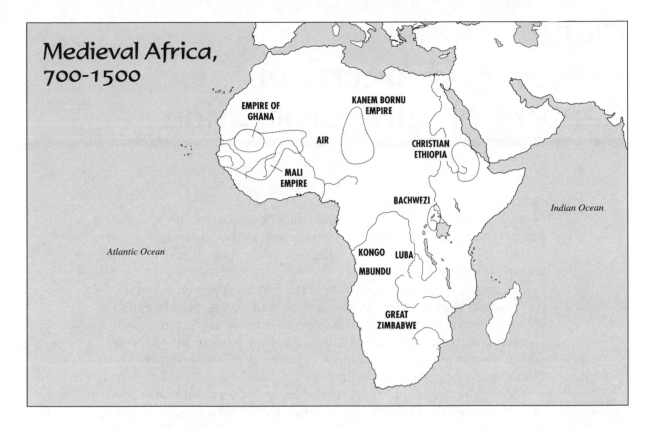

Medieval Africa, 700-1500

EMPIRE OF GHANA

KANEM BORNU EMPIRE

AIR

CHRISTIAN ETHIOPIA

MALI EMPIRE

BACHWEZI

Indian Ocean

Atlantic Ocean

KONGO   LUBA

MBUNDU

GREAT ZIMBABWE

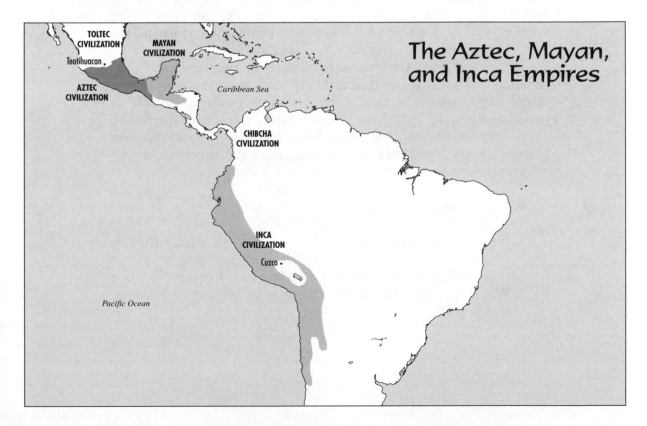

The Aztec, Mayan, and Inca Empires

TOLTEC CIVILIZATION

Teotihuacan

MAYAN CIVILIZATION

Caribbean Sea

AZTEC CIVILIZATION

CHIBCHA CIVILIZATION

INCA CIVILIZATION

Cuzco

Pacific Ocean

Unit 4
African and American Centers of Early Civilization

The Southern Hemisphere, which includes most of Africa and South America, developed civilizations shaped by distinctive geographic characteristics. Some societies made their home in rain forests, others in deserts.

The first African kingdom south of the Sahara appeared in Nubia, the modern Sudan. Here, as we saw in unit 1, the people called Kushites formed a nation heavily dependent on an Egyptian model. Once events took their toll on Kush, the East African kingdom of Axum, located in modern Ethiopia, replaced the Kushites as the region's most sophisticated civilization.

The origin of states in West Africa depended on the introduction of the dromedary to carry goods from the Mediterranean to the *sahel*, the geographic region that separates the Sahara from the western African rain forest. Trade in gold and salt made possible the first major kingdoms of West Africa, as Muslim merchants and native Africans established centers in Ghana and Mali.

In the Americas, Mexico and Peru were the two centers of civilization, for both regions held a variety of plants that could support large populations. The lack of large animals, however, capable of domestication inhibited growth in this part of the world. The failure to use the wheel, and to develop a writing system known to anyone except priests, in addition to the isolation of the Americas, meant slower progress for the American Indians.

While reading the following selections, ask:

1. What enabled the trans-Saharan kingdoms of West Africa to prosper?
2. Is it possible to compare the Aztec and Inca Empires?
3. Was it a good thing for the Americas to be isolated from the Old World?

CHAPTER 19
Early Africa Below the Sahara: How Did the First Kingdoms Emerge?

Archaeological remains and written documents are rare, but not completely absent, for ancient African history. In chapter 3 (selection 6), for example, we have already encountered evidence for the important kingdom of Kush in the Upper Nile region, a neighbor and sometimes a rival of the ancient Egyptian civilization. We also know that knowledge of iron smelting was widespread in sub-Saharan Africa at about the same time—around 1000 B.C.—that this important technological advance was transforming the history of the Southwest Asia.

Much evidence for ancient African history, however, comes from linguistics, folklore, and physical and human geography. Analyzing this evidence, historians believe that some two thousand years ago the Bantu people began to expand from their original homeland in present-day Nigeria and Cameroun. Mastery of ironworking and the introduction of certain high-energy foods such as bananas, cassava, and taro that had originated in Southeast Asia are believed to have aided the Bantu expansion. Relatively quickly, the Bantu spread, first across the Sudan to East Africa and then southward. Eventually they occupied most of sub-Saharan Africa. Indigenous peoples whom the migrating Bantu discovered were either absorbed or displaced into areas that were less desirable from the standpoint of human habitation—for example, the Pygmies into the central African rain forest or the Khoi Khoi (Bushmen) into southwestern Africa's deserts. As a result, most present-day blacks of sub-Saharan Africa speak one of more than two hundred languages of the Bantu family, including Swahili, today the common tongue of East Africa.

The selections in this chapter suggest something of the range of evidence on which historians can piece together the story of early African history. These sources encompass oral traditions (selection 3), African kingdoms' written records (selection 2), Muslim visitors' accounts (selections 1, 4, and 5), and geographical evidence (selection 6). As you read, ask yourself how historians have learned about early African civilization.

SELECTION 1:

Ancient Ghana

The interior of West Africa was the original Bantu homeland. The earliest written accounts of this region date from the tenth and eleventh centuries A.D., when Arabic-speaking Muslim traders crossed the Sahara desert in camel caravans. They were seeking gold, for which West Africa was a major source, and which the West Africans were willing to trade in exchange for salt, cloth, and various utensils.

The Muslims found flourishing towns and indigenous kingdoms in West Africa dependent on agriculture. Peoples' religion centered on the worship of natural forces, which the Muslims rejected as idolatry. Soon, however, some native people began to convert to Islam and to form separate communities.

Ghana was the oldest West African kingdom to be visited by Muslim traders. This state has nothing in common, except for the borrowed name, with the modern Republic of Ghana, on the coast of West Africa. The ancient kingdom of Ghana lay in the interior, on the grassland south of the Sahara, in what is now the Republic of Mauritania. The most detailed account of it was written about A.D. 1067 by a resident of Islamic Spain, Ubaydallah al-Bakri. He was not an eyewitness, but gathered from others oral and written reports, which he assembled in his library in the Spanish city of Córdoba. His account demonstrates that Ghana was already a well-organized kingdom.

The city of Ghana consists of two towns in a plain. One of these towns is inhabited by Muslims. It is large with a dozen mosques in one of which they assemble for the Friday prayer. . . . Around the town are wells of sweet water from which they drink and near which they cultivate vegetables.

The royal town, called al-Ghaba ["the grove"], is six miles away [from the Muslim town], and the area between the two towns is covered with houses. Their houses are made of stone and acacia wood. The king has a palace and conical huts, surrounded by a wall-like enclosure. In the king's town, not far from the royal court of justice, is a mosque where pray the Muslims who come there on missions. . . .

Around the king's town are domed huts and groves where live the sorcerers, the men in charge of their religious cult. In these are also the idols and the tombs of their kings. These groves are guarded, no one can enter them nor discover their contents. The prisons of the king are there, and if anyone is imprisoned in them, no more is ever heard of him. . . .

Their religion is paganism and the worship of idols. When the king dies, they build a huge dome of wood over the burial place.

After reading this selection, consider these questions:

1. Why did the Muslims live in a separate town in Ghana?

Al-Bakri, quoted in Nehemia Levtzion, *Ancient Ghana and Mali*, vol. 7 of *Studies in African History* (London: Methuen, 1973), pp. 22–23, 25.

2. Why would the sacred groves be off-limits to ordinary people?

3. What would a Muslim think of Ghana's religion?

SELECTION 2:

The Rock Churches of Lalibela

The Ethiopian people of northeastern Africa are not Bantus, but represent a fusion of Semitic and dark-skinned Hamitic ethnic groups. The modern state of Ethiopia is the successor to a long series of ancient and medieval kingdoms that traded with both Egypt and southern Arabia. In the fourth and fifth centuries A.D., Christian monks from the Mediterranean world reached the rich kingdom of Axum, which controlled both northern Ethiopia and adjacent parts of southern Arabia, and converted it to Christianity. However, the Muslim conquest of Egypt and Nubia cut off Axum and later Ethiopian kingdoms from the rest of Christendom. The Ethiopians retained their version of Christianity, which differed in some respects from the Byzantine and western European faiths, and turned their expansive energies southward. In the early thirteenth century, Emperor Lalibela (ca. 1185–1225) ordered ten Christian churches to be sculpted out of living rock, carved by persevering masons. In this selection, an Ethiopian chronicle describes what Lalibela ordered and how it was carried out. According to the chronicler, God had taken the king to heaven and showed him models of what he wanted; as the passage opens, God himself speaks.

"The time has come to construct churches like those which I showed you; arm yourself with the courage and energy necessary to accomplish this great work because souls will be saved by these churches! Hurry up and build them. I have ordered my angels to lend their help!"

[The chronicler, who was obviously immensely impressed by the churches, describes their construction in the following passages:]

Lalibela ordered the manufacture of a large number of iron tools of all kinds, some to cut out the stone, others to hew it, as well as many others for the construction of a temple in the rock. From that moment Lalibela no longer thought of his own needs or those of his wife, but fortified in everything by the Holy Spirit, dreamt each day of constructing the churches on the model of those which he had seen in Heaven. After having made the tools necessary for this work he ordered everyone to assemble and spoke to them, saying: "You who are all gathered together there, tell me what wages you want to help build these churches which God has ordered me to erect; let every man, stone mason and excavator of the soil alike, inform me as to the wage which he requires. Speak up, all of you, and what you ask of me I will give you so that you will not say that I made you work against your will, for I do not want your labor to be without recompense nor that you should murmur."

Richard K.P. Pankhurst, ed., *The Ethiopian Royal Chronicles* (Addis Abbaba: Oxford University Press, 1967), pp. 9–12.

Each person thereupon made known what he wanted and the king paid what he had promised. He did this without fail from the day the construction of the churches began till the day when it was finished. He gave wages to everyone, to those who cut the stone, to those who fashioned it, and to those who carried away the debris resulting from the cutting.

[Describing the method of work and the assistance rendered by the angels, the chronicle continues:]

The angels who were with the king made the measurements, indicating the required dimensions for all the churches, large and small. The land where the churches were to be built he purchased with gold, which was a great kindness on his part, for if he had wished to take it without payment who could have prevented him since he was king?

He first built a church resembling the one which God had shown him, an admirable work of art which a man could not create without divine wisdom; he embellished the inside and outside and gave it beautiful latticed windows. In front of this church he made two others, each with its own exit and separated inside by a partition provided with a door. Behind this he erected another large church which he adorned not with gold or silver, but with sculptures cut in stone; this latter church had seventy-two pillars. . . . To the left and right of this first church he dug out two others.

He named the first church Beta Maryam (House of Mary), the two in front Dabra Sina (Mount of Sinai) and Golgotha, that on the right Beta Masqal (House of the Cross), and that on the left Beta Danagel (House of the Virgins); he thus grouped together five beautiful churches cut from the same rock.

Near to these five churches he built two others which were very beautiful, but of a different construction; they were separated from each other by a partition wall; he called one Beta Gabriel (House of Gabriel) and the other Beta Abba Matae. He thus united these two churches, surrounding them with a single wall, and separated them within by a partition. He also built two other very beautiful churches, again of a different design; he called one of them Beta Marqorewos (House of Mercury) and the other Beta Amanuel (House of Emmanuel). Having grouped these two latter churches together, he built another, isolated church; it was constructed in a different way in the form of the cross, as the angels had indicated to him when they were making their measurements on the land; he gave it the name of Beta Giyorgis (House of George). He thus completed the construction of ten churches, each with different architecture and appearance.

[Claiming that all ten churches were an exact reproduction of those in Heaven that God had shown Lalibela, the chronicler goes on to assert that the greater part of the work had actually been effected not by men but by angels.]

When he began to construct these churches angels came to help him in each of the operations; there were thus a company of angels at work as well as a company of men, for angels joined the workers, the quarry men, the stone cutters and the laborers. The angels worked with them by day and by themselves by night. The men would do a cubit's work during the day, but would find a further three cubits completed on the morrow for the angels worked throughout the night. Seeing this the workers exclaimed, "How wonderful! We did a cubit yesterday and today we have four!" They doubted whether angels were doing this work because they could not see them, but Lalibela knew, because the angels, who understood his virtue, did not hide from him; the angels were his companions and for that reason did not hide from his sight.

After reading this selection, consider these questions:

1. What was special about Lalibela's churches?
2. How did the king learn how to build the churches?
3. What advantage would a church built by angels confer?

SELECTION 3:

Sundiata Creates Prosperity for Mali

At about the same time that Lalibela was ruling Ethiopia, a king named Sundiata (d. 1255) founded the empire of Mali. Like Ghana, Mali covered a large area in the interior of West Africa. But unlike Ghana, Mali was an Islamic state whose power rested on the wealth of trading clans and the support of the Malinke people, the ethnic group to which Sundiata belonged. After seizing power from earlier rulers, Sundiata built an efficient military machine with which he could undertake a great expansion of Mali's borders. Mali was the greatest power in West Africa until the early fifteenth century, and although thereafter its boundaries gradually shrank, it endured until the mid–sixteenth century.

Nominally a Muslim, Sundiata made himself acceptable to the non-Muslim majority of the people he ruled by appealing to ancient West African traditions—above all, the traditions of the native Malinke. His fame as a djata *(ruler) still endures in the region's folklore, as the following tale reveals. Such a tale would have been passed on by* grigots, *or storytellers, to which the following selection makes a reference.*

The villages of Mali gave Maghan Sundiata an unprecedented welcome. At normal times a traveler on foot can cover the distance from Ka-ba to Niani with only two halts, but Sogolon's son with his army took three days. The road to Mali from the river was flanked by a double human hedge. Flocking from every corner of Mali, all the inhabitants were resolved to see their savior from close up. The women of Mali tried to create a sensation and they did not fail. At the entrance to each village they had carpeted the road with their multi-colored *pagnes* [robes] so that Sundiata's horse would not so much as dirty its feet on entering their village. At the village exits the children, holding leafy branches in their hands, greeted Djata with cries of "Wassa, Wassa, Aye."

Sundiata was leading the van. He had donned his costume of a hunter king—a plain smock, skin-tight trousers and his bow sling across his back. At his side Balla Fasséké was still wearing his festive garments gleaming with gold. Between Djata's general staff and the army Sosso Balla [a rebel son] had been placed, amid his father's fetishes. But his hands were no longer tied. As at Ka-ba, abuse was everywhere heaped upon him and the prisoner did not dare look up at the hostile crowd. Some people, always ready to feel sympathy, were saying among themselves:

"How few things good fortune prizes!"

"Yes, the day you are fortunate is also the day when you are the most unfortunate, for in good fortune you cannot imagine what suffering is."

The troops were marching along singing the "Hymn to the Bow," which the crowd took up. New songs flew from mouth to mouth. Young women offered the soldiers cool water and cola nuts. And so the triumphal march across Mali ended outside Niani, Sundiata's city. . . .

D.T. Niane, *Sundiata: An Epic of Old Mali*, G.D. Pickett, trans. (London: Longman, Green, 1965), pp. 80–82.

In their new-found peace the villages knew prosperity again, for with Sundiata happiness had come into everyone's home. Vast fields of millet, rice, cotton, indigo and fonio surrounded the villages. Whoever worked always had something to live on. Each year long caravans carried the taxes in kind to Niani. You could go from village to village without fearing brigands. A thief would have his right hand chopped off and if he stole again he would be put to the sword.

New villages and new towns sprang up in Mali and elsewhere. *Dyulas*, or traders, became numerous and during the reign of Sundiata the world knew happiness.

There are some kings who are powerful through their military strength. Everybody trembles before them, but when they die nothing but ill is spoken of them. Others do neither good nor ill and when they die they are forgotten. Others are feared because they have power, but they know how to use it and they are loved because they love justice. Sundiata belonged to this group. He was feared, but loved as well. He was the father of Mali and gave the world peace. After him the world has not seen a greater conqueror, for he was the seventh and last conqueror. He had made the capital of an empire out of his father's village, and Niani became the navel of the earth. In the most distant lands Niani was talked of and foreigners said, "Travelers from Mali can tell lies with impunity," for Mali was a remote country for many peoples.

The griots, fine talkers that they were, used to boast of Niani and Mali saying: "If you want salt, go to Niani, for Niani is the camping place of the sahel [trans-Saharan] caravans. If you want gold, go to Niani, for Bouré, Bambougou and Wagadou work for Niani. If you want fine cloth, go to Niani, for the Mecca road passes by Niani. If you want fish, go to Niani, for it is there that the fishermen of Maouti and Djenné come to sell their catches. If you want meat, go to Niani, the country of the great hunters, and the land of the ox and the sheep. If you want to see an army, go to Niani, for it is there that the united forces of Mali are to be found. If you want to see a great king, go to Niani, for it is there that the son of Sogolon lives, the man with two names."

After reading this selection, consider these questions:

1. How did Sundiata celebrate his victories?
2. Compare the triumph of Sundiata with that of Pompey (see chapter 10).
3. What were the characteristics of Sundiata's rule?

Selection 4:

Ibn Battuta Describes Mali

One of the world's great travelers was the Moroccan Ibn Battuta (1304– 1368), whose journeys took him into many parts of the world. He holds the record for miles traveled in the fourteenth century. One of his destinations was Mali, and the following selection is his account of that visit. He speaks of the ruler of Mali as sultan, for the rulers were all Muslims.

On certain days the sultan holds audiences in the palace yard, where there is a platform under a tree, with three steps; this they call the *pempi*. It is carpeted with silk and has cushions placed on it. [Over it] is raised the umbrella, which is a sort of pavilion made of silk, surmounted by a bird in gold, about the size of a falcon. The sultan comes out of a door in a corner of the palace, carrying a bow in his hand and a quiver on his back. On his head he has a golden skull-cap, bound with a gold band which has narrow ends shaped like knives, more than a span in length. His usual dress is a velvety red tunic, made of the European fabrics called *mutanfas*. The sultan is preceded by his musicians, who carry gold and silver guimbris [two-stringed guitars], and behind him come three hundred armed slaves. He walks in a leisurely fashion, affecting a very slow movement, and even stops from time to time. On reaching the *pempi* he stops and looks round the assembly, then ascends it in the sedate manner of a preacher ascending a mosque-pulpit.

As he takes his seat the drums, trumpets, and bugles are sounded. Three slaves go out at a run to summon the sovereign's deputy and the military commanders, who enter and sit down. Two saddled and bridled horses are brought, along with two goats, which they hold to serve as a protection against the evil eye. Dugha [the royal interpreter] stands at the gate and the rest of the people remain in the street, under the trees. . . .

I was at Mali during the two festivals of the sacrifice and the fast-breaking. On these days the sultan takes his seat on the *pempi* after the midafternoon prayer. The armor-bearers bring in magnificent arms—quivers of gold and silver, swords ornamented with gold and with golden scabbards, gold and silver lances, and crystal maces. At his head stand four amirs driving off the flies, having in their hands silver ornaments resembling saddle-stirrups. The commanders, qadi, and a preacher sit in their usual places. The interpreter Dugha comes with his four wives and his slave-girls, who are about a hundred in number. They are wearing beautiful robes, and on their heads they have gold and silver fillets, with gold and silver balls attached. A chair is placed for Dugha to sit on. He plays on an instrument made of reeds, with some small calabashes at its lower end, and chants a poem in praise of the sultan, recalling his battles and deeds of valor.

The women and girls sing along with him and play with bows. Accompanying them are about thirty youths, wearing red woolen tunics and white skull-caps; each of them has his drum slung from his shoulder and beats it. Afterwards come his boy pupils who play and turn wheels in the air, like the natives of Sind. They show a marvelous nimbleness and agility in these exercises and play most cleverly with swords. Dugha also makes a fine play with the sword. Thereupon the sultan orders a gift to be presented to Dugha and he is given a purse containing two hundred *mithqals* of gold dust, and is informed of the contents of the purse before all the people. The commanders rise and twang their bows in thanks to the sultan. The next day each one of them gives Dugha a gift, every man according to his rank. Every Friday after the 'asr prayer, Dugha carries out a similar ceremony to this that we have described.

After reading this selection, consider these questions:

1. How did the kings of Mali attempt to impress their citizens?
2. What did Ibn Battuta think of his stay in Mali?
3. What role did music play in Malian celebrations?

Ibn Battuta *Travels in Asia and Africa*, H.A.R. Gibb, trans. (London: Routledge and Kegan Paul, 1929), p. 326.

SELECTION 5:

A Judgment on Mali

*The contemporary American historian Ross Dunn has written a study of what Ibn Battuta's travels reveal about the history of the world in the fourteenth century. Commenting, in this selection, on the Muslim globetrotter's account of Mali, Dunn notes that he was much offended by the failure of the ruler, Sulayman, to pay him sufficient attention. An earlier but still famous ruler of Mali, Mansa Musa (1307–1332), was much more to Ibn Battuta's liking. (*Mansa *is a title, not a name.) In reading Dunn's account, notice the interaction of Muslim and Malinke traditions, both of which the Malian rulers had to balance.*

Finally, on the advice of Dugha, he [Ibn Battuta] made an appeal to Sulayman, brashly raising the issue of the *mansa*'s prestige among the Muslim rulers of the world:

> I have journeyed to the countries of the world and met their kings. I have been four months in your country without your giving me a reception gift or anything else. What shall I say of you in the presence of other sultans?

In all probability Sulayman could not have cared less what this wandering jurist said of him. At first he sublimely disavowed having even known that Ibn Battuta was in the town. But when his notables reminded him that he had received the Moroccan a few months earlier and "sent him some food," the *mansa* offered him a house and an allowance in gold. Notwithstanding the sultan's desultory effort to put things right, Ibn Battuta never got over the indifferent treatment he received, concluding in the *Rihla* that Sulayman "is a miserly king from whom no great donation is to be expected" and that Mansa Musa by contrast had been "generous and virtuous."

Ibn Battuta ended a sojourn of a little more than eight months in the capital in a state of am-

bivalence over the qualities of Malian culture. On the one hand he respected Sulayman's just and stable government and the earnest devotion of the Muslim population to their mosque prayers and Koranic studies. "They place fetters on their children if there appears on their part a failure to memorize the Koran," he reports approvingly, "and they are not undone until they memorize it." On the other hand he reproached the Sudanese severely for practices obviously based in Malinke tradition but, from his point of view, either profane or ridiculous when set against the model of the rightly guided Islamic state: female slaves and servants who went stark naked into the court for all to see; subjects who groveled before the sultan, beating the ground with their elbows and throwing dust and ashes over their heads; royal poets who romped about in feathers and bird masks. Ibn Battuta seems indeed to be harsher on the Malians than he does on other societies of the Islamic periphery where behavior rooted in local tradition, but contrary to his scriptural and legal standards, colored religious and social practice. We may sense in his reportage a certain embarrassment that a kingdom whose Islam was so profoundly influenced by his own homeland and its Maliki doctors was not doing a better job keeping to the straight and narrow.

After reading this selection, consider these

Ross E. Dunn, *The Adventures of Ibn Battuta* (Berkeley and Los Angeles: University of California Press, 1986), pp. 303–304.

questions:
1. Why did Muslim travelers want to visit West Africa?
2. How did the Malinke tradition blend with Islam?
3. Why do you think Ibn Battuta was not offered better hospitality in Mali?

SELECTION 6:

The Swahili Coast

East Africa's historical experience was very different from West Africa's. The Indian Ocean provided the people of East Africa with access to Southwest Asia, India, China, and present-day Indonesia. Trade in commodities and ideas around the Indian Ocean's vast rim was brisk.

The Swahili—the indigenous people of East Africa—depended on the monsoons that in the Indian Ocean basin start blowing from the northeast in early November and become intense between December and February. The wind is hot and dry, allowing traders from India and Arabia to steer their sailing ships to Africa. Then the wind changes, blowing from the southwest, bringing heavy rain. The Swahili people knew the pattern well, and organized their economic life around it.

Keep in mind the importance of the Indian Ocean trade while reading the following selection, by the modern scholar John Middleton.

The Swahili coast, although divided into these several ecological and culturally differentiated stretches, is nonetheless a single entity in which land and ocean are intimately linked. . . . Swahili civilization is essentially a maritime one. The coast itself, as a fertile stretch of soil that can be used for productive farming, is very narrow, in most places no more than ten miles wide. Most Swahili settlements have been in the same few fertile and well-watered places for centuries. Many settlements are towns in the sense of closely built-up places with permanent houses and streets; others are larger villages, also usually closely built-up but with no more than a handful of permanent houses. Between settlements most soils are sandy or of broken coral, both of which

carry crops, although only with continuous labor. Behind the coastline much of the land is not very fertile, although parts of it have supported productive grain plantations and have been a source of copal, orchella, aromatic woods and resins, and other export items. There are extensive mangrove forests in the tidal estuaries and mud flats, and sandy soils carry coconut palms. The areas of deeper and better soil, especially along the Nyali and Mrima coasts and on the islands of Zanzibar and Pemba, produce rice, grains, cloves, citrus, and many other fruits. The Swahili are gardeners and fishermen rather than farmers, and in the larger towns also traders. Their land has been closely cultivated for centuries, and except for the mangroves almost all its vegetation is man-made, most of the bush land being secondary woodland. A main factor in the recent decrease of cultivation and the decline in population in the more remote settlements was the abolition of

John Middleton, *The World of the Swahili: An African Mercantile Civilization* (New Haven, CT: Yale University Press, 1992), pp. 10–12.

slavery around the turn of the [twentieth] century. Almost everywhere in the now empty bush land, all that remain to mark the sites of former settlements are clusters of untended mango trees.

The ocean trade brought the Swahili wealth, luxury, and on occasions power, and the coast itself has produced enough for most everyday needs. Many of their food plants and trees came originally from Indonesia and India. In return there was a reverse diffusion of African plants to India and beyond. The staple food of most wealthier communities has been rice, grown on the larger islands and in parts of the mainland, using both natural swamps and some irrigation; today much is imported. Poorer people (and formerly slaves) depend on other staples, mainly sorghums, millets, maize, and cassava, grown in fields set outside the settlements under various forms of bush fallow. Trees are economically of great importance and the islands in particular grow spices. Tobacco, kapok, and many other plants are cultivated, and various gums and resins are collected wild. Contrasted to the land behind the coast itself, mainly savanna bush, much of the Swahili coast is one vast garden that has provided a firm productive base for the merchant towns dotted along it.

Part of the coast is the sea: the two cannot be separated. The Swahili are a maritime people and the stretches of lagoon, creek, and open sea beyond the reefs are as much part of their environment as are the coastlands. The sea, rivers, and lagoons are not merely stretches of water but highly productive food resources, divided into territories that are owned by families and protected by spirits just as are stretches of land. The Swahili use the sea as though it were a network of roads. They have long known the compass, but a good captain of a sailing vessel relies more on his own skill and knowledge of the coast and its islands—and on magic—to make his ship fast and safe. The Swahili are, and seem always to have been, highly competent shipbuilders, and their sailing vessels and canoes are still made and repaired at several places along the coast.

There has always been continual movement of traders and settlers up and down the coast. The coastline and sea provide a basic map in terms of which the Swahili conceptualize their society and

its history. The key to this map is the existence of the ocean monsoons. The monsoon winds cover most of the western Indian Ocean as far south as Madagascar, and the ocean trade has been organized around them as far back as historical knowledge goes. The northeast monsoon starts to blow in early November, is strong between December and February, and comes to an end by March. The weather is hot and dry, without rain. This is when the dhows [traditional Indian Ocean sailing craft] come from Arabia and India carrying salt fish and many kinds of consumer goods. At the end of the monsoon come the heavy rains, and then a period of storms and turbulence when only coastal sailing is possible. The southwest monsoon begins soon afterward and is at its strongest from July until September, when ships sail north with grain, mangrove poles, and other produce, and in the past with slaves and ivory. Then there come light breezes until the beginning of the next northeast monsoon; the sea is calm but with winds that are uncertain for sailing. The basic pattern is unchanging and reliable, summed up in the saying *Kasakazi mja naswi, Kusi mja na mtama* ("The northeast wind comes with fish, the southwest wind comes with sorghum"). . . .

The Swahili towns, set along this coast and its islands, have been the points of exchange between merchants who came by sea and by land. But the exchanges were virtually never direct transfers of goods between the two kinds of merchants. Merchants to and from Asia have carried their goods by ship, taking note of the monsoons, the need for ballast, and the internal organizational requirements of a merchant ship (the captain, the merchant himself, the crew, and water, food, and repair of ships). The owners of the very large ships have generally been Arab and Indian merchants, but Swahili merchants have owned vessels, using both Swahili and Arab crews. A trading expedition, which can take several months to cross the ocean and return, requires considerable financing that has not usually been available to the Swahili, whereas Indian and Arab merchants have been more readily given credit by Indian financiers. The African side of the trade was organized along much the same lines as the ocean side, with armed food caravans, often of several hundred porters, taking the place of sailing vessels. It was run mainly by African traders from the hinterland and interior, not by the Swahili merchants themselves. (Many nineteenth-century caravans were an exception; they were run by Arab and Swahili traders from Zanzibar and used well-marked trade routes and permanent encampments in the interior). Today, however, most of the traditional long-distance trade has gone and the middleman role of the Swahili towns has faded, although it is still remembered by older members of Swahili merchant families and remains the basis of Swahili views of their civilization.

The Swahili have lived along this coast and its islands for over a thousand years, and there were communities before that which must have been very similar to theirs except for adherence to Islam and use of the Swahili language. Swahili society has derived its main characteristics from four factors: the nature of the coast; the trade between Africa and Asia in which the Swahili have played the role of middlemen; their long subjection to colonial exchange and political systems; and their ethnic composition and the complex historical formation of their society.

The formation of a society such as this raises many problems of obtaining and interpreting information about the past. There are gaps in the archeological record and few reliable figures for the Indian Ocean trade. The difficulties of interpretation are rather more subtle, but in general are based on the tensions within present-day Swahili society. As in any hierarchically stratified society, the members of the higher strata wish to see the present as validated by the past. . . . Most [historians] have asked three important but sociologically somewhat inadequate questions: Is Swahili civilization an African one or a transplanted Asian one? In what ways do past historical processes of migration and incorporation relate to and so validate the distribution of present-day "communities"? And what has been the historical relationship between Islamic and pre-Islamic cultural elements? A fourth question . . . is: What have been and are the social and cultural characteristics of this society?

Swahili origins, in the cultural rather than the racial sense, reflect the relations over a very long period between various African and Asian cultures. A problem is that Swahili notions of hierarchy and social differences are permeated by the view that race and culture are coterminous, whereas in social and historical reality they are not. Both outside observers and members of the socially superior Swahili groups have long held that Swahili culture was transplanted from Asia, and this view has been translated into terms of ethnic origins. More recently it has been suggested that the African component is far greater than had been thought, even though there have been many immigrant groups from Asia. Each has at first claimed to be different from those it found already settled, but over time these distinctions have become blurred through intermarriage, concubinage, and by the adoption of Swahili language and custom. In order to differentiate themselves, immigrants and those already settled have shown an intense concern with nuances of dialect and speech, religious behavior, deportment, dress, house adornment, and other cultural traits. Their settlements along the long and narrow coastal strip, often separated by many miles, have over the centuries grown to be very distinctive. Each part of the coast has its own name, its own traditions and myths of origin and ancestry, its own dialect, and its own set of moral values within the basic moral system provided by Islam. Yet together they form a single society with a single underlying structure, within which are several deep-rooted axes of contradiction: that between claimed and imputed origins in Africa or Asia appears to be the most pervasive, most internal competition being phrased in its terms.

After reading this selection, consider these questions:

1. What is a monsoon, and how does it affect East African life?
2. How did the Swahili ocean trade differ from the commerce of the West African interior?
3. What explains the many differences among the cities of the Swahili coast?

CHAPTER 20
The Americas Before Columbus: What Civilizations Did European Intruders Find?

The Western Hemisphere is indeed a "new world" if we are considering the history of human evolution. As we have seen in chapter 1, human beings emerged from their hominid ancestry in Africa and eventually spread throughout Asia, Europe, and even Australia, but they do not seem to have inhabited the Americas until comparatively recently. The most widely accepted view has been that human habitation of the Western Hemisphere began about twelve thousand years ago. Some evidence, however, suggests that the date should be pushed back as far as forty thousand years ago.

All reputable authorities agree that late in the most recent Ice Age, Alaska and the easternmost tip of Siberia were connected by a land bridge, which had been created when sea levels dropped because large amounts of ocean water were frozen in the great ice caps covering much of North America and Eurasia. Due to sparse precipitation, the land bridge itself was not glaciated. Over this land bridge Paleolithic hunters wandered, pursuing caribou and other big game. Then, as the global climate warmed and as a gap opened in North America's continental ice cap, hunting bands moved south into the Western Hemisphere. A long-established view held that this happened about 10,000 B.C., but there may have been earlier openings as well, permitting an earlier migration. Very recently, DNA and linguistic evidence has been enlisted in the debate, which lends support to arguments for older migrations.

Whenever they came to the Western Hemisphere, the new natives had to adapt to environments ranging from subarctic tundras to tropical rain forests. Eventually, in the temperate regions of the highlands of central Mexico, settlement became relatively dense. As in Southwest Asia and northern China the Neolithic revolution occurred, whose most important features were the discoveries of agriculture and animal husbandry. The Neolithic revolution came to Mexico sometime before 6500 B.C.—not long after it began in the Old World. And in the third and second millennia B.C., there was an independent Neolithic revolution in Peru. From these beginnings, agriculture later spread to most parts of North and South America where natural conditions would allow crop cultivation. In California and the Pacific Northwest, however, agriculture never developed because oak forests or the sea provided enough food to support relatively dense populations without the necessity to cultivate the soil.

There were some important differences between the Neolithic revolutions in the Americas and those of the Old World, however. Corn (also called maize) was the native grain cultivated by the people of the Western Hemisphere and in Peru and adjacent lands, potatoes were the mainstays. Eurasian staples such as wheat, rye, oats, barley, and rice were unknown in the New World. The large animals that Eurasians were able to domesticate, especially cattle, sheep, and horses, had perished in the New World before the Neolithic revolution occurred, victims not only of climate change but also of efficient Paleolithic hunters. The lack of large domesticated animals (llamas in the highlands of Peru were the only exception), had profound consequences for the native American civilizations because there was no incentive to develop the wheel—no "horsepower" was available to pull the wagons and plows that otherwise they might have developed. The impressive cities that Mexicans and Peruvians built were put together solely with human muscle power. Keep this in mind as you read the selections in this chapter. Consider, indeed, how these Western Hemisphere civilizations compared with the Old World civilizations we have encountered.

SELECTION 1:

Teotihuacán

The greatest American Indian city was Teotihuacán, near the site of modern Mexico City. It flourished, by European reckoning, about A.D. 500— that is, when Rome was crumbling before German attacks on its borders. Since its inhabitants had no writing, it is from archaeological discoveries that their way of life must be reconstructed. In this selection, American historian Ross Hassig describes Teotihuacán's rise and decline.

Teotihuacán reached its peak around A.D. 500 with a population of 200,000 people, approximately one-third of whom were economic, political, and religious specialists and not farmers. The city also underwent an increase in militarism, especially in the final century before the city's collapse (A.D. 650–750), when many martial depictions appeared in murals and ceramics. Significant changes took place in Teotihuacán's military, affecting armaments, organization, and tactics. Some of these changes merely reflect lacunae in the data, but others are certain and all indicate increasing military pressures, whether internal or external. There was no significant change in arms—thrusting spears and atlatls [spear-throwers] continued to dominate—but innovations in armor had broad repercussions. . . .

[The decline and fall of the city is not easy to explain.]

The sketchy data available suggest that Teotihuacán fell of its own weight. It had dominated vast stretches of Mesoamerica but was incapable of militarily incorporating every independent city into a Teotihuacán empire. Although it could mount the largest army, Teotihuacán nevertheless lacked the manpower required to conquer and control all the cities: Mesoamerica's far-flung cities presented a serious logistical obstacle that could not be overcome with the technology of the day, nor did Mesoamerica's relatively low population density permit an organizational solution to this problem.

Conquests at any significant distance were exceptionally costly and, even if achieved, control was difficult to maintain. Only by garrisoning troops and settling peoples in these distant centers could Teotihuacán exercise any significant and sustained domination over them, yet garrisons were expensive to maintain under the manpower and logistical limitations of the Classic period. Accordingly, Teotihuacán established colonies and military enclaves only in selected centers. Nearby areas could be controlled directly from

the capital, but colonies offered the surest way to maintain control in distant areas. From these secure centers, Teotihuacán's influence extended into the surrounding areas, either alone or in alliance with local groups who also benefited by the arrangement. Through this mechanism, Teotihuacán dominated production and trade throughout much of Mesoamerica.

Part of the rational for Teotihuacán's expansion was to control the production or trade of culturally important items. Teotihuacán did not achieve this position simply because it produced some of these goods (notably obsidian) and consumed others (such as exotic minerals). It expanded its own production to levels far greater than that of their sites, both absolutely and per capita, but to benefit by so doing, control of a stable and predictable market was essential. And this is what it sought, spurred, no doubt, by the insistence of the elites whose elevated welfare depended on the acquisition of wealth and exotic imported goods.

Teotihuacán did not compete with other major empires, but expanded under conditions in which it had no real competitors. The greatest brake on Teotihuacán's expansion was the friction of distance, but expansion also generates its own opposition. Teotihuacán unquestionably benefited from its vast trade network, but so did other centers that were tied into it. Teotihuacán's trading partners received goods that bolstered the positions of their local elites, so that Teotihuacán's economic success also led to the growth of increasingly sophisticated and powerful centers, both allied and independent, which contained emergent elites who increasingly competed for local goods. As a result, the trade network not only produced exotic goods and provided a market for Teotihuacán products, it also created competitors. These competitors were not restricted solely to Teotihuacán's trade partners; as each center grew and extended its influence, it also brought more of the surrounding area and towns under its influence and effectively removed these areas as trade partners for Teotihuacán. This was not a military competition, however. Man to man, Teotihuacán soldiers could probably have defeated any competitor, but the great costs of trans-

Ross Hassig, *War and Society in Ancient Mesoamerica* (Berkeley and Los Angeles: University of California Press, 1992), pp. 82, 86–87.

portation in Mesoamerica meant that, generally, the farther away the target, the smaller the army that could reach it. While Teotihuacán maintained overall military superiority until its demise, it could not maintain local superiority everywhere and thus could not dominate numerically inferior forces at great distances.

As distant cities achieved local military superiority, especially non-allied cities, their elites usurped local goods that Teotihuacán sought and did so with impunity. Teotihuacán may have been able to defend its colonies and merchants even under these circumstances, but it did not have the military dominance to compel trade.

After reading this selection, consider these questions:
1. What do murals and ceramics depict in the last century of Teotihuacán?
2. How does the author account for the decline of the city?
3. What was essential for Teotihuacán's economic progress?

SELECTION 2:

Mayan Civilization

Following the demise of Teotihuacán, a new civilization arose in what is now southern Mexico, Guatemala, and nearby Central American states. It is unique in that many of its centers were in a tropical rain forest environment. This society is known as the Mayan, and its accomplishments in art, crafts, architecture, and mathematics rank it among the highest of world civilizations. An American authority on Mesoamerican history, Shirley Gorenstein, discusses Mayan life in the following selection.

Lowland Maya centers appear to have been built according to a basic plan. The buildings were located around courts and plazas, and the sculptured monolithic monuments, the stelae and altars, were used as adjuncts to the main constructions. Commonly, terraces, platforms, and truncated pyramids were used as substructures to support superstructures which rested on an intermediate building platform. The substructure consisted of a core of rubble and outer walls of masonry and had at least one steep stairway either projecting from or inset into it. The superstructure always contained interior space and was roofed by a vault which was created by sloping two masonry walls inward and upward until they met or could be bridged by a capstone. Not infrequently roof combs or crests were carried above the roof line.

Perhaps the major art of the Lowland Maya was the monumental carving exemplified in stelae and altars. The stelae were large, sometimes as high as three meters, and were limestone slabs, usually with figures depicted on one side and hieroglyphs on the other. They were set up in the courts of the centers and either commemorated historical or ritual events or served as markers for a calendrical time period. Altars were round or rectangular and have often been found in association with the stelae. Low-relief carvings of lintels and panels and wall paintings were also important art forms.

Ceramic vessels of many forms were produced

Shirley Gorenstein, *Not Forever on Earth* (New York: Charles Scribner's Sons, 1975), pp. 78–86.

to serve different purposes. Polychrome pottery was made throughout the period from the fourth to the ninth century A.D. The earlier designs show cranes, flying parrots, and men encircling the vessels. The later vessels have even more brilliant colors, achieved through special firing techniques, and present wonderful narrative scenes.

While ceramic figurines are important throughout the region, probably the most remarkable ones are those found at Jaina, an island off the coast of Campeche. The island contains one of the largest cemeteries known, and the figurines seem to have been manufactured there as grave goods. The greatest number of the figures are of men, whose facial expressions, body stances, and dress are touchingly true to life. In some cases the costumes, although also made of clay, are separate from the figures; perhaps dressing these forms served some ritual purpose.

Information on the intellectual achievements of the Maya comes from the few surviving native books and from wall paintings, stone sculpture, and ceramic decoration. The interpretation of these is aided by post-conquest accounts of native life. Nevertheless, the reconstructions are only fragmentary since thousands of books and artifacts were either destroyed by zealous Christians determined to convert the heathen or fell as natural prey to time.

The heart of Mayan intellectual life was religion, and their major achievements—writings, numeration, and the calendar—were not only inextricably bound with one another but also functioned mainly to express the tenets of the religion and to carry out rituals. . . .

We do not know how advanced mathematics was among the Maya, but their numeration would certainly have permitted them to do arithmetic with ease.

The Mayan calendar was built on an earlier Mesoamerican calendar in which the 260-day cycle formed the basis for all calculations. This earlier calendar was based not only on solar and lunar reckonings but also on an understanding of the related revolutions of the planets. Within the 260-day cycle were 13 units of 20 days each. Running concurrently with the 260-day cycle was a 365-day cycle consisting of 18 units of 20 days each and 5 days at the end. It would take 18,980 days for the two cycles to return to the same numbers and days, and this cycle, of 52 "years," was considered a sacred unit.

After reading this selection, consider these questions:

1. What were the major Mayan constructions?
2. How do you explain the Mayan interest in the passage of time?
3. What was the role of religion in Mayan life?

SELECTION 3:

The Aztec Political System

After the Mayan empire passed into history, the Aztecs began a new page. Coming into the Valley of Mexico as nomadic warriors about A.D. 1325, they founded their capital, Tenochtitlán, on an island in Lake Texcoco. Soon their numbers increased until they could build an empire, with tribute and taxes in kind coming from neighboring peoples. A modern historian analyzes the Aztec Empire's success in this selection.

The organization of the soil, thus established, formed the basis on which the Mexican state reposed. It was not merely the chief source of wealth, as in the ancient kingdoms of the Old World; there was really no other form of durable property. The principal means of exchange—cacao beans and small mantles—were no lasting substitute for a metal currency. Admittedly, small axe-shaped copper sheets and gold dust in quills were also used for monetary purposes in parts of Mexico; however, hoarding of these does not seem to have occurred on a large scale.

Land-holding thus provides the key to the social order; by taking the lion's share of the broad acres of the newly conquered, the ruler and nobles assured for themselves a firm basis of economic power, independent of the communal organizations. They were thus free to pursue their dreams of further conquest, unfettered by the fears or inhibitions of the masses. Whatever its original structure, the Mexican state was now in essence a tightly controlled oligarchy.

At the top of the social pyramid was the ruler (*tlatoani*). He was always chosen from the same family and was usually a son or brother of his predecessor. He was advised in the first place by a council of four, from the ranks of which his successor was normally chosen. These four councilors additionally played a major part in the choice of a new ruler, though elders and warriors, as well as the allied rulers of Texcoco and Tacuba, also took part, in order to give added ceremony to the occasion. The key council of four members probably came into formal existence at the time of Itzcóatl. Supreme power was thus very much concentrated in the hands of the royal family, to which the four councilors, as eligible to succeed to the throne, naturally belonged. There also existed a larger council, called the Tlatocan, variously described as having from twelve to twenty members; in addition, there was a war council to advise on military matters.

Thus, as an elective monarch, assisted by different bodies, the *tlatoani* was not absolute. However, his personal power tended to increase,

owing to a gradual process of centralization, culminating in the reign of Moctezuma I. In a state dedicated to conquest, the ruler must receive huge quantities of tribute, and his power will automatically be augmented at the expense of his subjects.

Next below the *tlatoani* in the social order, at one remove, stood the hereditary nobility, restricted in numbers, and perhaps mainly of royal descent. They were well endowed with land, but not on the vast scale of their European counterparts. Service to the state was obligatory, and they were expected to participate actively in war, to justify the retention of their privileged position.

In addition to this select few, a much larger upper, or leading, class existed—the distinguished warriors—based chiefly on meritorious service; in principle, they enjoyed their rank and land for their own lifetime. Often, however, such privileges tended to pass from father to son.

Equally to be taken into account were the priests. They formed an important and numerous caste—an intellectual élite more to be classed with the rulers than the ruled. In some respects they are hardly to be distinguished from the nobility, for the ruler himself was of priestly rank. They also went to war and took captives. The distinction between priests and warriors is not an absolute one. They performed the important additional task of educating the upper classes in the privileged schools (*clamecac*). The rest of the population went to what was virtually a college for military training (*tepochcalli*), which existed in each clan.

A smaller, but significant, group was the officials and judges; from the accounts of Sahagún [a sixteenth-century Spanish author on Aztec life] and others, it can be seen that in Tenochtitlán justice was meted out to rich and poor alike with severe impartiality. In addition to other special classes, there existed the merchants. . . . They constituted a group apart, and enjoyed many privileges, such as their own law courts.

Below these favored sectors stood the common people. Of these, the most important category was the freemen (*macehuales*), who formed the basis of the clan organization. The relative lowliness of their situation was defined by rigor-

Nigel Davies, *The Aztecs* (London: Abacus Press, 1977), pp. 79–81.

ous sumptuary laws; only the upper classes were permitted to wear cotton clothes or to drink cocoa. The elaborate attire, the fine jewels and sumptuous food of the nobles were taboo for the people; the latter were unceremoniously killed if they dared to indulge in such luxuries.

Next as a group came the serfs, bound to the nobles' hereditary lands. And last of all were the slaves. The institution was less highly developed than in the Old World, partly because prisoners of war were usually sacrificed. People lost their freedom chiefly as a consequence of certain crimes, or of unpaid debts; men could voluntari-ly sell themselves into slavery, and equally could be redeemed by a stipulated payment. Slaves were mainly used in domestic service, and as carriers in the absence of pack animals.

After reading this selection, consider these questions:
1. How did the Aztecs assess wealth?
2. What were the classes of Aztec society?
3. Compare the role of the Aztec emperor with that of the Egyptian pharaoh (see chapter 3).

SELECTION 4:

Human Sacrifice Among the Aztecs

The Aztecs are famous in history for their bloody practice of human sacrifice. The killing of human beings to please divinities or natural forces is not uncommon in human history, including the civilizations of the Maya and other ancient Mexican cultures, but probably no developed civilization carried the practice to Aztec extremes. Even the sixteenth-century Spanish invaders of Mexico, who themselves had no compunction about shedding innocent human blood, were revolted by the Aztec ceremonies they witnessed—and used the gory practice to justify their own brutal conquests. In the following selection, contemporary American historian Brian Fagan demonstrates the centrality of human sacrifice to the Aztec way of life.

The offering of human blood was perhaps the most profound of religious acts. Human sacrifice was the touchstone of all Aztec virtue, the key to their understanding of the spiritual world. The gods themselves had originated the rite of sacrifice by immolating themselves to nourish the Fifth Sun. Humankind had an equal responsibility to feed the sun. The Aztecs believed that they had acquired the custom from the gods themselves, a lineage sufficient to clothe it with powerful divine sanction.

Sacrifice renewed not only the god to whom it was offered, it provided an ultimate test of manhood for the victims. Human beings counted in the cosmic order only insofar as their offerings nourished the gods. The more valorous the offering, the more the gods were nourished. It followed that the blood or the heart of an elite warrior was much more nutritious than that of a

Brian M. Fagan, *The Aztecs* (New York: W.H. Freeman, 1984), pp. 229–31.

slave. Every captive was the property not of his captor but of the god to whom he was destined to be sacrificed. Often the victim was painted and dressed in the god's regalia so that he or she became a symbolic god sacrificed to the god himself or herself. Elaborate rituals surrounded the more important of these sacrifices. The flawless young man chosen to impersonate Tezcatlipoca assumed the role of the god for a full year. He walked around in divine regalia, playing the flute. A month before his death, he was married to four young priestesses who impersonated goddesses and who sang and danced with him as he walked around the capital. On the day of sacrifice, the young man climbed willingly and alone to his date on the sacrificial stone. His decapitated head was displayed on the skull rack that stood in the plaza below the temple. On occasions like this, human sacrifice was not an earthly, but a divine, drama.

The Aztecs knew of many varieties of human sacrifice, including death by arrows, burning, and beheading. Then there was autosacrifice, a form of blood offering involving self-mutilation, the piercing of limbs and other parts of the body with maguey thorns and/or sharp pointed bones and collecting the blood on slips of paper that were presented to the god. Sometimes the entire community indulged in such blood-letting rites in a collective orgy of self-offering.

The most common sacrifice was the extraction of the heart, a practice unique to Mexican civilization. The priests painted the sacrificial victims with red and white stripes, then reddened their mouths and drew black circles around them. They glued white down on the victim's heads. The priests then marshaled the victims at the foot of the temple pyramid steps before escorting them up the staircase one by one. At the summit, each prisoner was thrust backwards over the *techcatl*, the sacrificial stone. . . . Some authorities speculate that the entire sacrificial rite was symbolic. The climbing prisoner was the young sun rising to his zenith at the moment of sacrifice. The tumbling body was the setting sun returning to the earth.

No one knows exactly how many human victims the Aztecs sacrificed. Cortes estimated that fifty people were killed at every temple annually, which would mean that some twenty thousand persons died for the gods throughout Aztec domains every year. Several early chroniclers agree that Tlaxcala sacrificed eight hundred captives in most years and a thousand every fourth year, the divine year. But the highest numbers were counted in Tenochtitlan, where as many as eight hundred victims for one festival alone have been spoken of.

After reading this selection, consider these questions:

1. What was the purpose of human sacrifice among the Aztecs?
2. What impelled individuals to willingly accept the role of a sacrificial victim?
3. How do modern people regard sacrifice?

SELECTION 5:

The Economy of the Incan Empire

Civilization had been taking shape in Peru since the first millennium B.C. A series of advanced cultures arose, culminating in the empire estab-

lished by the Inca people between about A.D. 1200 and 1400. By the time the Spaniards arrived in South America, in the early 1530s, the Inca Empire reached from modern Ecuador to central Chile. Inca was the title of the ruler, but the name also became attached to the empire itself and to its dominant ethnic group. Like the Aztec Empire in Mexico, its contemporary, the Inca Empire exacted tribute from dozens of other Indian states. Although the heart of the empire was in the highest part of the Andes Mountains, it was held together by a remarkable network of roads, maintained by conscripted local labor and over which relays of imperial couriers ran on foot.

The Inca Empire's remarkable economic foundations—a combination of compulsion and welfare—are described by the contemporary historians Craig Morris and Adriana von Hager in this selection.

As in most premodern states, the Inka did not strive for an appearance of separation between the political and economic aspects of their relations with the people they ruled. On the contrary, gifts and state hospitality involving large quantities of goods were a basic element of Inka power. . . . The state distributed large quantities of food and maize beer to accompany activities in the impressive public section of the city. Written sources tell of massive issues and gifts of cloth to state officials, the army, and newly conquered or incorporated peoples.

The major problem facing the state economy was how to provide for these enormous outlays of hospitality and the living costs of increasingly large numbers of leaders, bureaucrats, and others who served the state. In theory the state functioned without tribute of goods. Its revenues were based on labor given by the subjects to till the state's fields, care for its herds, make its cloth, and build its roads, bridges, and cities. Lands throughout the empire were divided into several classes. Lands of local communities provided subsistence for the great majority of the people; lands linked to religion provided goods related to various cults; state lands of various kinds supported the Inka rulers, their armies, and the massive labor forces who worked for the state. How much land belonged in each category is not known, nor do we have many details about the acquisition of state and religious lands. It seems clear that some of the land that passed into state use must have been used for local purposes before the Inka expansion. Additional land for farming was created or greatly improved by the Inka through terracing and irrigation projects as the state devoted some of its labor revenues to projects that increased production.

The labor tax was an outgrowth of Andean principles, probably centuries old, whereby leaders received labor from the people of their communities. In return, the leader was expected to support the people generously while they worked for him. Such support usually was not limited to mere subsistence rations. Instead, people did their work in a festival context with food, drink, and music. In this way, economics, politics, and religion were wrapped in an elaborate package of work, ritual, and festival. The evidence for feasting and drinking found at Huánuco Pampa exemplifies the state's enlarged version of these principles played out against the backdrop of an imperial city.

Most of the labor for the state came from ablebodied male heads of household, who served the state in turns. This rotating labor system, called *mit'a*, was used to cultivate the state's fields and to carry out its many construction projects.

After reading this selection, consider these questions:

Craig Morris and Adriana von Hager, *The Inka Empire and Its Andean Origins* (New York: Abbeville Press, 1993), pp. 169–70.

1. What was the major concern of the Inca economy?
2. How were taxes paid in the Inca Empire?

3. Do you see any connection between the Inca economic system and American capitalism?

SELECTION 6:

The Inca Child Tribute

A narrative of the Spaniard Bernabe Cobo gives further information about the way of life among the Incas. He devotes part of his narrative to the custom whereby the Inca required that young women be taken to Cuzco to become wives of the emperor or to marry into nobles' families. Young men were trained for service to the state.

The apportionment of this tribute in children that the king ordered his subjects to pay every year was no more limited than the other contributions; it depended on what the Inca desired. All these children had to be from nine to ten years old or younger, and all the males gathered in this way were sacrificed; and they were killed by strangulation with a cord, or by a blow with a club, and then they were buried, and sometimes they got them drunk before having them killed.

The number of girls that were gathered was much larger than the number of boys, as can be seen by the assignments the girls were given. The method of gathering them was as follows. A judge or commissioner named by the Inca was dispatched to each province, and his only responsibility was this matter of collecting girls, watching over them, and sending them to Cuzco when they were the right age, and this official was called *apupanaca*. He wandered about the towns within his jurisdiction, and he had the authority to pick out any girls that seemed to him to have beauty, a good figure, and a good disposition, if they were between eight and nine years of age or

younger; these girls were called *acllas*, which means "chosen women"; they were brought to the house of the *mamaconas*, and for this reason it was called *acllaguaci*, which means "house of the chosen women"; and there was one of these houses in the capital of every province. The young girls were raised in these houses until they were fourteen years old; they remained in the company of the *mamaconas*, who were the cloistered women, dedicated to the service of their gods in the manner of nuns or like the vestal virgins of Rome. The *mamaconas* taught these girls all of the women's work and activities such as spinning, weaving wool and cotton, preparing food, making their wines or *chicas*, as well as other jobs that are appropriate for women. There was income designated for their support which came from the fields belonging to Religion, and there were also overseers who were in charge of supplying them with what they needed and watching over them very carefully with the object of protecting their virginity.

Every year at the time of the fiesta of Raymi, the commissioner who chose this tribute took from these houses of seclusion the girls who were thirteen or fourteen years old or older, and with no less watchfulness than had been used up to that point, he took them to Cuzco, according to

Father Bernabé Cobo, *History of the Inca Empire*, Roland Hamilton, trans. (Austin: University of Texas Press, 1979), pp. 235–37.

the number that each province had to send that year. Once the girls that were sent from all the provinces, which was an excessively large number, were gathered together in that city, they were placed in the presence of the Inca, who distributed them immediately, according to the present need, in the following order. Some were assigned to the monasteries of *mamaconas* to replace the number of those that died, and these took the vows of that order, living always in confinement and chastity, occupied in the service of the temples of the Sun, Thunder, and the other gods that were served by women.

The Inca took another considerable number aside and ordered that they be kept to be killed in the sacrifices that were made during the course of the year; these sacrifices happened often and for many different reasons, such as for the health of the Inca, when he got sick and when he went to war in person; and in case he died, those that were to be sent to the other life in his company would be killed; and for many other occasions they felt a need for this sacrifice, because they were under the influence of the devil. And it was a necessary prerequisite that the girls for these sacrifices be virgins. The Inca assigned the most noble and beautiful girls to be his servants and concubines, and gave a large number of them out to his captains and kinsmen, remunerating with this kind of prize the services that they had rendered to him; and for the same reason, he gave some of these virgins to other people when he wanted to do them a special favor, and receiving one of these virgins from the Inca personally was considered to be an extraordinary favor. This is because these Indians do not value anything as highly as having many wives, and other than their legitimate wife, they could not have another except as a special favor from the king, and he would normally give these women out for different reasons, that is to say, for someone being eminent in some art or for having exhibited special skill in something pertaining to the public welfare or for having done some brave deed in a war.

After reading this selection, consider these questions:
1. What was the purpose of the child tribute of the Incas?
2. What was the education of the young girls taken to the house of the *mamaconas*?
3. What were the possible options for the *acllas*?

Acknowledgments

UNIT ONE

Chapter 1:

Selection 1 Excerpted from Bernard Wood, "The Oldest Whodunnit in the World," *Nature*, vol. 385, iss. 6614, January 23, 1997, p. 292, by permission. Copyright 1997 Macmillan Magazines Ltd.

Selection 2 Excerpted from Adam Goodheart, "Mapping the Past," *Civilization*, vol. 3, no. 2 (March/April 1996), pp. 40–47, by permission of the publishers.

Chapter 3:

Selection 4 Excerpted from R.B. Parkinson, *Voices from Ancient Egypt*; ©1991 the British Museum, British Museum Press. Reprinted with permission of the British Museum Press.

Selection 5 Excerpted from *Ancient Nubia*, by P.L. Shinnie (New York and London: Kegan Paul International, 1996), with permission from the publishers. Copyright 1996 by Peter Shinnie.

Chapter 4:

Selection 1 Excerpted from Jonathan Mark Kenoyer, "The Ancient City of Harappa," *Asian Art and Culture*, vol. 9, no. 1 (Winter 1996), pp. 86–89, by permission of the author and publishers.

Chapter 5:

Selection 3 Excerpted from *Lustful Maidens and Ascetic Kings: Buddhist and Hindu Stories of Life*, by Roy C. Amore and Larry D. Shinn. Copyright ©1981 by Oxford University Press, Inc. Used by permission of Oxford University Press, Inc.

Chapter 6:

Selection 5 Reprinted with the permission of The Free Press, a division of Simon & Schuster, from *Chinese Civilization and Society: A Sourcebook*, by Patricia Buckley Ebrey. Copyright ©1981 by The Free Press.

Chapter 7:

Selection 5 From *Women Poets of China*, by Kenneth Rexroth and Ling Chung. Copyright ©1973 by Kenneth Rexroth and Ling Chung. Reprinted by permission of New Directions Publishing Corp.

UNIT TWO

Chapter 8:

Selection 2 From *Women and law in Classical Greece*, by

INDEX